**Investment
A Practical Approach**

The M & E Handbook Series

Investment
A Practical Approach

David Kerridge
Principal Lecturer at Bristol Polytechnic

Revised Edition

Pitman Publishing
128 Long Acre, London WC2E 9AN

© Longman Group UK Ltd. 1987, 1988

First published in Great Britain 1987
Revised edition 1988

British Library Cataloguing in Publication Data

Kerridge, David
 Investment: a practical approach.—Rev. ed
 —(M & E handbook series).
 1. Great Britain. Investment
 I. Title
 332.6'0941

 ISBN 0-7121-0978-1

All rights reserved. No part of this publication may be reproduced,
stored in a retrieval system, or transmitted, in any form or by any
means, electronic, mechanical, photocopying, recording and/or otherwise,
without the prior written permission of the publishers. This book may
not be lent, resold, hired out or otherwise disposed of by way of trade
in any form of binding or cover other than that in which it is published,
without the prior consent of the publishers.

Founding Editor: P. W. D. Redmond

Typeset, printed and bound in Great Britain.

Contents

Preface viii
The purpose and structure of this book xi

Part one The background to personal investment decisions

1 The investment scene   3

2 The investor's needs   8
   The investor's circumstances; Taxation and investment

3 Investment in cash assets   17
   Selecting cash investments; Forms of cash investment; A review of cash investments

Part two Direct investment in stocks and shares

4 Investment in shares   31
   Stocks and shares – the different types; Buying stocks and shares on the Stock Exchange; The securities markets; Investment in shares issued to raise finance for companies; New issues; Rights issues; Capitalization issues; Takeover situations; The rights of shareholders; The redemption of company shares; Stock market indices

5 The selection of shares   70
   The criteria for share selection; Fundamental analysis; The *Financial Times* 'London Share Service'; Using available

Contents

information to assess a company's prospects; The use of Extel cards; Technical analysis; The efficient market hypothesis; **Appendix to Chapter 5:** The analysis of a company's annual report and accounts; The chairman's statement; The profit and loss account and balance sheet; Source and application of funds statement; Other important measures; Priority percentages; Current cost accounting

6 Investment in gilt-edged and fixed-interest securities   115
Gilt-edged and fixed-interest securities; Gilt prices and yields; Main considerations when investing in gilts; Special types of gilt investments; How to buy and sell gilts; Investment in other fixed-interest securities

7 Warrants, traded options and futures   140
Investment in warrants; Investment in traded options; Investment in conventional options; Investment in futures

Part three Investment in professionally managed funds

8 Investment in unit trusts   161
The nature of unit trusts; The range of unit trusts; Investors' considerations when selecting unit trusts; Buying and selling; The Personal Equity Plan (PEP)

9 Investment in investment trusts   181
The nature of investment trusts; The advantages and disadvantages of investment trusts; Sources of information on investment trusts; Investors' considerations when selecting investment trusts; Other investment trust securities

10 Life assurance linked investments   198
The link between life assurance and investment; What are the main types of life assurance?; The taxation of life assurance linked investments; The merits of life assurance investments for different investors; Investors' considerations when selecting life assurance linked investments; Other types of insurance linked investments

11 Other investments 219
Investment in land and property; Investment in commodities; Investment in precious coins and chattels

Part four The successful selection of investments

12 Portfolio planning 233
Taxation and the selection of personal investment portfolios; Investments for children; Investments for retired people; Portfolio planning and risk

13 The protection of investors 241

14 The state of the economy and investment 247
Economic influences on share and bond prices; Summary

15 Prospects for investment in the world's stock markets 256
Prospects for investment in the US; Prospects for investment in the UK; Prospects for investment in West Germany; Prospects for investment in Japan; Further reading

16 1988 update on the world's stock markets 275
The United States; The United Kingdom; West Germany; Japan

17 Investment for trust funds 284

18 Personal pensions 291
The provision of pensions by the private sector

19 Recent developments in investment 301
Giving investment advice; Investor protection; Other developments in investment

Appendices 315
1 The 1988 Budget; 2 Passing examinations on investment; 3 Examination questions; 4 Useful addresses; 5 The investment advice question

Index 343

Preface

Who should read this book?

If you are a student following a syllabus on investment, this book is for you. I had particularly in mind the Institute of Bankers Diploma Course Stage 2 Investment syllabus as I wrote the book, and have endeavoured to cover all the topics that occur on it. However, students on a wide variety of professional courses like the Stock Exchange examinations, BTEC and degree-level courses should find it helpful.

If you are looking for a book that surveys the personal savings and investment scene at a level which is neither too superficial and anecdotal nor too academic and mathematical, this is for you. Whether you are an investor, or involved in investment management and advice, I hope you will find it helpful.

How does this book provide a practical approach?

The book is structured to give a practical analysis of an investor's requirements. It starts with identifying the aims and needs of the investor, and recognizes that some investors want to be actively involved in investment decisions while others would rather hand over most of these decisions to professional investment managers. It therefore begins its analysis of alternative investments with an examination of stocks and shares for those who want to be directly involved. It then examines the many alternative fund management services available for investors who want to leave most of the

Preface ix

investment decisions to professional managers.

Only information that is necessary to assist in investment decisions is provided. Descriptive material of the City and its institutions which does not influence actual investment decisions is at a minimum.

The book attempts to give you a flavour of the findings of academic research which have a bearing upon practical investment decisions. However, it does not attempt to discuss academic points in detail nor to use analysis requiring specialist mathematical skills.

Having surveyed the investment alternatives, the final section reviews the economic influences that cause stocks and shares to rise or fall in price and the investment prospects in the major world markets. These chapters cover topics not usually found in alternative books. However, their subject-matter is at least as important as all of the preceding chapters. A practical study of investment requires not only knowledge of the investment alternatives available, but also how to assess whether stocks and shares are likely to go up or down, and which of the world markets is likely to provide the greatest profits.

In addition to a careful reading of the text, I would suggest the following ways of consolidating your knowledge.

Read as many as possible of the magazines to which I have referred in the text. These will provide you with more information and keep you up-to-date.

Select the investments you would make if you had capital available – say £30,000. Now monitor the progress your investments would have made. If you would have selected some shares, obtain and study the latest annual report and accounts. If you would have selected investment trusts or unit trusts, write off to their managers for their latest reports. Fill out some of the coupons in the advertisements in the financial press inviting you to write for further information about the services provided by varous financial advisory and investment companies. This type of involvement will bring the subject to life for you and teach you an enormous amount.

Keep a notebook or file for a summary of the information you glean from the daily press and magazines about particular economies, stock markets, companies and other investment topics. Avoid collecting information that will be out of date within a few days or weeks, e.g. monthly statistics. You will find quarterly,

x Preface

semi-annual and annual data more helpful. For ease of reference, keep all this information under specified subjects headings, e.g. US economy, the Personal Equity Plan.

Having shown you what to look for in these chapters, I hope you will be better able to keep yourself up-to-date with what is happening on the investment scene and why.

The book's approach is practical in that nearly all examples are real investment ones. They are also explained in such a way that you can then refer to the financial pages of a newspaper, e.g. the *Financial Times*, and repeat the analysis for yourself using up-to-date figures or other examples. Many practical hints and specific examples are scattered through the book's pages. However, it is not intended to give specific investment advice, and the author disclaims responsibility for the performance of any investments you might select.

David Kerridge
1987

The purpose and structure of this book

This book will look at investment from the standpoint of the small investor and those in positions where they give advice to small investors.

In *Part 1*, *Chapter 2* reviews the considerations that should be taken into account before taking any investment decisions, while *Chapter 3* examines the alternative cash investments available.

Part 2 covers the situation where the investor wishes to retain control over the selection and management of investments.

Chapters 4 and 5 review direct investments in shares and *Chapter 6* in gilt-edged and other fixed-interest securities. *Chapter 7* examines ways in which the level of risk of these investments can be increased or reduced by the use of warrants, traded options and financial futures.

Part 3 covers the situation where the investor wishes to hand over responsibility for the day-to-day investment decisions to professional fund managers. *Chapters 8, 9 and 10* review investment in unit trusts, investment trusts and various insurance-linked investments.

Part 4 is a review of the factors which affect share and bond prices and the investment prospects in the world's major stock markets.

Part one
The background to personal investment decisions

1
The investment scene

1. The nature of personal investment. Personal investment involves the acquisition of assets by the investor in return for the lending of savings or money capital. There are three types of assets available to investors:

(*a*) *Cash assets* – maintain a constant value in money terms and earn interest. Examples are building society and bank deposits.

(*b*) *Financial assets* – like stocks and shares, fluctuate in price and may not guarantee to pay a specific income. The dividend income from shares, for example, depends upon the profits earned by the company whose shares are owned by the investor.

(*c*) *Real assets* – like land, buildings and commodities also fluctuate in price. They may provide an income, like property rented to a tenant, or may not, as in the case where the property is occupied by its owner.

Thus the income earned from investments may be fixed or variable. The size of the income expected from an investment is dependent upon its risk and the length of time of the investment. The higher the risk, the higher the rate of return expected by the investor to compensate for the risk. Similarly, the longer the period of time that the investor hands over access to the cash, the higher the rate of return that is required.

2. The role of financial institutions. Financial institutions like banks, building societies, insurance companies and the Stock Exchange play important roles in the field of personal investment.

(*a*) They act as *financial intermediaries*, bringing together the savings of lenders and investors with the borrowers who seek their funds. Most investors do not invest directly in real assets, but lend their money to financial institutions. For example, they deposit their cash with banks and building societies in return for the payment of interest and the security and ability to withdraw their deposits when required. The institutions in turn lend the savings at a higher rate of interest to borrowers who may require a mortgage loan to buy a house or finance to expand their business. By this means the investors' savings are ultimately invested in real assets which provide a financial return to both the borrower and the lender.

(*b*) Financial institutions also provide *secondary markets* which make financial assets marketable. The Stock Exchange and its members is an example. This is a market where the UK government and industrial and commercial companies can borrow money by selling financial assets to investors. The British government borrows billions of pounds each year by selling gilt-edged stocks which provide the investor with a fixed rate of interest income until the year specified for their redemption (*see* Chapter 6). Companies also borrow fixed-interest redeemable loans by selling loan stocks or debentures. Alternatively, they issue shares which are neither redeemable nor give a fixed rate of return, but a share of the profits paid to the shareholders as a dividend (*see* Chapter 4). The Stock Exchange is not only a market where these borrowers can raise new capital, but also provides a market for their paper assets once they have been issued. Investors who have bought stocks and shares and want to sell them for cash cannot sell them back to the government or the company which issued them. They must use the Stock Exchange to sell them to other investors who have spare cash and who are willing to buy them.

(*c*) Financial institutions also fulfil an important role by 'packaging' investments to make them more attractive to investors. By identifying the specific needs of borrowers and lenders, and designing investment 'vehicles' or 'packages' to meet them, financial institutions can increase the flow of saving and investment and hence the liquidity and efficiency of the financial system.

Some examples of this type of service provided by financial institutions are:

(*i*) The management of *unit trusts* and *investment trusts*. These

1. The investment scene

are professionally selected and managed investment portfolios of shares and fixed-interest investments. Private investors can buy a share in these portfolios as an alternative to selecting shares for themselves. The availability of unit trusts and investment trusts make it easier and less risky for the small investor to invest in the shares of both British and foreign companies (*see* Chapters 8 and 9).

(*ii*) The provision of savings schemes for retirement and the provision of capital or income in the event of death, accident or illness. Life assurance companies provide a variety of savings and investment schemes linked with different types of insurance. They are also responsible for the management of pension funds which receive and invest the regular contributions which people make towards the payment of their pensions when they retire (*see* Chapter 10).

The financial institutions therefore have a vital role to play in the channelling of the savings of investors efficiently and cheaply into the hands of the borrowers who need them. It is this flow of funds that provides the capital for keeping industry and commerce efficient and competitive in world markets.

The total size of the flow of personal savings and investment in any year is both a cause and a consequence of the size of the wealth produced in the country during that year, called Gross National Product (GNP). Greater investment by firms in productive assets financed by the public's savings not only creates jobs and income, but also increases the capacity to produce future wealth. The increased income that results from investors' savings and companies' investments then in turn increases the ability of people to save and invest more.

The importance of the financial institutions to the British economy has been increasingly assisted by the position of London half-way between Tokyo and New York. This has made it the location of the third leg in a global market stratgegy for the big US and Japanese investment banks. The New York Stock Exchange is open from 2.30 p.m. to 9.0 p.m. GMT while the Tokyo Stock Exchange opens at midnight and closes at 6 a.m. GMT. Positioned almost precisely between these two periods of trading, the London market is helping to make 24-hour trading a reality, and British financial institutions have expanded to compete in these markets.

6 Personal investment decisions

3. The rise of institutional investment. One measure of the success of the financial institutions in meeting the needs of investors is the extent to which their importance has increased relative to the private investor in the use made of the Stock Exchange. Between the spring of 1983 and mid-1986, the proportion of the value of total equity turnover accounted for by individual investors declined from 28.4 per cent to 18.6 per cent. In the medium and long-dated gilt market, the proportion of total turnover by value accounted for by individual investors declined from 19.8 per cent to 6.6 per cent. The changes in the personal investment market that will result from the Building Societies Act 1986, which allows building societies to market investment products, and the start of the Personal Equity Plan on 2 January 1987 are likely to result in a continued growth in the relative importance of institutional investment. Nevertheless, the privatizations of large industries like British Telecom, British Gas and British Airways will result in an increase in the total number of investors who own shares.

Another important factor that has contributed to the growth of investment in the products of the financial institutions rather than direct investment in stocks and shares has been the distortions in the financial markets created by the taxation system. For example, until the budget in March 1984, premiums paid into life assurance linked savings schemes were eligible for tax relief (*see* Chapter 10). Pension schemes are still exempt from all taxes on the income and gains made by the pension fund. Unit trust and investment trust managers can still buy and sell shares within their funds without incurring a liability to capital gains tax (*see* Chapters 8 and 9).

4. Is personal saving investment, speculation or gambling? Saving by placing cash deposits in a bank or building society is investment because it will earn a specified rate of return and the sum invested is secure. Speculation and gambling imply risk which requires a prospective investor to take a view on the probability of the occurrence of the different events that might cause the value of the investment to increase or decrease.

We also speak of investment in stocks and shares because when these securities are issued, they supply the funds for investment in capital equipment by the companies issuing them. Thus the investor is indirectly investing in real assets which increase the country's

1. The investment scene

wealth. The intended period of the investment is important. In the long run, it is assumed that the value of stocks and shares will increase with growth in the economy, so a long-term purchase is called an *investment*. However, the person who purchases a new issue of shares like the TSB issue in anticipation of a quick rise in price and a quick profit is called a *speculator*.

Gambling implies a high level of risk because the gains of the winners are paid for by the losses of the losers. Investment in stocks and shares is not gambling because when investors gain from an increase in the value of their investments, it is not at the expense of other investors. In a bull market when all financial assets are rising in price, all investors can gain. However, special investment markets like traded options and futures can be used to gamble since the gains of one investor are the losses of another. Even so, these markets cannot be described as sophisticated casinos, for these same markets can be used to 'hedge' or reduce risk (*see* Chapter 7).

2
The investor's needs

The investor's circumstances

Before making an investment, whether of a lump sum or regular savings out of income, an investor should first consider the following:

(a) How much money can the investor afford to invest?

(b) How long is the period of time for which this investment is to be made?

(c) How much risk is the investor prepared to take that the investment might make a loss?

(d) Is the investor looking primarily for income or growth in capital values?

(e) What is the investor's personal tax position?

(f) How much responsibility does the investor want to take for the day-to-day decisions concerning the selection of investments, the reinvestment of income, and the switching between different investments? Would it be preferable to have these decisions taken by professional investment managers?

Let us now consider why these questions are important.

1. How much can the investor afford to invest? The income, expenditure and current investments of the investor should be taken into account as indicated by the following checklist.

(a) *Income (annual):*
  (i) Income from employment – both investor and spouse.
  (ii) Income from investments – both investor and spouse.

2. The investor's needs

(*iii*) Likely future level of earnings.

(*iv*) Security of earnings, e.g. likelihood of redundancy, the effect of accident or prolonged illness upon earnings.

(*b*) *Expenditure (annual):*

(*i*) Total expenditure on housekeeping, car, holidays, entertainment, etc.

(*ii*) Rent or mortgage repayments.

(*iii*) Other loan repayments – bank loans, hire purchase, and credit card commitments.

(*iv*) Life assurance premiums.

(*v*) Private pension contributions.

(*vi*) Likely changes in future commitments.

(*c*) *Value of assets and investments:*

(*ii*) Is the investor's home rented or owned? What is its market value?

(*ii*) Does the investor have any other savings or investments? If so, what form do they take, and what are their market value?

(*d*) *Other relevant information:*

(*i*) Does the investor intend to move house soon? If so, will this require more or less capital?

(*ii*) What provisions have been made for life assurance?

(*iii*) Does the investor participate in either an employer-related or a private pension scheme?

(*iv*) Are there other personal considerations, such as impending retirement, that are relevant to the investment decisions?

Having considered these points, the investor can decide on the minimum and maximum level of investment to undertake. It would usually be prudent for savings above the minimum level to be placed in investments which have a stable value and can be converted into cash very quickly and at little or no cost to the investor. These are called *cash investments*, and are reviewed in Chapter 3. We return to giving advice on pensions, life assurance, etc. in Chapter 11 after we have reviewed all the alternative types of investment that are available.

2. What is the length of time of the investment? If the investor is likely to want ready access to some investments, the following conditions should be met.

(*a*) No costs are incurred in buying and selling the investment. This applies to deposits made with banks and building societies, but with most other investments, including stocks and shares, investment trusts and unit trusts, a cost will be incurred when they are bought and sold. These costs are referred to as *transaction costs*. This means that the value of the investments must rise by more than these costs before a profit is made. In general, the larger the amount of the investment, the lower these transaction costs will be as a percentage of the sum invested.

(*b*) The investments can be converted back rapidly into cash. Some deposits can be converted back into cash on demand; others require a period of notice. In general, the longer the period of notice required, the higher the rate of return that can be earned. Stocks and shares and other investments take varying periods of conversion into cash (*see* 4:**11**, 6:**24**, 8:**24**).

(*c*) The investment maintains a stable value. Deposits in banks, building societies and National Savings investments all hold their capital value. The market price of most other investments, whether company shares, fixed-interest securities, unit trusts, investment trust shares or insurance-linked investments, can fluctuate, and this makes them risky for short-term investment.

3. How much risk is the investor prepared to take? The risk of an investment describes the range of possible rates of return that it might provide. An investment in National Savings Certificates is risk free because the investor will know in advance what the return will be and there is no possibility of a capital gain or loss. Investment in the shares of a company means that the investor will not know for certain either what the future dividend payments will be, or whether there will be a capital gain or a capital loss resulting from a change in the share price. The investor will have to decide whether to play safe with low-risk investments or increase potential return by holding a mix of low-risk and more risky investments.

The investor's risk can be reduced by holding a selection of low-risk and higher-risk investments. The combination of several investments is called a *portfolio*, and by ensuring that these are not concentrated in the same sector, e.g. all gold-mining shares, the diversification of the portfolio can decrease the range of possible rates of return. Diversification can be achieved not only by

2. The investor's needs 11

investment in several industrial sectors, but also at the international level by spreading investments between the UK, the US, Europe and the Far East.

It is important that the risk of the investment selected is appropriate to the investor's situation. The aim should be to achieve the highest expected return that is compatible with that level of risk. Money should never be placed in a high-risk investment if the investor cannot afford to lose it if things turn sour.

4. Investment for income or capital growth? If the investor does not currently need extra income, investments should be primarily for capital growth. This is because income received from the investment will be taxed at the investor's marginal rate of income tax while capital gains are free of tax until they are realized by the sale of the investment.

5. What is the investor's tax position? This is a crucial factor in an investor's choice of investment. The two taxes that will affect the selection are income tax and capital gains tax (*see* **7** and **8**).

6. How much responsibility does the investor want to take for the selection of investments? Investors have a wide choice concerning the amount of responsibility that they take for their investments and the amount they can hand over to professional managers.

(*a*) *Retention of maximum control*. The investor decides the composition of an investment portfolio and how much is invested in cash assets, shares and fixed-interest securities.

(*b*) *Retention of partial control*. The investor selects investments like unit trusts or investment trust shares where the day-to-day decisions concerning the selection of particular shares and the reinvestment of income are taken by professional investment managers. However, the investor may decide to switch from one unit trust or investment trust to another specializing in a different world market.

(*c*) *Investment responsibility given to professional managers*. If investors do not want to be involved in investment decisions at all, they can either invest in a general unit trust or investment trust where the fund's managers have responsibility for selecting the

12 Personal investment decisions

investments which they consider have the best prospects worldwide, or they can employ one of the firms of investment advisers to select their investments for them. These services are offered by many stockbrokers, merchant banks, high street banks, insurance brokers, and members of the Financial Intermediaries Managers and Brokers Regulatory Association (FIMBRA) (*see* 8:**17**, 10:**14**).

Taxation and investment

The selection of investments is affected by income tax and capital gains tax.

7. Income tax. All income received from investments, whether interest or dividends, is liable to income tax at the investor's marginal rate. The tax rates are subject to change by the government and, for each tax year which runs from 6 April to the following 5 April, are announced by the Chancellor of the Exchequer in his annual budget speech. The income tax rates for different levels of income for the latest year are shown in Appendix 1.

All dividends and interest payments are paid to investors after the standard rate of income tax has been deducted, except for National Savings investments and payments received from abroad. Dividend and interest payments from which the standard rate of income tax have been deducted are said to be *net* of tax; payments without deduction of tax are paid *gross*. Building society and bank deposit interest are paid after deduction of "composite rate tax". This represents an estimated average tax rate for all investors in interest-earning bank and building society deposits. It is intended to raise the same tax revenue as would have been collected had taxpayers paid the standard rate and non-taxpayers paid nothing. The taxpayer is credited with having paid the standard rate of income tax even though the composite rate of only 25.25 per cent has been deducted.

The following points should be noted:

(*a*) Investors not liable to income tax should not invest in bank and building society deposits which deduct composite rate tax as it cannot be reclaimed from the Inland Revenue. They should invest in National Savings investments or overseas bank deposits which pay interest gross (*see* 3:**7**, 3:**9**). The tax that has been deducted from

2. The investor's needs

the dividends paid on shares and unit trusts can be reclaimed. If gilt-edged stocks are bought through the Post Office from the National Savings Stock Register, their interest is paid gross. If gilts are bought on the Stock Exchange, interest is paid net but can be reclaimed from the Inland Revenue (*see* **6:27**).

(*b*) Investors paying the standard rate of tax should compare net yields. They benefit from the implicit subsidy of bank and building society deposit rates which are credited with the deduction of the standard rate of income tax when only the lower composite rate tax has been deducted.

Any income received gross will have to be declared on the annual tax return and the standard rate will be collected by the Inland Revenue, but the investor has the use of these funds until this time.

(*c*) Investors liable to higher rates of income tax will have to pay the Inland Revenue the extra tax on their income from all of these investments. The extra tax payable will be the difference between that payable at the marginal rate and the amount already collected.

EXAMPLE: Net dividends received: £7,100
The investor's marginal rate of income tax: 50 per cent
Standard rate of income tax: 29 per cent

(*a*) Calculate the gross value of the dividends received.

$$\text{Gross dividends} = \text{Net dividends} \times \frac{1}{1 - \text{Standard rate of income tax}}$$

$$= £7,100 \times \frac{1}{1 - 0.29}$$

$$= £7,100 \times \frac{1}{0.71}$$

$$= £10,000$$

(*b*) Calculate total tax payable.

Total tax payable = Marginal rate of income tax × Gross dividends
= 50 per cent × £10,000 = £5,000

14 Personal investment decisions

(c) Calculate the tax already paid.

Tax already paid = Gross dividends − Net dividends
= £10,000 − £7,100 = £2,900

(d) Calculate higher rate tax payable.

Higher rate tax payable = Total tax payable − Tax already paid
= £5,000 − £2,900 = £2,100

8. Capital gains tax. A capital gain is made when an investment is disposed of at a higher price than that for which it was bought. Part of this gain is taxable at the rate of capital gains tax which is announced by the Chancellor of the Exchequer annually in his budget. The calculation of taxable gains is affected by the indexation allowance, the annual exemption limit and losses on the sale of investments.

(a) *The indexation allowance.* The indexation allowance measures the amount of the gain in value of the investment that can be attributed to the rate of inflation. The rate of inflation is measured by the Retail Price Index (RPI) which is calculated monthly by the Central Statistical Office to show the rate of price increases experienced by the average consumer. The indexation allowance is applied by increasing the acquisition price of the asset in the capital gain calculation as follows:

$$\text{Adjusted purchase price of investment} = \text{Purchase price of investment} \times \frac{\text{RPI at date of disposal}}{\text{RPI at date of purchase (or 31 March if later)}}$$

$$\text{Taxable gain} = \text{Sale price of investment} - \text{Adjusted purchase price of investment}$$

If the date of purchase of the investment was earlier than 6 April 1982 when the allowance was first introduced, the investor can apply the indexation allowance to the higher of the original cost or its value at 31 March 1982. This increase in value due to inflation is then added to the original purchase price of the investment, and the taxable gain is found by subtracting them from the sale price. The

2. The investor's needs

figures for the RPI are published monthly by HMSO in their statistical review *Economic Trends* and reported in the press, e.g. the *Daily Telegraph* publishes a table monthly in their Saturday edition giving the indexation factor for each month since March 1982.

(b) *The annual exemption limit.* The Chancellor announces an annual exemption from capital gains tax in his budget. *See* Appendix 1 for the latest exemption limit.

(c) *Losses on the sale of investments.* If an investment is sold at a loss, then the amount of the loss can be offset against gains in the same tax year, or carried forward to be offset against gains in future years.

EXAMPLE:
Purchase price of investment in February 1983: £25,000
Sale price of investment in July 1986: £50,000
Annual exemption allowance for 1986/87: £6,300
Rate of capital gains tax: 30 per cent

$$\text{Indexation allowance} = \frac{\text{RPI July 1986}}{\text{RPI February 1983}} = \frac{384.7}{327.3} = 1.175$$

Adjusted purchase price = £25,000 × 1.175 = £29,375
Taxable gains = £50,000 − £29,375 = £20,625
Less annual exemption allowance = £20,625 − £6,300 = £14,325
Tax payable = 30 per cent × £14,325 = £4,297

The following investments are exempt from capital gains tax:

(a) Transfers between husband and wife.
(b) Life assurance policies.
(c) National Savings Certificates, National Savings Bonds.
(d) Gilt-edged securities.
(e) UK corporate bonds acquired after 13 March 1984.
(f) The principal private residence.
(g) Private cars and other wasting assets that deteriorate over time.
(h) Personal belongings that are worth less than £3,000 at the time of acquisition and disposal.

Future capital gains tax liabilities can be avoided or reduced by ensuring that the annual exemption allowance is used. Unused allowances cannot be carried forward to future tax years. The realization of capital gains for this purpose is sometimes called *bed and breakfasting*. It requires that the investor sells some of the investments showing gains at the end of a Stock Exchange account and instructs the broker to buy them back at the beginning of the next account. Reduced commission is usually charged for this type of transaction. Losses can also be realized in this way to offset against other gains made by the investor.

3
Investment in cash assets

Selecting cash investments

1. Important considerations. Investors must decide how much of their investments need to be of a type that is safe and readily accessible. Their decision should be influenced by three considerations:

(*a*) Their anticipated expenditure needs plus a little extra for the unexpected ones!

(*b*) The rate of return obtainable from cash assets compared with alternative investments. If share or bond prices are expected to rise strongly, they should economize on the amount of their investments held in liquid form. If security prices are expected to fall, they should increase their holdings of cash assets.

(*c*) The current rate of inflation and the expected rate over the next twelve months. If the annual rate of inflation exceeds the rate of interest obtainable from cash investments, their real rate of return is negative and investors should economize on cash investments and look for index-linked alternatives. The 1980s have so far been a decade of positive real interest rates, so they will not incur losses due to the falling purchasing power of money by holding cash investments.

2. Taxation and cash investments. The selection of cash investments must not be based upon a comparison of their gross yields, but the investor's net yields. An investment's net of tax yield can be calculated by multiplying its gross yield by one (1) minus the marginal rate of income tax.

18 Personal investment decisions

EXAMPLE:
Gross yield = 11.5 per cent
The investor's marginal rate of income tax = 29 per cent
The investor's net yield = 11.5 per cent × (1 − 0.29)
= 11.5 per cent × 0.71
= 8.165 per cent

To calculate the net yield for an investor paying a higher than standard rate of income tax on an investment paying interest net of composite rate tax (CRT), it is necessary to calculate the gross yield first.

EXAMPLE:
Quoted rate net of CRT = 6.5 per cent
The investor's marginal rate of income tax = 60 per cent

(*a*) Calculate the gross yield on the investment. Remember that, although CRT is less than the standard rate of income tax, when calculating the gross yield it is assumed that the standard rate has been deducted.

$$\text{Gross yield} = \text{Net yield} \times \frac{1}{(1 - \text{Standard rate of income tax})}$$

$$= 6.5 \text{ per cent} \times \frac{1}{1 - 0.29}$$

$$= 9.155 \text{ per cent}$$

(*b*) Calculate the investor's net yield on the investment.

$$\text{Net yield} = \text{Gross yield} \times (1 - \text{Investor's marginal rate of income tax})$$

$$= 9.155 \text{ per cent} \times (1 - 0.6)$$

$$= 3.662 \text{ per cent}$$

3. Published information on net yields. There are several publications which regularly compare the net of tax yields on cash investments for different marginal rate taxpayers.

(*a*) Weekly publications. The Saturday editions of the *Financial Times*, *The Times*, *Daily Telegraph* and *Guardian*; *Investors' Chronicle*.

(b) Monthly publications. *Money Management*, *Planned Savings*, *What Investment*, *Money Magazine*, *Money Observer*.

The investor should look for these publications and study their tables carefully. It should be noted that some of the rates change frequently. Table 3A illustrates the range of cash investments available. This table compares the net of tax returns for 0, 29, 40, 50 and 60 per cent taxpayers and will be used as the basis for comparison between the alternative cash investments reviewed in **4–10**.

Forms of cash investment

4. Bank deposits. There are four main types of bank deposits available with high street and City banks:

(a) Current accounts: provide instant access but earn no interest.

(b) Deposit accounts: require seven days' notice of withdrawal but have no minimum investment requirement. The interest is paid net of composite rate tax (CRT) which cannot be reclaimed from the Inland Revenue by non-taxpayers. Hence the net yields for non-taxpayers and standard rate taxpayers shown in Table 3A are the same.

(c) High-interest cheque accounts: provide instant access and a cheque book, but require a minimum investment. The interest is paid net of CRT. Details of the accounts that are available and their minimum investment are found near the back of the *Financial Times* headed 'Insurance, Overseas and Money Funds'. Under the headings 'Money Market Trust Funds' and 'Money Market Bank Accounts', the interest rates on a large number of alternative accounts are shown.

(d) Term deposits: although the interest payable on deposit accounts and high-interest cheque accounts is variable at short notice, the rate of interest on a term deposit is fixed for the period of the deposit. While this may be an advantage at a time of falling interest rates, it will already be reflected in the interest rate offered. The terms available are 1, 3, 6 and 12 months, and money cannot be withdrawn during the period of the deposit. Interest is paid net of CRT.

20 Personal investment decisions

Table 3A Available interest rates (10 October 1986). Reproduced by kind permission of the Investors Chronicle

Investment type		0%	Percentage return for taxpayers at 29%	40%	50%	60%	Amount invested min.	max.	Withdrawal (days)
Clearing bank (a) deposit account		4.30	4.30	3.63	3.03	2.42	None	None	7
term deposit 1 month		6.50	6.50	5.49	4.58	3.66	£2,500	£24,999	30
3 months	(b)	7.31	7.31	6.18	5.15	4.12	,,	,,	90
6 months		7.50	7.50	6.34	5.28	4.23	,,	,,	180
12 months		7.69	7.69	6.50	5.42	4.33	,,	,,	365
Building societies									
ordinary shares (c)		5.25	5.25	4.44	3.70	2.96	£1	£250,000	—
high interest access account (d)	(b)	7.25	7.25	6.13	5.11	4.08	£500	No max.	—
90 days' notice or penalty (c)		8.00	8.00	6.76	5.63	4.51	£500	£250,000	90
National Savings Bank									
ordinary account (e)		6.0/3.0	4.3/2.1	3.6/1.8	3.0/1.5	2.4/1.2	£1	£10,000	—
investment account		10.75	7.63	6.45	5.38	4.30	£5	£100,000	31
income bonds		11.25	7.99	6.75	5.62	4.50	£2,000	£100,000	90(f)
deposit bonds		11.25	7.99	6.75	5.62	4.50	£100	£100,000	90(f)
indexed-income bonds		8.00	5.68	4.80	4.00	3.20	£5,000	£100,000	90(f)
National Savings Certificates (f) (g)									
31st issue cashed in after: 1 year		5.76	5.76	5.76	5.76	5.76	£25	£10,000	8
2 years		6.21	6.21	6.21	6.21	6.21	,,	,,	,,
3 years		6.74	6.74	6.74	6.74	6.74	,,	,,	,,
4 years		7.28	7.28	7.28	7.28	7.28	,,	,,	,,
5 years		7.85	7.85	7.85	7.85	7.85	,,	,,	,,
General extension rate		8.01	8.01	8.01	8.01	8.01	—	—	—

3. Investment in cash assets

Index-linked savings certificates (4th issue) (f) (g)							
real return after: 1 year	3.00	3.00	3.00	3.00	3.00	£25	£5,000	8
2 years	3.25	3.25	3.25	3.25	3.25	,,	,,	,,
3 years	3.50	3.50	3.50	3.50	3.50	,,	,,	,,
4 years	4.50	4.50	4.50	4.50	4.50	,,	,,	,,
5 years	6.00	6.00	6.00	6.00	6.00	,,	,,	,,
compound real return over 5 years in addition to inflation-proofing	4.04	4.04	4.04	4.04	4.04	,,	,,	,,
TSB deposit account	4.25	4.25	3.59	2.99	2.39	£1	None	7
premium account } (b)	7.00	7.00	5.92	4.93	3.94	£1,000	,,	28
term deposits	6.00	6.00	5.07	4.23	3.38	£1,000	,,	365
Finance house fixed notice deposits (b)	6.35–6.73	6.35–6.73	5.37–5.69	4.47–4.74	3.58–3.79	£500	£25,000	30–365
Money funds (b)								
Allied Arab Bank	7.57	7.57	6.40	5.33	4.26	£5,000	£100,000	—
Citibank (Money Market)	7.00	7.00	5.92	4.93	3.94	£2,000	£3000,000	—
M&G Kleinwort Benson (h.i.c.a.)	6.73	6.73	5.69	4.74	3.79	£2,500	No max.	—
Phillips & Drew (h.i.c.a.)	7.00	7.00	5.92	4.93	3.94	£2,500	No. max.	—
Charterhouse Japhet (sterling a/c)	7.10	7.10	6.00	5.00	4.00	£2,500	No max.	7
British government stocks (net redemption yield)								
Treasury 3% 1989	8.56	7.62	7.26	6.93	6.61	None	None	—
Treasury 13% 1990	11.33	7.66	6.27	5.01	3.74	,,	,,	—
Gas 3% 1990/95	7.06	6.03	5.63	5.28	4.92	,,	,,	—
Treasury 14% 1996	11.33	7.64	6.24	4.95	3.67	,,	,,	—

(a) Lloyds Bank. (b) Adjusted for 25.25% composite rate tax, credited as net of basic rate tax. No tax credit to nil taxpayers. (c) Abbey National. (d) Woolwich (Prime Account) £5,000–£10,000 7.5%, £10,000+ 7.8%. (e) First £70 interest tax free; 6% paid on balance kept at £500 or more for each calendar month if £100 min for whole of 1986. (f) Penalties for withdrawal in first year. (g) Tax free. (h) First year return – then adjusted for inflation and guaranteed for 10 years.

INVESTORS CHRONICLE 10 October 1986

22 Personal investment decisions

5. Building society deposits. There are a very large number of building societies offering a wide choice of types of deposit facilities, all of which pay interest after the deduction of CRT. Ordinary share accounts provide withdrawal facilities upon demand and require a minimum investment of only £1. To earn higher rates of interest, investors must either invest larger sums (similar to the banks' high-interest accounts and money funds) or accept a minimum period of notice before withdrawal, e.g. 28 or 90 days.

To compare the differences in rates offered by alternative building societies, the investor should examine the table of building society investment rates published each Saturday in the *Financial Times*. The monthly magazines *Money Management*, *Planned Savings*, *What Investment*, *Money Magazine* and *Money Observer* also include similar tables.

6. Finance house deposits. Finance houses are the companies that provide the credit for hire-purchase contracts. Most of them are subsidiaries of commercial banks and hence financially sound. They are also required by the Banking Act 1979 to register with the Bank of England and this provides some additional protection to investors. Deposits are usually for a fixed term of 1, 3, 6 or 12 months, and the rates obtainable, net of CRT, are higher than those from comparable term deposits with banks.

7. National Savings Bank investments. There are a wide range of National Savings investments available from the Post Office, each targeted at a different type of investor. They all provide excellent value for the investor for whom they are intended.

(*a*) *National Savings Bank ordinary account.* Interest is paid gross at 6 per cent per annum provided the balance in the account exceeds £500 for a complete calendar year, otherwise the rate is 3 per cent per annum. The first £70 per annum is tax-free for all taxpayers. Certain banking services are also provided.

(*b*) *National Savings Bank investment account.* This account pays interest gross at a much higher rate than the ordinary account, but 31 days' notice of withdrawal is required. The minimum investment is only £5, so this is the ideal 'deposit account' for the non-taxpayer.

(*c*) *Income bonds.* These bonds pay a monthly income gross at a

3. Investment in cash assets

rate of ½ per cent higher than is obtainable from the investment account. The minimum investment is £2,000 and three months' notice of withdrawal is required. The high interest rate and the payment of interest gross makes this an ideal investment for non-taxpayers seeking a high risk-free income. The rate of interest can be varied by the National Savings Bank after six weeks' notice.

(*d*) *Deposit bonds.* These bonds earn the same gross interest rate as income bonds, but the interest is added to the value of the investment rather than distributed as income. The minimum investment is only £100 but the same three months' notice of withdrawal is required. This is an ideal investment for non-taxpayers seeking to accumulate a high risk-free rate of return.

(*e*) *Indexed-income bonds.* If the investor is concerned about the effect of inflation upon the rate of return on cash investments, the indexed-income bond is one alternative which should be considered. (Others are index-linked savings certificates (*see* (*g*) below) and index-linked gilts (*see* 6:**22**). These bonds provide an index-linked income payable monthly for ten years. The interest is paid gross and is initially 8 per cent. Each year, the annual interest payments are increased by the rate of inflation in the previous year. However, the investor's capital, which can be withdrawn on three months' notice, is not protected by index linking.

(*f*) *National Savings Certificates.* Like deposit bonds, the interest earned is not paid out, but is accumulated in the value of the certificate. The rate quoted applies if the certificates are held for five years. If they are surrendered within the five-year period, a lower rate of return is earned, as shown in Table 3A. If they are held for more than five years, they qualify for the 'General extension rate' also shown in Table 3A. The notice of withdrawal required is only eight days. The minimum investment is £25 and the maximum per issue is £10,000. A new issue is brought out when the National Savings Bank considers the rates offered by the current issue are out of line with other interest rates available to investors.

One of the main features of National Savings Certificates is that the rate of return quoted is tax free. This makes them an extremely attractive investment for investors liable to pay the higher rates of income tax.

EXAMPLE: The 31st issue of National Savings Certificates yields

7.85 per cent net for all taxpayers if they hold them for five years. Thus for 60 per cent taxpayers this is equivalent to a gross rate of return of

$$7.85 \text{ per cent} \times \frac{1}{1 - 0.6}$$

$$= 7.85 \text{ per cent} \times \frac{1}{0.4}$$

$$= 19.625 \text{ per cent}$$

This calculation is known as the *grossed-up net redemption yield*. It shows the gross rate of return that an investor must seek to equal the same net rate of return. The formula for its calculation is:

$$\frac{\text{Grossed-up net}}{\text{redemption yield}} = \frac{\text{Net yield to}}{\text{redemption}} \times \frac{1}{1 - \text{Investor's marginal rate of income tax}}$$

(g) *Index-linked savings certificates.* The index-linked savings certificate rises in value each year in line with the Retail Price Index plus a rate of interest that increases for each year that they are held up to the fifth year. The certificates do not benefit from the index linking until they have been held for one year. They are sometimes referred to as 'granny bonds' as originally they were only available to retired people., As with ordinary National Savings Certificates, the minimum investment per issue is £25 and the maximum £5,000. The notice of withdrawal required is eight days. Their income which is not distributed is also tax free. Their relative attraction compared to the ordinary National Savings Certificate therefore depends upon the rate of inflation.

(h) *The yearly plan.* This is a monthly savings scheme which allows an investor to invest between £20 and £200 a month at a rate of interest that is fixed for a five-year-period at the start of the savings contract. The rate of return is reduced if investors either stop their monthly payments or withdraw their savings. The rate of interest earned is not distributed but, as it is tax free, this is a very attractive investment for investors paying the higher rates of income tax.

8. Foreign currency deposits. Investors may want to open a bank

3. Investment in cash assets

account in a foreign currency to protect their savings against a fall in the value of sterling. This can be arranged with the high street banks but, as with high-interest cheque accounts, a minimum deposit is required. Interest is paid after deduction of CRT. A cheque book foreign currency high-interest account with no charges and denominated in either US dollars, Deutschmarks, Swiss francs or Japanese yen is offered by Charterhouse Japhet in London. Details can be found in the list of 'Money Market Bank Accounts' at the back of the *Financial Times* which was referred to in 4(*c*).

9. Offshore bank deposits. If investors are non-taxpayers they can also avoid composite rate tax by opening a bank account offshore where interest is paid gross. Any of the high street banks can arrange for an account to be opened for an investor in one of their branches either in the Channel Islands or the Isle of Man. These accounts may be denominated in sterling or a foreign currency.

10. Offshore currency funds. Many high street and merchant banks also operate currency funds offshore in the Channel Islands. These resemble unit trusts in that the investor purchases units (shares) in a fund which invests in short term bank deposits and very liquid assets (*see* Chapter 8). There is usually no bid offer spread for the units and very low management charges. The funds provide a range of foreign currencies and sterling, and switches between currencies can usually be arranged at money market rates, i.e. on the same terms available to banks. Rothschild Asset Management's 'Old Court Currency Fund' offers deposit facilities in no less than fifteen different currencies and a managed currency fund. For details of the banks offering this service, study the page at the back of the *Financial Times* headed 'Insurance, Overseas, and Money Funds'.

One word of caution is necessary. There are two types of currency funds available, those with distributor status and those without. Since January 1984, the Inland Revenue has applied income tax to both the income and capital gains made from investments offshore unless the fund applies to it for distributor status. To qualify, the fund must distribute at least 85 per cent of the income from investments that it receives. Investors in funds which have qualified for distributor status pay income tax on their dividends or interest payments, but capital gains tax on any increase in the value of their units when they sell them. The capital gains are eligible for the annual exemption limit and indexation allowance. Thus most UK residents are likely to pay less tax if they buy units in a fund with distributor status. Some banks like Rothschilds and Lazard Brothers and Co offer both funds with distributor status and funds which accumulate interest in the price of the unit. These accumulator units will be attractive to non-residents and wealthy higher-rate taxpayers resident in the UK who do not intend to sell their units until they have retired when their marginal rate of income tax will fall and they may even move abroad.

11. British government stocks. While these are listed in the 'Available interest rates' shown in table 3A, they will not be discussed until Chapter 6 as they are not liquid investments. The reason for this is that the price of these securities will fall if interest rates rise, inflicting a capital loss on investors if they have to sell immediately afterwards and before redemption.

A review of cash investments

12. The differences between individual cash investments. The investments described above vary in six ways other than the rate of interest payable.

(*a*) The amount of notice required for withdrawal in cash. Instant withdrawal is available from ordinary and high-interest cheque accounts with banks, the ordinary share account and high-interest access accounts with building societies, and the ordinary account of the National Savings bank. Three months' notice of more is required on several National Savings investments and term deposits with banks, finance houses and building societies.

(*b*) Whether or not a penalty is imposed for early withdrawal of the investment. If National Savings Certificates are surrendered in the first five years, a lower rate of return is earned.

(*c*) Whether or not the investments are protected against the effects of inflation upon the purchasing power of the investment.

(*d*) The frequency of payment of interest. This is not shown in Table 3A taken from the *Investors Chronicle* but is shown in other

3. Investment in cash assets

tables such as the one produced weekly in the Saturday edition of the *Financial Times*. If interest is paid monthly, the rate of return is higher than if the same annual rate is paid quarterly, every six months, or annually. This is because the interest paid can be added to the capital invested and so also earn interest.

(*e*) The income tax rules relating to the investment. Investors should examine Table 3A and similar up-to-date tables in the financial press to work out which investments offer them the highest net of tax rate of return.

(*f*) Whether or not the interest rate is fixed or variable. The interest rate is fixed on term deposits and the National Savings Certificates, the yearly plan and indexed-income bonds. In all other cases, it is variable after a period of notice.

Progress test 3

1. How much of an investor's assets should be kept in liquid form? (**1**)
2. How is the net yield from an investment calculated? (**2**)
3. If you are given the net yield from an investment, how do you calculate the equivalent gross yield? (**2**)
4. Where would you look to find the comparative rates of return available from:
   (*a*) cash investments?
   (*b*) different building societies? (**3**)
5. What types of fund apply for distributor status? To whom is this important and why? (**10**)
6. What cash investments are suitable for an investor worried by:
   (*a*) a rise in the rate of inflation?
   (*b*) a possible fall in interest rates? (**4–11**)

Part two
Direct investment in stocks and shares

In this second part of the book, we shall examine the opportunities for direct investment in securities like stocks and shares, leaving to Part three the alternative of investment in professionally managed portfolios such as unit trusts, investment trusts and insurance-linked investments.

We start this part with an analysis of investment opportunities on the stock market and how this type of investment can be undertaken. We shall then look at the methods available to help investors choose the securities in which to invest. The last two chapters will examine fixed-interest investments and the management of risk by the use of the traded option and financial futures market.

4
Investment in shares

Stocks and shares – the different types

1. Stocks. A stock in the UK is a security issued by the government, a local authority or company usually in return for a loan. The certificate specifies the interest rate payable and the date of redemption. (Some confusion occasionally arises because both in the US and the UK the name is sometimes applied to company shares.) The main types of stocks available are as follows:

(*a*) British government or gilt-edged stocks: certificates issued by or underwritten by the UK government in return for loans (*see* Chapter 6).

(*b*) Local authority bonds (*See* 6:**31, 32**).

(*c*) Company debentures and loan stocks: loan certificates which may be either secured against specific company assets, e.g. land and buildings (called *mortgage debentures* or *fixed debentures*) or against the general assets of the business (called *floating debentures*) or unsecured (called *simple* or *naked debentures*). The company must appoint a trustee to the issue to safeguard the investors' interests ensuring that the company acts in accordance with the trust deed of the issue, e.g. the trust deed may limit further borrowing by the company unless the debentures are redeemed (*see* 6:**34**).

(*d*) Convertible loan stock: loan certificates convertible into ordinary shares on terms and at times specified when issued (*see* 6:**37**).

(*e*) Bulldog bonds: loan certificates issued by foreign governments and international agencies (*see* 6:**4**).

2. Shares. A share is a security issued by a company conferring

32 Stocks and shares

part-ownership on the holder. There are several types of shares that may be issued by companies:

(*a*) *Ordinary shares.* Investors in these certificates are entitled to share the profits of the company after all prior charges arising from the expenses of the business and the payment of interest have been met. The ordinary share has a nominal value, usually 5p, 10p, 12.5p, 25p, 50p or £1, and when this is multiplied by the number of shares issued, this gives the amount of nominal share capital in the balance sheet of the company's accounts. This is the equity capital of the company and hence shares are sometimes called *equities*. The market price of a share is separate from its nominal value, being determined by the relationship between the demand for and supply of the company's shares on the Stock Exchange. Dividends are declared and paid usually twice a year and are received by shareholders net of the standard rate of income tax.

(*b*) *'A' ordinary shares.* These are share certificates whose holders are entitled to the same dividends as ordinary shareholders but are not entitled to vote at shareholder meetings. The issue of this type of security has now ceased, and those still outstanding are gradually being given the same rights as ordinary shares.

(*c*) *Preference shares.* This type of security pays a fixed dividend expressed as a percentage of its nominal value, e.g. ICI 5 per cent. Preference shares with a nominal value of £1 pay net dividends equivalent to 5 pence gross per share each year in two instalments. Holders of this type of security rank before ordinary shareholders but after the providers of loans for the repayment of their capital in the event of the liquidation of the company. Special types are:

   (*i*) Cumulative preference shares – if a dividend is passed in any year, the investor will be compensated as soon as profitability is restored and before the ordinary shareholder receives a dividend.

   (*ii*) Participating preference shares – entitled to a share in the profits of the company as well as the fixed annual dividends.

   (*iii*) Convertible preference shares – convertible into ordinary shares during a time period and at a price specified at issue.

(*d*) *Warrants.* These are issued by companies at the time of an issue of shares or loan stock as a sweetener to make their purchase more attractive. A warrant confers on the holder the right to purchase ordinary shares from the company at a fixed price within a specified time period (*see* 7:**1**).

4. Investment in shares

Buying stocks and shares on the Stock Exchange

3. The system before the 'big bang'. Before 27 October 1986, the mechanism for buying or selling stocks or shares on the Stock Exchange involved the following stages:

(*a*) Investors contacted a stockbroker or bank to give their purchase or sale instructions. Commercial banks would act only as an intermediary in this process, passing on the instructions to a stockbroker, but the small investor frequently felt this way more convenient.

(*b*) Instructions were in the form of either to buy or sell 'at best' (i.e. the best price obtainable at the time the instruction was executed), or a limit was placed on the price (i.e. a maximum price for a purchase, a minimum for a sale).

(*c*) The broker then acted as an agent for the investor and carried out the investor's instructions by dealing on the floor of the Stock Exchange with one of the *jobbers*. Jobbers acted as wholesalers dealing with brokers (they would not deal directly with the public). The broker would ask the jobber for the price of the share without indicating whether his client was a buyer or a seller. The jobber would give two prices, the higher being the price at which he was prepared to sell and the lower that at which he was prepared to buy. The difference was called the 'jobber's turn'. Having obtained quotations from the different jobbers making a market in the share for which he had received instructions, the broker returned to the one making the most favourable quotation for his client and made the deal.

EXAMPLE: Investor wants to deal in ICI ordinary shares.

Jobber A quotes 947–951
Jobber B quotes 948–952
Jobber C quotes 946–950

If the investor wants to buy, the broker will deal with Jobber C at 950.
If the investor wants to sell, the broker will deal with Jobber B at 948.

The system where the broker and jobber fulfilled separate roles was called the 'separation of capacity'. Its advantage was that the broker always acted as an agent on behalf of the investor, never as a principal. This meant there was no conflict of interest, as would occur if the broker was selling shares already in his possession.

(*d*) The broker charged his client commission for the transaction based upon a minumum scale laid down by the Stock Exchange. There were separate scales for gilts and company shares, and slightly higher rates if the commission was shared with a bank introducing the business. Brokers also operated a minimum charge which was mostly in the range £7–20 with the cheapest terms offered by the country brokers and the highest by the larger City brokers. The charges paid by the investor included VAT on the commission and 1 per cent stamp duty on the purchase of shares. (Stamp duty was reduced to 0.5 per cent from 27 October 1986.)

4. Criticisms of the old dealing system. An investigation into the operation of the Stock Exchange by the Office of Fair Trading in 1983 found that many of its rules contravened the provisions of the Restrictive Practices Act 1976 as they had the effect of reducing the level of competition there. The three main criticisms were:

(*a*) The 'separation of capacity' whereby both brokers and jobbers acted in a 'single capacity' and kept to their distinct roles.

(*b*) The fixed commission system which prevented brokers competing on price.

(*c*) The restrictions on membership of the Stock Exchange that prevented outsiders from having more than a 29.9 per cent interest in any one member firm.

The government was also worried about the ability of London to retain its position as one of the world's leading financial centres because:

(*d*) The rules of the Stock Exchange permitted only individuals to become members. This had the effect of denying membership to the big US and Japanese broking firms which all had corporate status. Since they were excluded, it gave them the incentive to deal off the Stock Exchange in the stocks and shares required by their own investing clients. As they were not members of the Stock Exchange, they were not bound by the minimum commission system

4. Investment in shares

and could therefore offer a more competitive price. Hence, 'parallel markets' to the Stock Exchange were developing.

(e) A secondary market in British shares had already developed in New York by the use of American Depository Receipts. (An ADR is a bearer certificate entitling the holder to ownership of shares deposited for safekeeping with a bank in the US.) Since fixed commissions had been abolished in New York in 1975, it was cheaper for institutions to deal in UK securities in New York than in London. The turnover of the shares in the largest UK companies was therefore sometimes bigger on the New York Stock Exchange than the London Stock Exchange.

(f) The increase in the size of bargains as institutional purchases and sales became much greater than those of private investors placed a strain upon the capital resources of jobbing firms. The advent of new technology in the dealing rooms of Stock Exchange participants also required that jobbing and broking firms had better access to capital than was possible with the partnership system which was obliged by law to distribute most of the profits each year. The result was a decline in the number of both broking and jobbing firms, which was particularly serious among the latter as having only two or three firms making a market in a company's shares reduced the level of competition.

(g) The Stock Exchange had failed to respond to the challenge of the growth of the Eurobond market. This market consists of the issue, resale and purchase of long-dated loan stocks with a fixed or floating rate of interest. The bonds are issued by sovereign governments, international organizations and multinational companies and can be denominated in any of the world's major currencies (*see* 6:**6**). Since the Stock Exchange did not participate in the development of this market, trading in these securities does not take place there but between the world's international banks, most of which have a branch in London. London has become the world centre of the Eurobond market and turnover in 1985 was some $2,250 billion compared with some $475 billion for equities and gilts on the London Stock Exchange.

5. The need for change. The stock market is particularly important to the government as the volume of gilts traded exceeds that of other securities. To ensure that the Stock Exchange is able to continue as a market place for government securities, it was important that the market participants should be adequately capitalized.

For all of these reasons, an agreement was reached between the Stock Exchange Council and the government in June 1983 that reforms would be introduced to allow wider participation in the Stock Exchange and that minimum scales of commission would be removed by December 1986 in return for exemption from the restrictive practices legislation.

6. Changes prior to the 'big bang'. In the period up to the 'big bang' in October 1986, four important changes took place in the organization of the Stock Exchange.

(*a*) With effect from March 1986 the Stock Exchange rule restricting the outside ownership of member firms to 29.9 per cent was removed, and the first outsider to take advantage of this change was the Union Bank of Switzerland which increased its stake in Phillips and Drew, Stockbrokers, to 100 per cent.

(*b*) Also from March 1986, the Stock Exchange started to admit corporate members. The first outsiders to take advantage of this rule change were the US broking firm Merrill Lynch and the Japanese investment house Nomura.

(*c*) A whole series of mergers and takeovers took place as firms combined to gain financial strength to be able to compete effectively and provide a whole range of financial services after the 'big bang'. Some examples of these changes were:

(*i*) Barclays Bank + de Zoete & Bevan (stockbrokers) + Wedd Durlacher Mordaunt (jobbers) + Barclays Merchant Bank = Barclays de Zoete Wedd.

(*ii*) National Westminster Bank + Fielding Newson Smith (stockbrokers) + Bisgood Bishop (jobbers) + County Bank (merchant bank) = National Westminster Investment Bank.

(*iii*) Kleinwort Benson (merchant bank) + Grieveson Grant (stockbrokers) + Charlesworth & Co (jobbers) = Kleinwort Grieveson.

(*iv*) Citicorp (US bank) + Vickers da Costa (stockbrokers) + Scrimgeour Kemp-Gee (stockbrokers) + Seccombe Marshall & Campion (discount house) = Citicorp Investment Bank.

4. Investment in shares

(*d*) Faced by the continuing threat that the US and other foreign banks and brokers making a market in UK shares would bring about a decline in its importance, in September 1986 the London Stock Exchange merged with the opposition – the International Securities Regulatory Organisation (ISRO). This body represented all the foreign security houses making a market in international equities and Eurobonds. The Stock Exchange was renamed the International Stock Exchange of the United Kingdom and the Republic of Ireland. It is responsible for making markets in gilt-edged stocks, domestic and international equities, and traded options, but not Eurobonds (*see* 13:3).

7. The 'big bang' changes. The 'big bang' on 27 October 1986 saw the introduction of three main changes in the way the Stock Exchange operated.

(*a*) The abolition of single capacity. The distinction between brokers and jobbers where each had a specialist role to play ended. In its place, there are now three types of Stock Exchange participants:

(*i*) Broker dealers who are market makers. These firms undertake to quote a two-way price at which they are prepared to buy and sell specified shares. Members of the public can deal directly with these brokers. Hence they combine both the original jobbing and broking functions and are said to be acting in a 'dual capacity'.

(*ii*) Broker dealers who are not market makers. These can deal for clients either with the market makers as an agent, or on their own account as a principal. The interests of their clients are protected by the requirement that the broker dealer always follows the 'best execution rule'. This rule permits the broker to act as a principal only when the price given their clients is as good as or better than the best price obtainable from a market maker.

(*iii*) Agency brokers. These firms continue to operate in a single capacity as an agent on behalf of their client and obtain the best price available for them from the market makers.

(*b*) The abolition of fixed-scale commissions. Since October 1986, the commissions charged by brokers have been open to negotiation and competition. As in the US when fixed commissions were abolished in 1975, big institutions are benefiting from large

38 Stocks and shares

savings. However, even the small investor is paying less as a result of the high level of competition between the market participants and the new technology which is lowering administration costs.

(c) The introduction of the Stock Exchange Automated Quotations System (SEAQ). This is an electronic price display and recording system covering some 3,500 securities and gilts. The equities are divided into four classes of shares:

(i) Alpha stocks. These are the most actively traded equities in which a continuous two-way price is quoted by the market makers and displayed on the screen. By turning to the relevant page on the screen for a particular share, a broker can see the prices quoted by each of the market makers, the best buy and sell prices displayed separately in a yellow band, the volume of trade during the day, and the price at which the latest transaction took place. All deals in these stocks must be reported promptly so that the running total and latest price data can be updated.

(ii) Beta stocks. These shares are traded less frequently than alpha stocks but continuous two-way prices are displayed by their market makers. The best buy and sell prices are displayed in a yellow band, but information on volume and latest trades are not published immediately.

(iii) Gamma stocks. These are less actively traded stocks, and while two-way quotes are shown, they can be indicative rather than firm prices.

(iv) Delta stocks. No prices are given on SEAQ for these least actively traded shares, only the names and telephone numbers of their market makers.

The SEAQ Equity Service provides three levels of service for its users.

(i) Level 1 – for the investment community which are not members of the Stock Exchange. This displays the best bid and offer prices for each security. In the case of alpha stocks, it also gives the number of trades reported in the last five minutes and the total volume of trades for the day.

(ii) Level 2 – for members of the Stock Exchange. This service shows all the competing quotes of market makers, the best quotes in a yellow band in the case of alpha and beta stocks, and volume and latest price information for alpha stocks.

4. Investment in shares 39

(*iii*) Level 3 – for market makers. This service provides the same information as level 2, but permits market makers to input the prices at which they are prepared to buy and sell, and the volume for which these quotes are binding. After each deal, the market makers must enter on their terminals the details of each trade so that the volume and latest price data can be updated.

8. The system after the 'big bang'. Purchases or sales of shares by investors take place in the following way. The investor contacts any of the three types of broker to obtain details of the best price available. The broker turns to the appropriate page of the viewdata system and gives the investor details of the best price quoted. If the investor decides to deal, the broker then contacts the market maker offering the best price on the screen and deals at that price. The broking firm may only deal on its own account as a principal in the transaction if its price is at least as good as the best market maker's price.

The investor is therefore protected against any impropriety by the 'best execution rule' and fixed quotes by market makers, details of which are widely available. Additional protection is provided by the requirement that the time at which all deals take place must be recorded and reported to the Stock Exchange. This allows a complaint by an investor to be investigated by the Stock Exchange. Records of all transactions will be kept by the Stock Exchange for five years.

SEAQ also provides a gilts service covering government stocks, bulldogs and corporate loan stocks. This service provides two displays. The first shows the two-way prices of the market makers in the gilts market. The second is an alphabetically listed index of securities against which are shown the names of market makers. This service is available to both members and non-members of the Stock Exchange.

Details of international equities are shown on SEAQ International. Market makers key in the bid and offer prices at which they are prepared to deal and this data is transmitted world-wide to participants.

9. Planned development of SEAQ. Two important developments of SEAQ that are currently being planned are:

(*a*) SEAQ Automatic Execution Facility (SAEF). This system will allow the broker dealer to execute his client's deal automatically with the market maker with the best price without having to telephone the market maker. This will apply to small transactions, leaving brokers and market makers more time to concentrate upon larger or more complex ones.

(*b*) Block Order Exposure (BLOX). A system is being devised for large purchase or sale orders to be displayed to institutions. This will give easier access for smaller brokers who are not market makers to larger trades and provide a wider audience for infrequently traded stocks which should improve their liquidity.

10. The gilt market after the 'big bang'. The main change in the gilt market has been the increased number of market makers. There are three participants in the gilt market.

(*a*) *Market makers* who provide continuous two-way prices which are displayed on the SEAQ gilts service. In return, they enjoy the same privileges as gilt-edged jobbers under the old system i.e. ability to borrow on favourable terms from the Bank of England and favourable tax treatment.

(*b*) *Inter-dealer brokers* who trade only with market makers and keep secret the identity of their clients. Their role is to redistribute risk by acting as an agent for a market maker who wishes to sell or increase particular holdings to alter their risk exposure.

(*c*) *Stock Exchange money brokers* who provide liquidity to the gilt market by lending funds to market makers when their holdings of gilts build up and they are short of cash, and invest their spare cash when they run down their holdings of gilts.

11. The settlement system on the Stock Exchange. Payment or settlement of the account with the broker is for cash in the case of British government and local authority stocks, but for company stocks and shares there is a special 'settlement day' or 'account day' following each Stock Exchange account. The year is divided into some 24 account periods, mostly of two weeks, starting on a Monday and ending on the Friday. The current dates are given in the *Financial Times* at the top of the page giving the market report on the London Stock Exchange. Account day is always the second

4. Investment in shares

Monday after the end of the account. *Same account trading* is the name given to the transaction that is undertaken and reversed within the same account period. Investors that expect share prices to rise during the account may purchase shares at the beginning of the account hoping to sell them at the end and show a profit. Conversely, investors expecting share prices to fall can sell shares at the beginning of the account in the expectation of buying them back cheaper later in the account. This type of trading benefits from the payment of only one commission but, since the 1986 budget, does not avoid stamp duty.

The period of the Stock Exchange account can be extended by two days by investors dealing in 'new time' by opening their position on the last Thursday or Friday of an account. By specifying that the transaction takes place in new time, it is treated as if it had occurred in the following week but, for this privilege, the price offered is less competitive.

12. The system for the transfer of ownership of shares. When the investor's shares are sold by brokers through market makers, the identities of the new investors may still be unknown. Before the Stock Transfer Act 1963 which lays down the current procedures, the process of the transfer of ownership was long and laborious. It required that both the seller and buyer sign a stock transfer form and both their signatures had to be witnessed. (This procedure still applies to new issues of partly paid shares.)

Since the 1963 Act, only the seller (transferor) needs to sign a stock transfer form which gives all the relevant details of the number and type of security. The transferor then returns this to the broker with the security certificates. In the case of gilts and shares where the new owner is known, e.g. a gift, the broker then completes the stock transfer form by writing in the name and address of the new owners and sending it with the certificate to the registrar. (In the case of gilts, the registrar is the Bank of England.) The registrar will then alter the records of security owners and issue another certificate to the new owner. If there is more than one new owner, the selling broker will complete a 'broker's transfer form' for each purchase instead of the relevant part of the stock transfer form and forward these to the registrar.

To try to simplify the transfer process further for company

securities, the Stock Exchange introduced in 1979 a system called TALISMAN (**T**ransfer **A**ccounting **L**odgement for **I**nvestors and **S**tock **MAN**agement for Jobbers). The seller receives a modified version of the stock transfer form transferring the shares to SEPON Ltd (**S**tock **E**xchange **PO**ol **N**ominees). This has to be signed and returned with the relevant certificate to the selling broker who delivers them to one of the TALISMAN centres. Purchasers of company securities receive them by transfer from SEPON. The TALISMAN computer system keeps records of all the purchases and sales by SEPON with each broker and at the end of the account, produces a statement for each broker of the transactions undertaken and transfer forms in buyers' names for delivery to the appropriate registrars. Figure 4.1 shows a stock transfer form and contract note.

The securities markets

13. Structure. Besides the main market in stocks and shares on the Stock Exchange, there are four other closely related markets in company securities.

(*a*) The traded option market.
(*b*) The unlisted securities market (USM).
(*c*) The over the counter market (OTC).
(*d*) The Third market.

14. The traded option market. This is part of the Stock Exchange and is discussed in detail in Chapter 7.

15. The unlisted securities market (USM). At the end of the 1970s, trading by brokers in smaller companies without a listing on the Stock Exchange increased. This was possible under Rule 535(2) of the Stock Exchange which permits occasional trades in unlisted companies. Realizing that there was a need for a 'nursery' for companies prior to a full listing, the Stock Exchange launched the unlisted securities market in November 1980. Since then it has grown rapidly and by the autumn of 1986, the number of firms which had obtained a quotation exceeded 500. Although it is called an unlisted securities market, the market is the Stock Exchange and the securities are traded by the same brokers. However, to obtain a

4. Investment in shares   43

712

TALISMAN SOLD TRANSFER

This transfer is pursuant to a Stock Exchange transaction, and is exempt from Transfer Stamp Duty

Above this line for Registrar's use only

| 8 | I24687B | | 29/02/88 | J(24) | Bargain Ref. No. | j245356 |

Name of Undertaking: BRITISH TELECOM

Certificate lodged with Registrar

Description of Security: ORD 25P

(for completion by the Registrars/Stock Exchange)

Amount of Stock or Number of Stock units or Shares or other Security in words

Hundreds of Millions	Tens of Millions	Millions	Hundreds of Thousands	Tens of Thousands
*****	*****	*****	*****	*****
Thousands	Hundreds	Tens	Units	Part Units
TWO	ZERO	ZERO	ZERO	

2000

In the name(s) of –

Name(s) of registered holder(s) should be given in full, the address should be given where there is only one holder

ANTHONY NIGEL INVESTOR
1 PROSPERITY VIEW
BANK TOWN
STERLINGSHIRE
ST12 6BA

Account Designation (if any)

If the transfer is not made by the registered holder(s) insert also the name(s) and capacity (e.g. Executor(s)) of the persons making the transfer

I/We hereby transfer the above security out of the name(s) aforesaid into the name of SEPON LIMITED and request the necessary entries to be made in the register

Bodies corporate should affix their common seal and each signatory should state his/her representative capacity (e.g. Company Secretary / Director) against his/her signature

Balance Certificate Required for (amount or number in figures)

Stamp and Firm Code of Selling Broker

PLEASE SIGN HERE ➡

1. _A. N. Investor_

712
Stock Beech & Co. Ltd.

The Bristol & West Building   Telephone 0272 20051
Broad Quay   Telex 44239
Bristol BS1 4DD   Telegrams Spry Bristol

2. _____

3. _____

4. _____

Date:

SEPON LIMITED is lodging this transfer at the direction and on behalf of the Member Firm whose stamp appears hereon ('the Original Lodging Agent') and does not in any manner or to any extent warrant or represent the validity, genuineness or correctness of the transfer instructions contained herein, or the genuineness of the signature(s) of the transferor(s). The Original Lodging Agent by delivering this transfer to SEPON LIMITED authorises SEPON LIMITED to lodge this transfer for registration and agrees to be deemed for all purposes to be the person(s) actually lodging the transfer for registration

Stock Exchange Operating Account Number (if applicable)

Figure 4.1   (a) A stock transfer form

Stock Beech & Co. Ltd.
Members of The Stock Exchange Established 1844

The Bristol & West Building
Broad Quay
Bristol BS1 4DD

Telephone 0272 20051
Telex 44739
Telegrams Spry Bristol

Date 29/02/88
Bargain No. J245356

Client Code I24687B
OAN
Office Reference JMP

ANTHONY NIGEL INVESTOR
1 PROSPERITY VIEW
BANK TOWN
STERLINGSHIRE
ST12 6BA

In order to expedite settlement of this transaction please sign the Transfer and tick one of the following boxes.
Should the Certificate(s) be held by your bank, please sign and forward to your bankers the attached Certificate Release Letter.

1. ☐ Already forwarded
2. ☐ Balance due from recent sale
3. ☐ To be forwarded by my bank (Release Letter sent to bank)
4. ☐ Enclosed herewith
5. ☐ Due from recent purchase
6. ☐ Authority held to request Certificate(s) from bank/solicitor

Stock Quantity	Net Proceeds	C.A.D.
2000	£ 1988.50	N

Stock Description
BRITISH TELECOM ORD 25P

CERTIFICATE RELEASE LETTER

Date 29/02/88
Bargain No. J245356

Client Code I24687B
Partner Responsibility JMP

Dear Sir

Please forward to my Brokers, Messrs. Stock Beech & Co. Ltd., The Bristol & West Building, Broad Quay, Bristol BS1 4DD, free of payment, certificate(s) for the undermentioned security that you hold on my behalf.

Yours faithfully

Security BRITISH TELECOM ORD 25P
Quantity 2000

Stock Beech
Members of The Stock Exchange Established 1846

The Bristol & West Building Telephone 0272 20051
Broad Quay Telex 447739
Bristol BS1 4DD Telegrams 'Sorv' Bristol

Wantford Court 75 Edmund Street
Throgmorton Street Birmingham B3 3HL
London EC2N 2AY 021 233 3211
01-638 8471

DIRECTORS
T.C.M. Stock (Chairman)
C.G.R. Carr-Ellison Elliston (Deputy Chairman)
R.M. Davidson (Managing)
P.S. Hertford
N.G.K. Matchen
C.J.L. Mooreon
P.W.P. Mooreon
C.M. Runacres (Secretary)

ASSOCIATE DIRECTORS
T.A.A. Abrahams
G.W.B. Austin O.B.E. A.F.C.
R.E.G. Austin
M.C. Bailey
E.R. Bowers
D.A. Chadwcott
J.S. Ellis
M.C. Harnage
R.L. Hart
F. Jephcott
D.H. Lambert
J. McFadden
R.J. Newton
J.G.F. Panzetta
J.E. Parkhouse
W.J. Reynolds
M.J.K. Robson
S.M. Weal
F.G. Wort

MANAGERS
K.W. Yeates
D.W. Marsfield

STOCK BEECH & Co LTD   Registered in England No. 2014426
Registered Office: Bristol & West Building, Broad Quay, Bristol BS1 4DD
V.A.T. Registration No. 139 7138 47

CONTRACT NOTE AND TAX INVOICE

A. N. INVESTOR ESQ
1 PROSPERITY VIEW
BANK TOWN
STERLINGSHIRE
ST12 6BA

Our Ref :

Notes for your attention :

By order of :- ANTHONY NIGEL INVESTOR

Bargain Date and Tax Point	Security	Client	Account	Contract ref.	Settlement Date
29 FEB 88	0875490	I24687B	J1(24)	J245356	11 MARCH

WE THANK YOU FOR YOUR INSTRUCTIONS AND HAVE SOLD ON YOUR BEHALF AS AGENTS
BRITISH TELCOM 25P ORD SHARES

Time	Quantity	Price	Consideration
15:30	1000	2.00	£ 2000.00
	1000		£ 2000.00
		COMMISSION	£ 10.00
		V.A.T. AT 15.00%	£ 1.50

TOTAL £ 1988.50

Subject to the Rules, Regulations and
Usages of The Stock Exchange

E & O E

Roderic R. Davidson
Managing Director

CAPITAL GAINS TAX. We recommend that Contract Notes be retained for future reference.

V.A.T. Invoice for services rendered. (N) = Not subject to V.A.T.

Figure 4.1 (*b*) *A contract note*

quotation, the company does not have to comply with such restrictive or expensive requirements as for a full listing.

16. Advantages of the USM for companies seeking a listing.

(a) The minimum percentage of equity to be held by the public is only 10 per cent for USM companies but 25 per cent for a full listing. This enables firms to raise outside capital without surrendering control. However, due to firms selling a percentage greater than the minimum on obtaining a quotation, subsequent rights issued and share-financed takeover bids, an average of 40 per cent of the equity of USM companies is in the hands of the public.

(b) The trading record of companies seeking a USM quotation is a minimum of three years compared with five years for a full listing.

(c) Companies seeking a USM quotation do not need to produce the detailed accountant's report required for a full listing. However, a fairly detailed report may be required by the company's sponsors. The period since the last audited accounts must not be more than six months for a full listing, but up to nine months is permitted for the USM. For a full listing, a letter to the Stock Exchange confirming the adequacy of the working capital of the company is also required.

(d) Advertising requirements are cheaper for a USM flotation: one box advertisement may suffice, while for a full listing, two advertisements for the full prospectus are required.

(e) The listing fees with the Stock Exchange are nil for companies quoted on the USM but up to £15,000 for a full listing. Subsequent annual charges are £1,500 for the USM, but up to £3,500 for a full listing.

(f) A more detailed undertaking on the disclosure of information to the Stock Exchange must be made for a full listing than for the USM.

(g) The charges made by professional advisers for a full listing are higher than for the USM.

(h) Cheaper alternatives to a full offer for sale with prospectus available to firms seeking a quotation on the USM are:

(i) An introduction. This is only possible where no new money is raised and at least 10 per cent of the equity is already in the hands of the public. This applies where the company's shares are already traded on the 'over the counter market' (*see* **19** below).

4. Investment in shares

(*ii*) A placing. Since October 1986, a placing of up to £2 million is permitted without any distribution outside the sponsor's own clients and up to £5 million without an offer for sale. Between £2 million and £5 million, 25 per cent of the issue must be made through other distributors or directly to the public.

17. Advantages of the USM for investors. The attraction of the USM for investors is the prospect of potential dramatic gains if the companies selected are the successful ones. Investment in the USM is more risky than investment in the large established companies in the main market. In 1985, 14 companies saw their share price rise by over 10 per cent while 47 shares halved in value. Price movements can be as much as 20 per cent in a week and an unexpected set of bad profit figures can wipe up to 50 per cent off the market value of the company.

These dramatic movements in individual shares are not reflected in the Datastream USM Index (printed daily in *The Times*) which has under-performed the *Financial Times* Actuaries – All Share Index (*see* **54**) since the commencement of the market in 1980. Particular factors can explain this. In the early years, the USM was dominated by oil and oil exploration companies which transferred from trading under Rule 535(2) to the new market. Their poor performance dominated the USM's results. Since then, the largest oil companies have obtained a full listing and the influx of a wide range of companies has removed the market's dependence upon this sector. However, the market was again depressed in 1985 by the poor performance of electronics and computing companies.

18. Important considerations. Potential investors in the USM should consider the following points.

(*a*) The higher level of risk. The market is both more variable and less liquid than the main market. Since there are less shares in the hands of the public, there may be very limited trading once the initial listing has taken place, and so the bid offer spread will be wider. Investors may consider that a managed fund would be appropriate to their needs. (The First Charlotte Assets Trust and the Throgmorton USM Trust are two investment trusts specializing in USM companies. The Temple Bar USM Trust managed by Guinness Mahon is the first authorized unit trust to be permitted by the Department of Trade and Industry to invest more than 25 per cent of its assets in USM stocks. However, because it is more risky and hence not intended for the ordinary investor, the minimum investment is £10,000. The MIM Britannia Unlisted Securities Market Fund is an offshore unauthorized unit trust fund run from Jersey. Unit trusts and investment trusts are discussed in detail in Chapters 8 and 9.)

(*b*) The market in which the company is trading and its prospects.

(*c*) The quality of the firm's management. Do the firm's original management still run the company and hold a sizeable financial stake?

(*d*) The reputation of the firm's backers, particularly its stockbroker, can be a guide to its potential performance.

19. The 'over the counter' (OTC) market. This is primarily a market in shares not quoted on the Stock Exchange. Until the new Financial Services Act comes into operation, its dealers have to apply to the Department of Trade and Industry annually for a licence to deal. There is no building in which the OTC market operates; it consists of telephone dealing with the licensed dealers making a market in some 230 companies' shares. The dealers quote a bid offer spread with no extra transaction charges to those implicit in the spread. Some dealers also quotre prices for popular new issues like British Telecom and TSB.

The companies in whose shares the licensed dealers make a market can be much smaller and riskier than those quoted on the USM or the main market of the Stock Exchange. Annual profits are likely to be a minimum of £100,000 with a track record of at least one year. The fact that there may be only one dealer prepared to trade in a particular company's share can also increase the share price volatility. Investors should also be aware that its dealers are not members of the Stock Exchange and so there is no access to the Stock Exchange's Compensation Fund in the event of dealer default.

One of the best-known operators in the OTC market, and now admitted as a member of the Stock Exchange, is Granville (formerly M J H Nightingale) which places a box advertisement each day in the *Financial Times* recording the prices and yields of the shares in which they deal. However, unlike other dealers in the OTC market like Harvard Securities, Prior Harwin or Afcor, they are not market makers dealing on their own account. Their policy is to match buyers with sellers for a commission. This means that an investor may not be able to deal immediately but might have to wait for another investor wanting to undertake the opposite transaction.

20. The Third market. The Stock Exchange introduced a third tier to the market in January 1987. To qualify for a quotation, a company must:

(*a*) be incorporated in the UK;
(*b*) not be involved in certain types of business

   (*i*) holding cash
   (*ii*) holding minority interests in other companies
   (*iii*) investment, property or commodity holding or dealing;

(*c*) have at least one year's audited accounts showing significant revenue flows or, if a 'greenfield venture', have fully researched projects or products with a prospect of significant revenue being generated within a short timescale;

(*d*) be introduced to the Stock Exchange by a member firm acting as a sponsor.

The role of the sponsoring broker is to assess the suitability of the company and ensure that it fulfils the requirements and rules of the Stock Exchange. It must usually arrange for at least two market makers to register to deal in the shares of the company. Additional brokers may also act as 'accredited dealers'. Such a firm would have an obligation to seek matching parties to any business brought to it, but would not be required to maintain two-way prices. All Third market shares will be initially classified as deltas on SEAQ although it is expected that some will later be reclassified as gammas.

21. The advantages of the Third market. The advantages for a company obtaining a quotation on the Third market rather than the USM will be:

(*a*) shorter trading record required;
(*b*) no initial charge for admission and no annual fees;
(*c*) only one box advertisement in a national newspaper is required;

(d) there is no minimum amount of equity that must be in the hands of the market, but the sponsoring broker must demonstrate to the Stock Exchange Council that sufficient shares will be in the public's hands for a reasonably liquid market to result;

(e) the trading of shares in BES companies will not cause investors to lose their eligibility for tax relief under the BES scheme.

22. Investor protection. To protect investors in Third market shares, brokers will be required under the Financial Services Act to exchange a customer agreement letter with the client which explicitly refers to Third market stocks before they may recommend them to their client or buy them if they have discretion over their client's portfolio. Clients must also be appraised of the riskiness of Third market securities before broker dealers can accept instructions to purchase a security.

The creation of the Third market and the requirement that sponsoring brokers must be members of the Stock Exchange has put pressure upon OTC dealers to apply for membership.

Investment in shares issued to raise finance for companies

23. The Business Expansion Scheme (BES). The Business Expansion Scheme which was introduced in 1983 provides for investments in the new equity of a company carrying on a qualifying trade to be eligible for income tax relief. The maximum investment eligible for relief in any one tax year is £40,000, so the cost of such an investment for a 60 per cent marginal rate investor is only £16,000. Qualifying companies must be incorporated in the UK and their shares must not be quoted on the Stock Exchange or USM. Qualifying trades excluded professional services, farming and property development until 19 March 1986. Since this date, farming and property development have become qualifying trades provided the value of the company's land and buildings does not exceed one-half of the value of its net assets (i.e. ordinary shareholders' funds). (The value of these fixed assets can, however, be reduced by the amount of long-term borrowings of the company.) Wholesalers and retailers of goods collected and held as an investment e.g. antiques and fine wines, have also been made non-qualifying trades from the same date.

To qualify for the tax relief, investors must hold the shares for at least five years. Trading of the company's shares on the Third market or OTC at the end of this period provides a way in which investors can take their profits. For shares issued before 19 March 1986, any capital gains above the full amount invested (including the tax relief) is liable for capital gains tax. However, a loss arising on disposal will not be allowable for capital gains tax purposes to the extent that BES relief was given on the issue of the shares. For shares issued since 19 March 1986, all gains are free of capital gains tax after the five-year qualifying period.

24. How to invest in the BES. There are two main avenues by which investors can invest in a BES.

(*a*) By direct investment, e.g. by subscribing to an issue advertised in the financial press.

(*b*) By investing in a business expansion fund managed by a merchant bank or broker like Granville. This relieves investors of the responsibilities of monitoring their particular investments and, like investments in unit trusts or investment trusts, spreads their risk over several companies.

New issues

25. Advantages of 'going public'. When a company's shares are quoted for the first time on the Stock Exchange, the company is said to have *gone public*. The issue of its shares is called a *Stock Exchange flotation*. The benefits arising from a quotation are:

(*a*) access to new equity capital through the market;
(*b*) greater prestige with customers and creditors;
(*c*) easier access to loans through the market and from banks;
(*d*) the shares of the company can be used to finance takeovers;
(*e*) the owners can realize some of their investment in the company.

26. Disadvantages of 'going public'. The disadvantages of a quotation for a company are:

(*a*) potential loss of control of existing owners and vulnerability to

52 Stocks and shares

a takeover;
  (b) the costs of the flotation;
  (c) additional pressures on the directors by new shareholders.

27. Conditions of obtaining a full Stock Exchange listing. To obtain a full Stock Exchange listing, a company must:

  (a) have produced a rising pre-tax profit record for the past five years;
  (b) ensure that at least 25 per cent of the shares of the company will be in the hands of the public after the issue and that their value exceeds £0.5 million;
  (c) sign the Stock Exchange's 'Listing Agreement' undertaking to comply with the Stock Exchange rules and regulations, e.g. to publish interim statements for the first six months of the financial year and to inform the Stock Exchange of events, such as bids or acquisitions, which are likely to affect the company's share price.

28. Methods of flotation. There are five main ways in which the shares of a company can be quoted for the first time on the Stock Exchange.

  (a) an issue by prospectus;
  (b) an offer for sale;
  (c) an offer for sale by tender;
  (d) a placing;
  (e) an introduction.

29. An issue by prospectus. The company draws up a prospectus, with the help of a stockbroker or a merchant bank which is a member of the Issuing Houses Association, giving all the information required by the Companies Acts and the Stock Exchange Regulations. The prospectus is published in at least two national newspapers and is intended to give investors the information they will require to assist them to come to a decision whether or not to apply for shares in the company. It contains information on the following:

  (a) A history of the company. The nature and location of its business. The names and addresses of its directors and its professional advisers.

4. Investment in shares

(*b*) Details concerning the age and experience of the directors and senior management of the company.

(*c*) The reasons for the issue and how the proceeds will be used.

(*d*) A summary of the financial position of the company.

(*e*) A profit forecast and a statement on dividend policy.

(*f*) A detailed 'Accountants' Report' containing five years' figures for the profit and loss account, balance sheet, and statement of source and application of funds. The latest accounts should be within three months of the report and, if more than nine months since the latest annual results, special audited interim accounts should be included.

(*g*) The amount of authorized and issued share capital and loan capital. Details of outstanding share options.

(*h*) The Memorandum of Association and the Articles of Association of the company.

(*i*) Details of subsidiary companies.

(*j*) The directors' interests in the company, service agreements, emoluments and executive share options.

(*k*) Details of any substantial shareholdings.

(*l*) Details of any outstanding litigation and claims.

(*m*) Details of principal properties and investments.

(*n*) A statement by the directors that the working capital available is considered sufficient.

(*o*) Details of the procedure for application for shares and the application form.

The company will arrange for the issue to be 'underwritten' to ensure that the shares are sold. Underwriters (merchant banks) agree to purchase any shares not taken up in return for a commission.

30. An offer for sale. The company sells the shares to the stockbroker or issuing house which then offers them for sale to the public. Otherwise, the procedure is very similar to the first method. A prospectus is drawn up and published in at least two papers for a full listing. The broker or issuing house will also underwrite the issue with other financial institutions to protect themselves against a failure.

One of the problems for an issuing house is pricing the new

shares. If the price is set too high, the issue will be under-subscribed and this will be bad for both the reputation of the company and the issuing house. If the price is set too low, the issue will be dramatically over-subscribed, the share price will rise rapidly to a large premium on the market, and the owners of the company will have sold their shares cheap. The aim is to set the price so that there is an opening premium to encourage marketability of the shares. When an issue is over-subscribed, the issuing house has to allocate the shares that are available. The usual procedure is to scale down the allocation given to investors with large applications and to hold a ballot to determine the allocation between investors that have made applications for smaller numbers.

'A 'letter of acceptance' is sent to successful applicants. This letter can be used to transfer title free of stamp duty for about six weeks when the company's registrar will send out share certificates.

The prospect of a quick capital gain arising if the share price should rise in the market to a premium over the issue price encourages some investors to apply for shares which they have no intention of holding beyond the first few days of active trading. Such investors are called *stags*. Investors considering stagging should bear in mind that a cheque must be sent with the application form, and this may be cashed before the allocation of shares takes place. Photocopies of the application form and multiple applications will be rejected.

31. An offer for sale by tender. One way in which issuing houses sometimes try to avoid the problem of under-pricing or over-pricing an issue is by making an offer for sale by tender. The issuing house will fix a minimum price and invite tenders at or above this. When all the applications have been received, the issuing house will fix a 'striking price'. All investors who have offered to pay this price or above will then receive the shares for which they have applied at the striking price, even though some offers may have been higher.

32. A placing. A cheaper method of issuing shares which may be more appropriate to smaller issues is their 'placing' by the issuing house or the stockbroker with a number of financial institutions, pension funds, insurance companies and their own private clients. On both the Stock Exchange main market and USM, one-quarter of the shares are allocated to other market makers. If investors are interested in this type of issue, they should discuss with their

4. Investment in shares

brokers the possibility of being added to their private clients' placing list.

33. An introduction. An introduction to the London Stock Exchange applies both to large overseas companies which are already quoted on an overseas stock exchange and British companies whose shares are traded on the OTC who want a Stock Exchange listing. No new shares have to be issued at the time of the introduction.

34. Further information. You should now look for and examine the prospectus of a new issue in the financial press. In the *Financial Times* on the page headed 'London Stock Exchange', you will find in the top right-hand corner the latest prices of recent new issues.

Sometimes shares are issued in 'partly paid form'. This means that an initial payment must be made upon application, and further instalments at specified dates. The most famous case of this was the British Telecom issues where the full price of the share at issue was 130 pence, but only 50 pence was payable upon application in November 1984 and the remaining 80 pence in two instalments of 40 pence in June 1985 and April 1986. The rise in the partly paid share price from 50 to 150 pence before the second instalment gave investors a gain of 100 pence on an outlay of 50 pence, or 200 per cent! Had the shares been issued at the fully paid price of 130 pence, the increase in price of 100 pence would have been a gain of only 77 per cent. This magnified gain which can result from the lower initial outlay is sometimes described as the consequence of *personal gearing*.

Rights issues

35. Definition. A rights issue is the means by which a company can obtain new equity capital from its shareholders. The company offers its existing shareholders new shares at a discount to their market price. The number offered each shareholder is in proportion to the number already held.

EXAMPLE: Existing share price = 240 pence
The company offers existing shareholders one new share at 190

56 Stocks and shares

pence for every four already held.

36. The effect on the price of shares. This offer to its shareholders is not such a bargain as may at first appear. The gain that shareholders make from the purchase of the new shares at a discount is usually offset by a fall in the price of those they already hold. In theory, the market price of the existing shares will fall to a weighted average of the old share price and the offer price of the new discounted shares. This weighted average price is called the *theoretical ex rights price*.

Continuing with the example

$$\text{Theoretical ex rights price} = \frac{(4 \times 240\text{p}) + (1 \times 190\text{p})}{5} = \frac{1{,}150\text{p}}{5}$$

$$= 230 \text{ pence per share}$$

Gain in price of new share = 230p − 190p = 40p
Fall in price of existing shares = 240p − 230p = 10p × 4 = 40p
Net gain = 0

37. Reasons for change in price of share. The market price of the share can diverge from this theoretical ex rights price for either or both of two reasons:

(*a*) Market influences – if the stock market is moving up or down at the time, the ex rights share price of the company is likely to move up or down with the market trend.

(*b*) Confidence of investors in the company's policies – if the investors see the rights issue as a sign of weakness in the company's prospects and do not believe that the company will use the new funds profitably, the ex rights price will fall below its theoretical price. Conversely, if the rights issue is viewed as a sign of opportunities for the company to expand into more profitable areas, the market price may rise above the theoretical price.

The market share price will tend to trade around its theoretical price when the shares are traded ex rights which is normally the day after the provisional allotment letter has been sent to existing shareholders.

4. Investment in shares

38. Choices open to investors. Investors who are existing shareholders have three choices when they receive their allotment letter.

(*a*) Subscribe for the new shares. This will increase their investment in the company and should only be undertaken if they can afford it and believe that the investment would be at least as good as any alternative.

(*b*) Sell their entitlement to the new shares 'nil paid' by signing the form of renunciation on the back of the provisional allotment letter and sending it to their stockbroker. The right to purchase the new shares at a discount to the market price has intrinsic value and hence can be sold until payment for the new shares is due – hence the term 'nil paid'. The theoretical value of a nil paid share is the difference between the theoretical ex rights price and the discounted offer price of the new share.

EXAMPLE:
Theoretical ex rights price = 230p
Offer price of new shares   = 190p
Value of nil paid share price = 40p

In theory, investors would neither lose nor gain by selling their nil paid shares, for the money they receive should equal the fall in value of their investment in the existing shares.

EXAMPLE:
An investor owns 1,000 shares
Fall in value of existing shares = 1,000 × (240p − 230p) = £100
Sale of 1,000 ÷ 4 = 250 nil paid shares @ 40p   = £100
Net gain or loss for investor   =   0

In practice, the value of nil paid shares will diverge from their theoretical price depending upon whether the rights price is well or badly received, as explained above.

(*c*) Do nothing. After the period in which investors have the right to buy the new shares has expired, the company will sell the rights not taken up and distribute the proceeds to the shareholders who did not apply for or sell their allotment.

Nil paid shares also provide investors with the opportunity to gain (or lose) from their implicit personal gearing (*see* **34**). For example, assume some good news caused the ex rights share price to rise on the market from 230 pence to 250 pence, a gain of 8.7 per cent. The value of a nil paid share would rise from 40 pence to 60 pence (250p − 190p), an increase of 50 per cent.

39. Further information. You should now look on the page at the back of the *Financial Times* headed 'The London Stock Exchange' and find on the right-hand side the box containing the prices of recent rights issue shares, fully paid or nil paid as appropriate. For further details of latest issues, see the Saturday supplement to the *Financial Times* on the second page headed 'Markets: Company News Summary'.

Companies choose the size of the discount on the new shares to try to ensure that they are all taken up. They may have the issue underwritten by City banks and institutions to guarantee their sale. This will be unnecessary if the issue is 'deep discounted', e.g. the National Westminster Bank rights issue in May 1986 to raise £715 million by a one-for-one issue at 200 pence when the market price before the issue was 860 pence. Deep discount rights issues have a serious disadvantage for investors who do not want to take up their entitlement to the new shares and propose to sell their rights. If the value of the rights sold is more than 5 per cent of the original investment, the excess is liable to capital gains tax. This is unlikely to occur when the discount is in the usual 10–20 per cent range, but will affect investors when it is very large.

Capitalization issues

40. Definition. Capitalization issues do not raise new capital for the company, but alter its balance sheet and the market price of its shares by increasing the number of issued shares. If the share price is considered heavy, i.e. expensive compared with other share prices on the market, the directors can propose to existing shareholders a 'scrip' issue or 'bonus' issue of a new share for each one or more existing shares held. This is usually approved and, when the shares are quoted 'ex cap' after the issue, the share price falls pro rata.

4. Investment in shares

EXAMPLE:
Old share price = £15
Scrip issue: 4 new shares for each share already held
'Ex cap' price = £15 ÷ 5 shares = 300 pence

On the balance sheet of the company, there is a restructuring of the composition of shareholders' funds. The issued share capital increases by the par value of each share times the number of new shares issued, and the reserves are reduced by the same amount.

Takeover situations

41. Forms of takeover. A takeover involves the assumption of the ownership and control of the victim company by the bidding company as a result of obtaining more than 50 per cent of the victim company's ordinary voting shares. A reverse takeover is where a smaller company takes over the control of a larger one. A *merger* involves the amalgamation of two companies to form a new one. A list of the latest takeover bids is given each Saturday on page 2 of the supplement of the *Financial Times* under the heading 'Markets: Company News Summary'.

42. The implementation of a takeover bid. When a bid is made, it is either agreed or rejected by the victim's board of directors. If it is agreed, the board's recommendation of acceptance is likely to result in the takeover being successful unless a higher bid should suddenly come forward. Investors in the victim's shares have the choice between accepting the bid or selling their holding in the market for a price that will be a few pence below the bid price.

If the bid is rejected the investors have to choose between the offer of the bidder and the advice of the victim's board to reject it. They should examine the bidder's offer carefully, paying particular attention to:

(*a*) The terms of the offer. Is it a cash offer for each share of the victim company, or is the bidder offering its own securities or a mixture of cash and securities? The securities offered by the bidder may be its ordinary shares, preference shares, loan stock or convertible loan stock.

(b) The market value of the offer. Does the price offered reflect the investor's view of the prospects of the company if it retains its independence? If the bidder is making a cash offer, this is the only important question. If the bidder is offering its own shares, the prospects of the new combined company have to be considered.

43. The public interest. Takeover bids sometimes raise questions affecting the public interest. In this situation, the Director General of Fair Trading can advise the Secretary of State for Trade and Industry to refer the proposal to the Monopolies and Mergers Commission. This is most likely when the new combined company will have a greater share than 25 per cent of a particular market. A referral will hold up a proposed takeover for at least six months and, more often than not, results in the withdrawal of the bid.

44. The City Code on Takeovers and Mergers. Takeover bids sometimes attract a rival bidder, resulting in a higher offer. To protect the interests of shareholders, companies are expected to abide by the rules laid down by the City Code on Takeovers and Mergers. This was first published in 1968 and is an example of self-regulation designed to remove the need for statutory intervention. Some of the main provisions of the Code are:

(a) Once an offer has been made, the board of the victim company must not take any action that would frustrate the offer without the approval of a shareholders' meeting.

(b) The directors must act only in the interest of their shareholders and employ outside independent advisers (a merchant bank).

(c) All documents for circulation to shareholders must be prepared to the same high standard as required for a prospectus.

(d) All the shareholders in the victim company must be treated identically and provided with the same information. This is intended to prevent the bidder from offering a higher price to some shareholders than others. In particular, if 15 per cent of the target company's shares have been accepted before the bid is made, the bid must be either for cash or contain a cash alternative of the highest price paid for the shares in the previous 12 months. Similarly, once 30 per cent of the shares have been acquired, a bid for the

4. Investment in shares

remainder must be made at the highest price paid in the previous 12 months.

(*e*) The bidder can increase its stake in the target company beyond 15 per cent by purchases in the market up to a further 10 per cent per week.

(*f*) The period of the offer made by the bidder is a minimum of 21 and a maximum of 60 days from the posting of offer documents. The terms of the bid may be improved provided there are 14 days remaining for shareholders to consider them. The bidder can seek permission from the Panel to extend the period of the bid. If the bidder improves the terms of the offer, the new terms can be accepted or rejected by the shareholders who have already accepted earlier terms. Acceptances can be withdrawn up to the time the bidder declares the bid 'unconditional', which occurs when a sufficient number of the shareholders who own a majority of the shares have accepted the bidder's terms.

Once the offer has been declared unconditional, the investor can either accept the terms offered as the bidder will invite late acceptances, or sell the shares in the market. One point to note is that if the investors accept a cash offer, they become liable to capital gains tax on the rise in price since purchase, whereas if they accept the securities of the bidder, liability to capital gains tax is deferred as the new securities are regarded as being a replacement for the original investment and not a consideration for its sale.

The rights of shareholders

45. The definition of a company. A company is a separate legal entity from the shareholders that own it. All the various Companies Acts that regulate companies were consolidated into the Companies Act 1985, though this has subsequently been amended. Public companies are specifically defined by the Act and are designated by the abbreviation 'plc' after their name. Any company that is not a public company is a private company, the appropriate abbreviation if limited being 'Ltd'. The major difference is that a public company's securities can be offered to the public at large.

46. The memorandum. When a company is formed or incorporated, it has to register *inter alia* its memorandum and articles of association with the Registrar of Companies. The *memorandum* states:

(*a*) the company's name;
(*b*) its status as a public company if appropriate;
(*c*) whether the company's registered office is situated in England, Wales or Scotland;
(*d*) the objects of the company;
(*e*) a statement that the liability of its members is limited; this means that shareholders cannot be required to contribute additional capital provided the shares they hold are fully paid and not partly paid;
(*f*) the amount of the company's authorized share capital and details of its division into shares and their nominal value;
(*g*) a statement by the proposed first members to the effect that they wish to form a company.

47. The articles of association. The *articles of association* details the relationship between the company and its members, and between members. It will generally provide for the following:

(*a*) the issue of shares and details of any restrictions on their transfer;
(*b*) the arrangement of meetings, voting and proxy votes;
(*c*) the appointment of directors, their powers, duties and removal;
(*d*) dividends and reserves;
(*e*) the accounts and their audit;
(*f*) the winding up of the company.

48. The rights of individual shareholders. The directors are responsible for the management of the company. The main rights of the ordinary shareholders are:

(*a*) to receive a copy of the company's annual report and accounts;
(*b*) to receive notification of company meetings, to attend, vote and speak;
(*c*) to appoint a proxy to attend meetings;

4. Investment in shares

(d) to share in the profits of the company whether in the form of dividends or an increase in reserves;

(e) to subscribe for any new share capital or convertible loan stock in proportion to their existing holdings;

(f) to transfer their shares freely, although in the case of a private company there will probably be a restriction on this right;

(g) to elect and remove the directors of the company.

The rights of preference shareholders and debenture holders are much more restricted. While they are entitled to receive a copy of the annual report and accounts, they are not normally allowed to attend the general meetings for shareholders. If their interests are affected by particular issues, a separate meeting called a 'class meeting' may be called at which they can vote.

Shareholders' interests are also protected by the Stock Exchange requirement that listed companies should publish more information than strictly required by law. In particular, they are required to provide an interim report covering the first six months of the financial year, and the directors must explain any departures from standard accounting practice or failures to meet published forecasts of profits.

49. Notification of interest. The Companies Act 1985 requires that investors acting individually or collectively who acquire more than 5 per cent of the nominal value of the issued voting share capital must notify the company in writing within five days. If the company believes that an investor is failing to reveal its interest, the company can require the investor to clarify the position. In the case of a nominee holding, the company can require the identity of the investor to be disclosed. This happened in the case of Westland plc after the 1986 takeover battle. If the investor refuses to provide the information required, the company can apply to the court to have the shares deprived of their voting and dividend rights.

50. Shareholders' meetings. An annual general meeting (AGM) must be held every calendar year and not more than 15 months since the previous one. At least 21 days' notice must be given and an agenda is sent to shareholders. The articles of the company will, in practice, differentiate as regards the ordinary and special business of meetings.

The *ordinary business* consists of:

(*a*) The consideration of the accounts, the auditors' and the directors' reports;

(*b*) the declaration of the final dividend; the directors can declare and pay the interim dividend without a meeting;

(*c*) the appointment of directors and the auditors.

Any other business is called *special business*. Business is transacted by resolutions, of which there are three types:

(*a*) *Ordinary resolutions* – these can be used for most routine matters and are passed by a simple majority of those voting at a meeting of which due notice has been given.

(*b*) *Extraordinary resolutions* – these are used in winding up the company. This type of resolution requires a majority of at least 75 per cent of the votes cast at a meeting of which due notice has been given.

(*c*) *Special resolutions* – these are used when the proposals involve a fundamental change in the company's structure. This type of resolution requires a majority of at least 75 per cent of the votes cast at the meeting, and 21 days' notice of the intention to propose the resolution must be given.

Meetings other than the AGM are called *extraordinary general meetings* and their business is generally designated by the articles of the company as special business. The directors can call such a meeting at any time and shareholders representing more than 10 per cent of voting shares can requisition one. The amount of notice required depends upon the type of resolutions to be proposed.

Voting at meetings is initially by a show of hands, but the directors can decide that a poll be taken and this can be demanded by five or more members representing 10 per cent of the voting capital.

A proxy cannot vote in a show of hands or, in the case of a public company, speak except to demand a poll. However, a proxy can vote on a poll and the voting is then based on one share, one vote. Rather than appoint a proxy, corporate shareholders can appoint a 'representative' who is given the rights of a member for the duration of the meeting. A member can appoint anybody as a proxy, but the directors generally specify those who are willing to act as such.

4. Investment in shares

The meeting must be quorate. The articles of association fixes the size of the quorum, which is usually two members.

The redemption of company shares

51. Changes since the Companies Act 1981. A company can redeem its shares subject to certain conditions to protect the position of creditors. Prior to the Companies Act 1981, only preference shares could be redeemed, but now the company can redeem any type of share if permitted to do so by its articles and if a resolution has been passed to authorize it. The redemption must be funded out of distributable reserves or a new issue, though in the case of private companies redemption out of capital is possible. If they are redeemed out of distributable reserves, an amount equal to the nominal value of the shares redeemed must be transferred to a non-distributable capital redemption reserve so that the amount of the non-distributable share capital is not reduced.

EXAMPLE: The General Electric Company has used some of its enormous cash reserves to buy in its shares. The reason for undertaking this action was that the increase in earnings per share for the remaining shareholders was greater than if the surplus cash was invested elsewhere.

Stock market indices

52. Definition. Stock market indices are used to monitor the direction and size of movements of the prices of quoted securities. They are also used as a test of the investment performance of the portfolios of both individuals and professional fund managers. The main stock market indices are as follows.

53. The *Financial Times* 30 share index. This is probably still the best-known and most quoted British Stock Exchange index. It was first calculated in 1935 but, since then, many of the original 30 companies whose shares were included in it have had to be replaced by others as they were either taken over or went into liquidation. In April 1986, for example, both the Imperial Group and Distillers had to be removed as a result of falling victim to takeover bids and

66 Stocks and shares

were replaced by Guinness and Royal Insurance. The index used to be criticized for being more representative of manufacturing industry than the market as a whole, but now that it contains shares like ASDA–MFI, British Telecom, BP, Boots, Grand Metropolitan, Marks and Spencer, Nat. West. Bank, Royal Insurance and Trusthouse Forte, this criticism has been much diluted.

The index is calculated at hourly intervals throughout the day by multiplying each of the 30 share prices together and taking the thirtieth root. This calculation is known as a *geometric mean* and has the advantage of giving equal weight to each company's share in the index rather than allowing the largest company to have the greatest influence. The index is sensitive to changes in market sentiment and is a good guide to the short-run performance of the share prices of large companies. However, it suffers from downward bias over the longer period of time which results from its method of calculation. This means that it is easier to out-perform this index than others not using a geometric mean and so should not be used for assessing long-term investment performance.

Details of *Financial Times* indices are shown in a box on the page in the *Financial Times* headed 'London Stock Exchange'. Four indices are shown: government securities, fixed interest, ordinary (this is the 30 share index) and gold mines. Underneath are shown the hourly values on the previous day. You should now look for these in the *Financial Times* and *see* fig. 4.2(*a*).

54. The *Financial Times* – Actuaries share indices. These indices can be found in a separate box at the bottom of the same page in the *Financial Times* (and *see* fig. 4.2(*b*)). The composition of the indices is determined by the Institute of Actuaries and the Faculty of Actuaries, and the daily prices and calculations are performed by the *Financial Times*. There are 40 separate sector indices, e.g. textiles (17) where the number in brackets represents the number of companies' shares in the index. The most important index is the all-share index which is based on 731 companies. This is an arithmetic mean of the share prices where the weights attached to each company's share depends upon the size of its market capitalization. It is the most representative of the market as a whole and, since it does not suffer from any statistical downward bias, is the index that should be used for judging investment performance.

4. Investment in shares

FINANCIAL TIMES STOCK INDICES										
	Dec. 3	Dec. 2	Dec. 1	Nov. 28	Nov. 27	year ago	1986		Since Compilation	
							High	Low	High	Low
Government Secs	81.55	81.23	81.13	81.75	81.77	83.79	94.51 (18/4)	80.39 (20/1)	127.4 (9/1/35)	49.18 (3/1/75)
Fixed Interest	88.58	88.41	88.38	88.55	88.55	89.33	97.68 (7/7)	86.55 (23/1)	105.4 (28/11/47)	50.53 (3/1/75)
Ordinary ♥	1,269.1	1,278.4	1,272.5	1,292.2	1,286.0	1,115.8	1,425.9 (3/4)	1,094.3 (14/1)	1,425.9 (26/6/40)	49.4 (26/6/40)
Gold Mines	317.0	322.9	331.8	314.5	302.2	276.3	357.8 (22/9)	185.7 (18/7)	734.7 (15/2/83)	43.5 (26/10/71)
Ord. Div. Yield	4.48	4.44	4.47	4.41	4.44	4.41	**S.E. ACTIVITY**			
Earnings Yld.%(full)	10.40	10.30	10.38	10.26	10.31	10.96	Indices		Dec. 2	Dec. 1
P/E Ratio (net) (*)	11.74	11.85	11.76	11.91	11.84	11.25	Gilt Edged Bargains		119.2	122.1
SEAQ Bargains (5pm)	25,431	27,395	29,647	28,875	28,696	—	Equity Bargains		238.5	258.5
Equity Turnover (£m)	—	962.86	896.35	1,146.02	750.20	745.74	Equity Value 5-Day Average		1946.2	1811.7
Equity Bargains	—	36,802	39,889	36,392	34,056	23,356	Gilt Edged Bargains		132.4	137.7
Shares Traded (ml)	—	379.6	385.7	362.1	355.9	342.8	Equity Bargains Equity Value		240.0 2027.4	241.0 2035.6

♥	Opening 1279.6	10 a.m. 1273.7	11 a.m. 1274.6	Noon 1266.6	1 p.m. 1264.9	2 p.m. 1267.9	3 p.m. 1268.3	4 p.m. 1268.7

Day's High 1279.6. Day's Low 1263.2.
Basis 100 Govt. Secs 15/10/26, Fixed Int. 1928, Ordinary 1/7/35, Gold Mines 12/9/55, SE Activity 1974 *Nil=11.27.

LONDON REPORT AND LATEST SHARE INDEX: TEL. 01-246 8026

Figure 4.2 *(a) Financial Times stock indices*

55. The *Financial Times* – Stock Exchange 100 index. When a Stock Exchange index that could be calculated every minute was required as the basis for trading in index-traded options and index financial futures (*see* 7:**15–17**) the *FT* 30 share index was rejected as being based upon too small a sample of shares, and the all-share index was rejected as being too large to calculate so frequently. Hence the *FT*–SE 100 index, referred to as 'Footsie', was devised, starting at 1,000 on 3 January 1984. Its sample of 100 shares is large enough to reflect the market as a whole, and yet is small enough to be constantly recalculated. The latest index values are shown at the bottom of the table of *FT*–Actuaries share indices in the *Financial Times* (and *see* fig. 4.2(*b*)).

56. Overseas share indices. The *Financial Times* has a daily page headed 'World Stock Markets' which shows all the main indices for the world's markets. Also of interest is the weekly table at the back of the *Economist* magazine.

The New York Stock Exchange is the largest in the world, followed by Japan and then the UK. The best-known New York Stock Exchange index is the Dow Jones industrial index followed by the broader-based Standard and Poor's composite index and the NYSE all common index. Similarly, in Japan, the Nikkei Dow

FT-ACTUARIES INDICES

These Indices are the joint compilation of the Financial Times,
the Institute of Actuaries and the Faculty of Actuaries

	EQUITY GROUPS & SUB-SECTIONS Figures in parentheses show number of stocks per section	\multicolumn{6}{c}{Wednesday December 3 1986}	Tues Dec 2	Mon Dec 1	Fri Nov 28	Year ago (approx.)
		Index No.	Day's Change %	Est. Earnings Yield % (Max.)	Gross Div. Yield % (ACT at 29%)	Est. P/E Ratio (Net)	xd adj. 1986 to date	Index No.	Index No.	Index No.	Index No.
1	CAPITAL GOODS (211)	675.06	−0.5	9.24	3.84	13.74	16.53	678.20	677.45	685.48	580.61
2	Building Materials (27)	844.33	−0.3	8.91	3.59	14.13	17.54	846.91	845.20	850.20	635.50
3	Contracting, Construction (29)	1148.77	−0.2	8.11	4.03	16.95	32.70	1151.22	1146.79	1152.23	944.12
4	Electricals (12)	1708.51	+0.3	8.69	4.94	14.90	54.84	1703.97	1703.68	1723.61	1584.74
5	Electronics (38)	1439.93	−0.5	10.00	2.86	13.35	29.90	1447.83	1472.89	1503.68	1474.40
6	Mechanical Engineering (61)	380.88	−0.5	10.45	4.37	12.17	10.89	382.86	380.31	382.04	327.32
8	Metals and Metal Forming (7)	349.26	−0.6	9.47	4.03	13.23	9.53	351.37	350.46	351.24	240.54
9	Motors (16)	269.03	−0.7	10.23	3.90	11.35	6.70	270.84	269.38	270.24	197.98
10	Other Industrial Materials (21)	1185.74	−0.6	7.57	4.60	15.68	30.33	1193.05	1173.46	1199.51	1015.77
21	CONSUMER GROUP (186)	923.72	−0.7	8.33	3.41	15.08	20.14	930.07	926.16	937.90	772.13
22	Brewers and Distillers (22)	915.44	−1.8	9.78	3.57	12.53	15.70	931.96	939.41	970.20	749.37
25	Food Manufacturing (24)	734.58	−0.3	9.27	3.83	14.06	17.96	737.14	729.50	731.27	572.12
26	Food Retailing (16)	1829.10		6.92	2.92	20.04	30.54	1829.49	1822.25	1839.64	1807.59
27	Health and Household Products (10)	1508.85	−0.7	6.31	2.52	18.47	26.19	1519.97	1506.59	1524.23	1201.67
29	Leisure (29)	966.20	−0.2	7.48	4.15	17.71	25.69	968.12	964.54	974.19	770.53
32	Publishing & Printing (14)	2653.33	+0.7	7.34	4.29	17.56	76.10	2635.46	2633.23	2667.22	1880.36
33	Packaging and Paper (14)	485.02	−0.4	7.17	3.43	18.06	11.74	486.95	480.97	483.08	373.11
34	Stores (38)	827.99	−1.0	7.68	3.23	17.68	17.37	836.57	832.11	841.65	796.35
35	Textiles (17)	535.33	−0.7	10.04	3.81	11.46	12.61	539.26	538.10	545.97	390.29
36	Tobaccos (2)	1261.64	−0.5	13.15	4.10	8.35	36.99	1267.42	1263.04	1272.21	801.53
41	OTHER GROUPS (86)	796.03	−0.5	8.55	4.07	15.04	17.65	799.70	793.09	800.40	730.43
42	Chemicals (20)	1014.79	+0.1	8.63	4.31	14.10	29.37	1013.67	995.11	1000.72	728.53
44	Office Equipment (4)	257.76	−0.5	7.21	4.13	16.77	7.55	259.28	256.27	256.07	226.57
45	Shipping and Transport (12)	1562.03	−0.3	7.67	4.34	16.62	44.94	1567.29	1559.32	1546.19	1351.78
47	Telephone Networks (2)	783.12	−1.0	11.09	4.72	12.26	16.67	791.00	781.04	792.07	926.01
48	Miscellaneous (48)	1104.14	−0.4	6.33	3.15	19.84	17.26	1108.16	1111.60	1125.28	900.91
49	INDUSTRIAL GROUP(483)	834.95	−0.6	8.61	3.68	14.71	18.83	839.77	836.07	845.80	718.95
51	Oil & Gas (7)	1405.67	−0.1	11.61	6.37	10.61	62.83	1407.33	1395.99	1395.56	1122.75
59	500 SHARE INDEX(500)	883.07	−0.5	8.97	4.00	14.06	22.31	887.68	883.38	892.41	753.84
61	FINANCIAL GROUP (118)	598.61	−0.8	—	4.76	—	18.25	603.58	601.08	607.08	521.67
62	Banks (8)	642.83	−1.7	19.58	5.69	7.01	23.94	653.94	650.06	657.02	527.42
65	Insurance (Life) (9)	855.43	+0.2	—	4.55	—	27.29	853.72	849.18	855.13	821.74
66	Insurance (Composite) (7)	449.27	+0.3	—	4.83	—	15.57	447.83	445.14	450.38	400.94
67	Insurance (Brokers) (9)	1172.82	−1.1	7.99	4.49	16.31	36.30	1185.33	1182.22	1194.23	1168.14
69	Merchant Banks (11)	338.53	−2.2	—	4.27	—	6.43	346.18	347.06	354.69	283.42
70	Property (50)	806.75	−0.6	5.77	3.57	22.51	17.24	811.63	809.31	813.82	678.02
70	Other Financial (24)	362.27	−0.5	9.08	4.41	13.43	9.43	363.95	363.76	366.86	300.43
71	Investment Trusts (98)	848.32	+0.6	—	2.69	—	15.44	843.56	839.28	840.96	630.28
81	Mining Finance (9)	325.27	−0.9	9.62	4.93	12.22	11.30	328.13	326.31	330.32	245.89
91	Overseas Traders (13)	755.56	−0.7	10.63	5.92	11.35	29.74	760.82	754.47	761.27	580.02
99	ALL-SHARE INDEX (731)	807.02	−0.5	—	4.09	—	20.95	811.28	807.41	815.34	685.29

	Index No.	Day's Change	Day's High	Day's Low	Dec 2	Dec 1	Nov 28	Nov 27	Nov 26	Year ago
FT-SE 100 SHARE INDEX ♦	1615.1	−10.4	1627.2	1608.9	1625.5	1617.8	1636.7	1632.5	1633.0	1415.6

Figure 4.2 (b) *FT – Actuaries indices*

index is the best known but is less broadly based than the Tokyo SE new index.

Progress test 4

1. Why was the 'big bang' planned, and what effect has it had on the small investor? (**4, 7**)

4. Investment in shares

2. What do the following mean:
(a) The Stock Exchange account
(b) Account day
(c) New time
(d) TALISMAN
(e) SEPON? (**11, 12**)

3. What opportunities do the USM, the OTC, the Third market and the BES offer:
(a) small companies
(b) investors? (**16–24**)

4. Describe the different ways in which a company may issue new shares. (**28–33**)

5. How should an investor in a company's shares respond to a takeover bid? (**42**)

6. What are the differences between the *FT* industrial ordinary index, the *FT*–Actuaries all-share index, and the *FT*–SE 100 share index? (**53–55**)

5
The selection of shares

This chapter reviews the main ways in which investors can evaluate shares and is intended to provide some guidance on how suitable shares for investment can be selected. The chapter is divided into the following sections:

(*a*) The criteria for share selection.

(*b*) Fundamental analysis.

(*c*) The use of information published daily in the 'London Share Service' page of the *Financial Times*.

(*d*) The use of Extel cards.

(*e*) Technical analysis.

(*f*) The efficient market hypothesis – is it possible to pick winners?

(*g*) The analysis of a company's annual report and accounts – appendix.

The criteria for share selection

1. Why invest in shares? Investment in shares is undertaken in the anticipation of obtaining:

(*a*) capital gains from a rising share price;

(*b*) a flow of income from the shares' dividend payments:

(*c*) protection from inflation by investing in the 'real' assets of the company so that both the share price and the dividend payments rise in step with inflation.

The relative importance of capital gains and income will depend

RICS Books

TITLE	INVESTMENT A PRACTICAL APPROACH
AUTHOR	D S KERRIDGE
PUBLISHER	PITMAN
SUPPLIER	OIPITO11

DATE INTO STOCK
21/02/91

PUBLICATION DATE
0/00/00

SP110133

5. The selection of shares

upon the personal circumstances of the investor which is something we discussed in Chapter 2.

2. What causes a share price to fluctuate? A share's price rises when a majority of investors expect the company's turnover and profits to increase at a faster rate giving rise to the expectation of larger dividends in the future. There are two sets of influences which affect a share price:

(*a*) *Market influences*: when investors believe that the economic and investment outlook is improving, they will increase their investment in shares in anticipation of higher future profits and dividends. Most share prices will then move upwards together. Conversely, a gloomy outlook causes most share prices to fall together.

(*b*) *Specific influences*: these are factors that affect investors' expectations of the future levels of profits of the particular company, but not all companies in the market, e.g. the anouncement of a large contract, a technical innovation, a strike.

Investing successfully in shares therefore involves two sets of decisions.

(*a*) Is the market likely to rise or fall? We shall discuss the factors that should be considered in the two final chapters.

(*b*) Which shares are likely to perform best?

Real success in investment requires not only correct answers to both questions, but correct timing of action. The investor needs to buy the shares with the best prospects *before* the share price is pushed up by everybody else getting the same idea.

3. The risk associated with investment in shares. Shares are a more risky investment than a building society deposit because their future rate of return cannot be forecasted with a high degree of certainty. The rate of return from an investment in shares is made up of two parts:

(*a*) the dividend payments received;

(*b*) the capital gain or loss resulting from the change in share price.

72 Stocks and shares

If the company has a record of a steady rate of growth of dividends, its future dividends can be estimated possibly with more certainty than its future share price.

As stated above, the causes of share price fluctuations can be either specific influences or market influences. Hence investment analysts have said that the total risk can be divided into specific risk and market risk.

(a) *Specific risk* – the name given to fluctuations in the rate of return attributable to factors affecting the particular company but not the market as a whole. Investment theory claims that if an investor holds a portfolio of at least 15 different shares, all from different sectors of the market, most of the specific risk is diversified away. This means that when a particular event causes one share in the portfolio to perform badly, there is probably another share where a different factor has caused it to perform better than expected. Thus it is safer to invest in a balanced portfolio of shares than just a few.

(b) *Market risk* – the name given to fluctuations in the rate of return of a share that are attributable to factors affecting the market as a whole. No matter how many shares are included in the investor's portfolio, there will be no reduction in market risk as a result of diversification.

Investors in shares expect to earn a rate of return greater than that available from risk-free investments like a building society account or a National Savings Bank account. The extra return required is a risk premium – compensation for expected fluctuations in the future rates of return from shares. Investment theory maintains that since specific risk can be reduced to very low levels by investors holding a diversified portfolio of shares, the risk premium that investors should earn from investment in shares should not be related to the share's total risk, but only its market risk. The market risk of a share should be thought of as being a measure of how dependent changes in the rate of return of that share are upon changes in the rate of return of the market. Some investment analysts try to measure the market risk of different shares. This is done by comparing fluctuations in the risk premium of the share with the risk premium that could have been earned from investing in the portfolio of shares that comprise the *FT*–Actuaries all-share index.

5. The selection of shares

This is shown in Figure 5.1 (remember, the risk premium is the rate of return earned over the risk-free rate, i.e. total rate of return minus the risk-free rate). The gradient of the line, b, which is called beta by investment analysts, is a measure of the share's market risk. The higher the value of beta, the greater the market risk, and hence the greater the required rate of return that should be demanded by investors.

Another factor affecting the risk of investment in a particular company's shares is its level of *gearing*. Gearing is a measure of the proportion of the company's long-term finance that is comprised of debt capital. The effect of high levels of gearing is to make the earnings available to shareholders much more volatile, as the example in Table 5A shows. This will make the price of the share more volatile and hence increase the risk of the shareholders' investment.

Table 5A *The effect of gearing upon earnings per share*

	Hi Gear Co Ltd £m	Lo Gear Co Ltd £m
12½% loanstock	80	20
Shareholders' funds (10p shares)	20	80
Capital employed	100	100

	Good year £m	Bad year £m	Good year £m	Bad year £m
Trading profit	50	20	50	20
Interest	10	10	2.5	2.5
Profit before tax	40	10	47.5	17.5
Tax at 35%	14	3.5	16.6	6.1
Profit after tax	26	6.5	30.9	11.4
EPS	13p	3.25p	3.9p	1.4p
The variation in EPS is shown by Good year / Bad year	4		2.79	

74 Stocks and shares

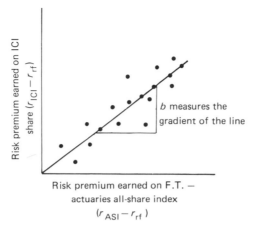

Figure 5.1 *The measurement of the level of market risk on an ICI share*

r_{ICI} = rate of return earned on an ICI share
r_{rf} = risk-free rate of return
r_{ASI} = rate of return earned on the *FT*–Actuaries all-share index

The risk premiums earned on an ICI share over a series of time periods are plotted against the risk premium earned from investment in the all-share index over the same time periods. A linear regression measures the relationship between the two risk premiums, and the equation of the line is:

$$(r_{ICI} - r_{rf}) = a + b(r_{ASI} - r_{rf})$$

By adding the risk-free rate to both sides, the equation identifies the investors' required rate of return for ICI shares.

$$r_{ICI} = a + r_{rf} + b(r_{ASI} - r_{rf})$$

Since we said earlier that the rate of return on a share should be the risk-free rate plus a risk premium dependent upon the level of market risk, the value of the intercept with the vertical axis, *a* in this equation, should tend to zero, otherwise there would be a third factor influencing the rate of return. Hence we are left with:

5. The selection of shares

r_{ICI} = risk-free return + risk premium dependent upon the size of beta, the measure of the market risk of ICI's share

$r_{rf} + b(r_{ASI} - r_{rf})$

This example is an illustration of *the capital asset pricing model* which is used by some investment analysts to estimate a share's required rate of return making allowance for its degree of risk.

Fundamental analysis

4. Definition. Fundamental analysis is the valuation of a company's share by the examination of its recent performance and the prediction of its future levels of profits and dividends. In theory, shareholders buy shares for the future stream of dividend payments that they will receive.

5. The calculation of the fundamental analysts. The current share price should be the present value of this future stream of dividends discounted at the required rate of return by its shareholders. The required rate of return from a share is affected by the riskiness of its future rate of returns, and the capital asset pricing model described in Fig. 5.1 is a theoretical model for defining the required rate of return for different shares. Thus we have:

$$\text{Current share price} = \frac{d1}{1+r} + \frac{d2}{(1+r)^2} + \frac{d3}{(1+r)^3} \cdots \frac{dn}{(1+r)^n}$$

where $d1 \ldots dn$ = dividends from years 0 to n
r = the required rate of return from investment in the company's shares

The further investors look into the future, the harder it becomes to predict the level of dividend payments. However, by assuming a constant rate of growth of dividends, g per cent, it can be shown that this model simplifies to:

76 Stocks and shares

$$\text{Current share price} = \frac{d1}{r-g}$$

e.g. $d1 = 5\text{p}$
$r = 20$ per cent
$g = 10$ per cent

$$\text{Theoretical share price} = \frac{5\text{p}}{20\% - 10\%} = 50\text{p}$$

These models are used by some analysts to evaluate a company's current share price. By comparing their estimated 'correct' share price with the current market share price, they can advise their clients whether the market price is cheap or dear.

The analysis of a company and the forecasting of its future dividends will involve a professional investment analyst in the examination of the company's accounts and also in research on its prospects together with those of its customers and its rivals. See the appendix to this Chapter for an analysis of a company's annual report and accounts.

The *Financial Times* 'London Share Service'

The 'London Share Service' is shown each day on the two penultimate pages of the *Financial Times*. It gives details of UK and some overseas company shares and fixed-interest securities which are quoted on the London Stock Exchange. The reader should find these two pages in a copy of the *Financial Times* and follow the analyisis in the text with the newspaper open.

6. The entry for the Burton Group plc. Under the heading 'Drapery and Stores' will be found the Burton Group, the company whose accounts are analysed in the appendix to this Chapter. At the time of writing, this was the entry:

1986 High	Low	Stock	Price	+ or −	Div Net	Cvr	Y'ld Gr's	P/E
354	242	Burton Group 50p	296	+2	4.4	3.1	2.1	21.0
(1)		(2)	(3)	(4)	(5)	(6)	(7)	(8)

5. The selection of shares

What does all this information on each company mean?

Column (1): the high and low for the year shows the range within which the share price has fluctuated. It is useful to compare with the present share price to discover its current strength or weakness. In the Monday issue of the *Financial Times*, the high and low prices for the year are replaced by the months in which the company's dividends are paid.

Column (2): the name of the stock or share, and its nominal or par value. Where no par value is shown against a share, it means its value is 25 pence. The par value is only of technical interest – what is important to investors is the market price.

Column (3): the market price of the share is 296 pence. This was the latest available price and represents a middle price between the bid and offer price. Investors should remember that the share price may well have changed since it was recorded on the previous day.

Column (4): this shows the rise or fall in the security's price on the previous trading day. On Mondays, this column shows the date when the security last went 'ex div'. A purchaser of a security 'ex div' will not receive the next dividend that will be paid shortly. With some shares changing hands very frequently, it is administratively necessary for a date to be fixed after which ownership will not entitle the holder to the next dividend. Hence a security will normally fall in price by the amount of the dividend to be paid at the start of business on the day that it is declared to be 'ex div'.

Column (5): 'div net' tells you the dividend in pence that has been paid in the latest year. Where possible, the *Financial Times* updates this figure to incorporate the latest half-yearly figures. It is called the *net dividend* because income tax at the standard rate has already been deducted. The *gross dividend* is found by dividing the net dividend by one minus the standard rate of income tax.

EXAMPLE:
The Burton Group
Net dividend = 4.4 pence
Standard rate of income tax = 29 per cent
One minus the standard rate of income tax = 71 per cent
Gross dividend = 4.4 pence $\times \frac{100}{71}$ = 6.2 pence

78 Stocks and shares

Column (6): cover is the number of times that earnings per share is greater than the net dividend per share. A very low level of cover tells you that the dividend is not very secure and the company is retaining little profit to invest in new projects for the future.

Column (7): the last two columns are probably the two most useful pieces of financial information for investors. The yield gross is found by dividing the gross dividend by the current share price. In the case of the Burton Group, the gross dividend was calculated from the net dividend to be 6.2 pence. Dividing the gross dividend by the current share price of 296 pence gives a gross dividend yield of 2.1 per cent. The advantage of calculating the gross dividend yield is that it can be compared with the gross yields of other shares and investments.

Column (8): P/E stands for the 'price earnings ratio'. This is calculated by dividing the current share price by the earnings per share shown in the latest year. The P/E ratio is therefore the number of times that the current share price exceeds the historical (most recently recorded) earnings per share. Putting it another way, it is the number of years of historical earnings that you pay for when you buy at the current share price. (The earnings per share figure for the Burton Group shown at the bottom of its profit and loss account for 1985 (*see* Table 5C in the appendix to this chapter) has been superseded by interim results and a scrip issue.)

7. The *Stock Exchange Daily Official List*. The *Financial Times* does not publish in their 'London Share Service' details of all the securities quoted on the London Stock Exchange. To obtain details on other securities, investors should consult the *Stock Exchange Daily Official List*, a copy of which is frequently available in larger public libraries.

This lists all stocks and shares quoted on the Stock Exchange and gives details of their quotation on the previous day, although this is wider than that which would actually be quoted by a market maker. It gives details of when the security last went 'ex div', when it was paid, when the last transaction took place in the security and its price. If the latest transactions were on the previous day, no date is given, but the prices at which transactions took place are recorded in ascending order. This record gives no indication as to volume, whether the transaction was a purchase or a sale, or how the price

5. The selection of shares 79

fluctuated within this range (*see* Fig. 5.2).

The major differences between the details available in SEDOL and those provided in the back pages of the *Financial Times* are:

(*i*) SEDOL provides a list of all the securities listed on the London Stock Exchange while the *Financial Times* lists only those which are most frequently traded.

(*ii*) SEDOL lists the prices at which trades took place on the previous trading day. Prices are listed in ascending order with each price given once only. However, it gives no indication of the volume of sales, nor whether each transaction was a purchase or a sale. Where no trade took place it gives the price and date on which the last transaction took place. The *Financial Times* records the prices at the close of business.

(*iii*) SEDOL gives a 'quotation' (which is composed of a bid and offer price) for each security except those listed on the USM. However, the spread is much wider than that obtainable from a market-maker and is not intended to represent prices at which investors can deal. Nevertheless, these prices are used as the basis of valuation for inheritance tax calculations, with the price selected for the calculation being one 'quarter up' from the lower price, i.e. the lower price plus 25 per cent of the difference between the two prices. The *Financial Times* does not give a spread but quotes a middle market price.

(*iv*) SEDOL gives details of when the security last went ex dividend, when that dividend was paid, and the amount of the dividend. The *Financial Times* provides this type of information only on Mondays.

(*v*) The *Financial Times* provides information of interest to investors not provided by SEDOL. This includes the dividend cover, the gross yield and the price earnings ratio for shares, and the interest yield and redemption yield for fixed interest securities. The *Financial Times* also records the change in price of the security on the previous trading day and the high and low prices of the security for the last year.

8. Comparison of dividend yields. If an investor is seeking income, then the dividend yield of alternative investments should be compared. The yield on shares is considerably lower than that obtainable on other investments, many of them less risky than

…

The Stock Exchange
Daily Official List

Friday 26 September 1986

Quarterly subscription £132.00 paper, £92.00 microfiche
By post £160.00 paper, £110.00 microfiche

Total number of bargains included 19192
Serial number 1409

Single copy £2.40 paper, £1.70 microfiche
By post £2.90 paper, £2.00 microfiche

Contents

- 2 British Funds, etc
- 3 Corporation and County Stocks
- 5 UK Public Boards
- 5 Commonwealth–Government
- 5 Foreign Stocks, Bonds, etc–(coupons payable in London)
- 22 Corporation Stocks – Foreign
- 22 Sterling Issues by Overseas Borrowers
- 23 Banks and Discount Companies
- 25 Breweries and Distilleries
- 27 Building Societies
- 27 Commercial, Industrial, etc
- 55 Financial Trusts, Land, etc
- 60 Insurance
- 61 Investment Trusts
- 67 Unit Trusts
- 67 Mines – Miscellaneous
- 68 Mines – South African
- 69 Oil
- 70 Property
- 73 Plantations
- 74 Railways
- 74 Shipping
- 74 Utilities
- 75 Water Works
- 79 Traded Options
- 83 USM Appendix

Dollar rates at 15.30

US $1.4355 per £1
Canadian $1.9940 per £1

FT–SE 100 Index

1557.7 at 15:30
1568.6–7.3 at close, CLOSE

Account dealing dates

Bargains for the following account are permitted during the last two business days of the current account

First dealings	Last dealings	Account days
15 September	26 September	6 October
29 September	10 October	20 October
13 October	24 October	3 November
27 October	7 November	17 November

Announcements

ERRATA

The following business done should not have been recorded in the DOL dated 25th September

Amstrad Consumer Electronics Ord p110 12, Chrysalis Group Ord p189, Dixons Group Ord p330, Firth (G.M.) (Hldgs) Ord p75, Hanson Trust Ord p180 200, London & Midland Industrials Ord p235, London International Group Ord p200, North Kalgurli Mines p47, North Kalgurli Mines New p44

The following business done should have been recorded at "special prices" in the DOL dated 25th September

Beatrix Mines Ord Shs of NPV p200, Premier Consolidated Oilfields Ord p22.7272,
Ranks Hovis McDougall 6¼% Uns Ln Stk (85/88) £90, Reed International 10% Uns Ln Stk (2004/09) £94,
Turner & Newall 11¼% Mtg Deb Stk (95/2000) £101, VG Instruments Ord p449, WPP Group Ord p530½z

Traded Options
The price shown for Distillers Co Ord is the Asserted price

Total turnover figures in equity stocks

Date	No. of bargains	Value(£'s)	No. of shares traded
22 September	12760	377384000	170300000
23 September	21304	525554000	233100000
24 September	17114	487358000	223400000
25 September	18003	527308000	241700000
19 September	16190	510994000	228200000

Figure 5.2 *The Stock Exchange Daily Official List* (a) *Details of contents*

Commercial, Industrial, etc

continued

xd	Pay	%	Code	C	Name, description		Quotation			Business done	
28Jy	5Se	p 1.3 (N)	427-041	27	**Hill & Smith Hldgs PLC** Ord 25p		p91-101		—	101‡Φ 98 9 100	
11Au	30Se	7	427-193	6	14% 1st Mtg Deb Stk 2000/03		£107-112		xd	108½ (18Au86)	
11Au	30Oc	p 2.3 (N)	427-267	51	**Hillards PLC** Ord 10p		p158-178		xd	173Φ 5Φ 8Φ 168 9 70 2 3	
12My	2Jy	p 3 (N)	427-870	49	**Hillsdown Hldgs PLC** Ord 10p	⁝⁝⁝	p290-310		—	299Φ 300Φ 3Φ 293 5 7 8 9 300 300‡ 2	
4Je	4Je	DM10 (Y)	S 430-168	68	**Hoechst Ag** DM50 (Cpn 50)	◕	£87-92	⊞	—	89¾ (24Se86)	7q
4Je	4Je	DM1 (Y)	S 430-180	68	Cdbr(Iss Warburg & Co)DM5		p870-920	⊞	—	895 (23Se86)	7q
—	—	—	S 430-191	68	Wts to sub for Shs of DM50 each		£170-220	⊞	—	DM676 (12Se86)	7q
12My	30Je	5	430-210	6	**Hoechst Finance PLC** 10% Gtd Uns Ln Stk 1990		£95-100		—	99 (13Je86)	
12My	30Je	5	430-124	8	10% Gtd Uns Ln Stk 1990 with Rts	☽	£320-340		—	280 (23Je86)	
11Au	1Oc	p 1.1 (N)	431-503	62	**Hollas Group PLC** Ord 5p		p38-48		xd	43Φ ½‡Φ 43 4‡ ½‡	
—	—	—	432-205	17	**Hollis PLC** Ord 2½p		p75-85		—	81Φ 78 9 81 ¾‡	
Au81	—	2.45 (N)	432-261	7	7% Cum Prf £1	✲	p90-100		—	—	
—	—	—	432-216	8	*252% Cnv Subord Ln Stk 1998 2½p* ◆		p76-86		—	—	
—	—	—	S 432-227	8	*252% CnvSubLnStk 1998 2½p(LA-26/9/86)* ◆		p76-86		—	81 (22Se86)	
11Au	30Se	p 2.5 (N)	432-722	75	***Holmes & Marchant Group PLC** Ord 10p*		p293-313		xd	300 (23Se86)	
12My	22Jy	$ 0.0135 (N)	786-087	44	***Holmes Protection Group Inc** Shs of Com Stk $0.01*		p108-128	⊞	—	111Φ 2Φ 4Φ 111 2 2‡ 3 3‡ 4‡	
12My	1Au	p 2.35 (N)	433-640	68	**Holt Lloyd International PLC** Ord 10p		p79-89		—	85Φ 86	
1Ap	30My	p 2 (N)	434-461	58	**Home Charm Group PLC** Ord 10p		—		—	£ 3.23 (7My86)	
15Se	23Oc	p 3.25 (N)	434-427	52	**Home Counties Newspapers Hldgs PLC** Ord 25p		p190-240		xd	200 (19Se86)	
1Ap	9My	p 1.15 (N)	434-546	49	**Home Farm Products PLC** Ord 10p		p90-100		—	90 2	
26Au	15Se	$ 0.5 q	S 435-185	35	**Honeywell Inc** Com Stk $1.50	◘	£52¼-54¼	⊞	—	44¾ (27Au86)	7q
23My	23My	Y 6	S 435-141	43	**Honda Motor Co Ld** Shs of Com Stk Y50		p533-553		—	577 (24Se86)	3w 7q
10Je	4Au	p 5.5 (N)	437-620	24	**Hopkinsons Hldgs PLC** Ord 50p		p268-288		—	275‡Φ 8Φ 82Φ 275 7 80 1 2 2‡ 3 3‡ 4‡ 5½‡	
Je	31Jy	p 2.625 (N)	437-664	7	5.25% Cum Prf £1		p60-70		—	65 (2Se86)	
Se	10Oc	p 0.88 (N)	437-909	48	***Horizon Travel PLC** Ord 25p*		p114-124		xd	120Φ 1Φ 118 9 20	
12My	31My	p 2.45 (N)	438-269	7	**Horne Bros PLC** 7% Cum Prf £1	✲	p53-63		—	53 (30Jy86)	
12My	31My	3⅞	438-281	6	7¾% Uns Ln Stk 95/2000		£75-80		—	77 (5Se86)	
30Je	25Jy	p 1.5 (N)	743-264	54	***Horne(Robert)Group PLC** Ord 20p*		p203-223		—	205Φ 210‡ 3	
30Je	25Jy	p 1.5 (N)	743-286	54	*Non-Vtg "A" Ord 20p*		p185-205		—	188Φ 195	
30Je	1Au	$ 0.165 q	S 439-314	76	**Hospital Corporation of America** Shs of Com Stk $1		£23⅞-25⅞	⊞	—	25⅛ (19Se86)	7q
28Jy	31Jy	p 1.575 (N)	440-123	7	**House of Fraser PLC** 4½% Cum Prf £1	✲	p95-105		—	40 (19My86)	
28Jy	31Jy	p 1.925 (N)	440-026	7	5½% Cum Prf £1	✲	p95-105		—	46 (19No85)	
28Jy	31Jy	p 2.625 (N)	440-048	7	7½% Cum Prf £1	✲	p95-105		—	115‡ ¼‡ (23My86)	
30Je	7Jy	4	440-101	6	8% Mtg Deb Stk 86/91		£88-93		—	91⅞‡ 2‡ (22Au86)	
30Je	31Jy	3	440-060	6	6% Uns Ln Stk 93/98		£65-70		—	67 (28Au86)	
30Je	31Jy	4⅛	440-082	6	8¼% Uns Ln Stk 93/98		£77-82		—	80½ (25Se86)	
1Ap	9Je	p 5.4 (N)	440-189	59	**House of Lerose PLC** Ord 25p	⁝⁝⁝	p145-165		—	155 (24Se86)	
—	—	—	440-747	53	***Howard & Wyndham PLC** Ord 5p*		p10-20		—	13 (24Se86)	
16Je	15Jy	9	440-576	6	18% Uns Ln Stk 76/91		£88-98		—	96 (8Se86)	
15Se	21Oc	p 0.7 (N)	440-769	18	**Howard Shuttering(Hldgs) PLC** Ord 10p		p37-47		xd	42 (25Se86) 43Φ	
1Se	1Oc	p 2.95 (N)	441-405	22	**Howden Group PLC** Ord Stk 25p	⁝⁝⁝	p90-100		xd	93Φ 6‡Φ 91 2 2‡ ½‡ 3 3‡ 4 4‡ ¼ 5‡	
14Ap	30Ap	3⅞	441-427	6	7¾% Deb Stk 86-91		£90-95		—	94‡ ¼‡ (23My86)	
14Ap	30Ap	4⅛	441-461	6	8¼% Deb Stk 86/91		£91-96		—	96‡ ¼‡ (23My86)	
15Se	30Se	1.75 (N)	441-643	7	**Hoyle(Joseph) & Son Ld** 5% Cum Prf Stk £1	✲	p37-47		xd	41 (9My86)	
30Je	31Jy	$C0.15 q	S 442-624	73	**Hudson's Bay Co** Ord Npv	✢	£12¼-14¼	⊞	—	12¾ 3 (10Jy86)	5y
31Jy	25Au	$ 0.02 q	S 442-884	22	**Hughes Tool Co** Com Stk $1	◘	£4¼-6¼	⊞	—	11‡ (21My85)	7q
2Je	1Jy	1¾	S 443-702	6	**Hulett Refineries Ld** 3½% 1st Mtg Stlg Deb Stk		£55-65		—	58 (19Au86)	
23De	24Ja	p 2 (N) (Y)	446-604	22	**Hunslet(Hldgs) PLC** Ord 25p	⁝⁝⁝	p185-225		—	203	

5. The selection of shares

Figure 5.2 (b) *A sample page*

Daily Official List

Friday 26 September 1986

+ For possible restrictions on transfer other than the normal restrictions on transfers of partly-paid shares, see S.E.O.Y-B
◊ For particulars/numbers refer to Quotations Department
∴ Conversion Rights have expired
:: Commission on these securities to be charged at the rates laid down in section A(e) of Appendices 39 and 41. The provisions of rules 207(1) and 208 may be applied
□ Company not subject to pre-emption requirements. Equity Capital may be issued for cash other than to existing shareholders by way of rights.
∗ On account of, or including arrears
× For year
● Net
q For quarter
ⁱ/₅₀ Participating dividend
ⁱ Including participating dividend
h For broken period
▪ This amount should be read in conjunction with the payment details in the W.O.I
♦ Dividend paid in cash or scrip at holder's option. For details see W.O.I
/ Special date
▼ Amount(s) actual of last payment
✕ Code number for the security in registered/bearer Form, for code number of security in bearer/registered form refer to the Master File Services Section of the Council
† For further details see S.E.O.Y-B
▷ Loan capital denominated in sterling to which the exemption from stamp duty on transfer does not apply
⦂⦂⦂ Double Taxation Relief. Company is prepared to operate the revised arrangement for application of taxation. See Council Notice No 52/73 and W.O.I page 108 of 18Feb74
○ These securities should be regarded as identical for the purpose of the Commission Rules.
● The rate of dividend expressed in the terms of issue or in the title of this security is affected by para 18 of Schedule 23 to the Finance Act 1972
⊛ C.S.I. levy not payable
◆ These securities may come within the conditions of Council Notice 50/80 for commission purposes.
△ Bargains done at Special Prices.
◇ Bargains done with a non-member or except to overseas markets
‡ Bargains done the previous day
u The documents of title for the bearer security have not been printed from engraved steel plates and do not therefore comply with The Stock Exchange's requirements
11 The "rate %" shown in brackets is the rate at which accrued interest should be calculated
1h Ex Dividend Action cancelled - See W.O.I
1k The amount payable by the purchaser is the bargain prices plus an amount equal to the gross interest accrued from the day after the last interest payment date to the settlement date for which the bargain was done or, in the case of transactions done 'ex interest' minus an amount equal to the gross interest accruing from the settlement date for which the bargain was done to the interest payment date
1r Royal Dutch - Co. has power to invalidate Br. secs. claimed to have been lost or stolen
1s Shell Transport & Trading - Dealings in Ord (Bearer) to be in amounts and multiples of 4 shares.
1x Refer to Announcements, Page 1
2a Armavir - Tovapbe Railway Gtd 4.5% Bds. of 09-13 (Gtd. by Russian Govt) (1999) 1909 issue due against Cpn 18. 1913 issue due against Cpn 11
2c Fees charged for registering transfers

6p Represented by Bonds - Notes to Bearer in denomn of FF5,000
6q Represented by Bonds - Notes to Bearer in denomn of NK 10,000
6r Represented by Bonds - Notes to Bearer in denomn of LF50,000
6s Represented by Bonds - Notes to Bearer in denomn of $A1,000
6v Represented by Bonds - Notes to Bearer in denomn of KD 5,000
6w Registered Notes of $1,000
6x Registered Notes of $1,000 and $10,000
7b BTR Nylex Ltd Ord $A0.50 for Checking use Code Number 6-437-129
7d Stamp Duty is chargeable on the 2p par value of the Alexander & Alexander Europe PLC associated Dividend shares.
7n Kakuzi Ltd. Payment of dividends to non-resident shareholders, to be made after necessary approval from Central Bank of Kenya
7q Overseas security for commission purposes - (see Council Notice 32/84)
7r Felixstowe Dock & Railway Co Pref units 3.25% half yearly payment, ex dividend 12th May 1986.
7v Dee Corporation Ex Rights (Rule 617.2) 4th June
7w St Modwen Properties PLC the dividend of 1.6625p payable 31st July 86, XD 30th June
86 Payment of all arrears. 9.975p, payable 31st July 86, XD 14th July 86
7y Safeway Stores Inc the dividends of $0.255, XD 26/08/86 & $0.17 XD 27/08/86, both payable 30/09/86
8k Combined English Stores Group Ex Rights(Rule 617.2) 26th Sept 86.
ve Vide Errata
XR Ex Rights
XC Ex Capitalisation
XS Ex Stock Distribution
XL Ex Liquidation Distribution
XE Ex Entitlement
XP Ex Repayment of capital
w With coupon
pm Premium
S Settled outside Talisman
C Eligible for settlement through the Central Gifts Office

Notes:
Code number - user should note when encoding the Code Number(s) must be prefixed by the lead digit '0'.
Only one bargain in any one security is recorded at any one price
Prices are shown in ascending order
Pending compliance with full listing requirements new securities are shown in italics

2g Dividend/interest payment not made Ex.
2j Oskarshamnsverkets Kraftgrupp Aktiebolag Retractable Bonds 1997 Retractable at par at the option of the holder on 1De85, 1De89, 1De93 and payable in full on 1De97. Interest to 1De85 15.75%, and thereafter as determined by the issuer.
3e The interest rate may be redetermined at the issuers option on specified dates before the final redemption date. The notes are retractable at the holders option at these dates. For details of current coupon and specified dates refer to Quotations Dept.
3n For code numbers of individual Short Term Notes refer to Master File Services Section of the Council.
3w Dealings normally in units of 1,000 shares
4f The Quotation is expressed in Deutsche Marks as a percentage nominal amounts of the Bonds at fixed rates as under:—
Ireland 7⅞ 79–88 DM 7.55(G)
Metropolitan Est & Prop.int.N.V DM 7 7⅝8
New Zealand 6.75% DM 11 1/9
Norwegian St. & Municipal Pow DM 9.65
Rothmans Int 6.25% DM 7.8
Turn (J) of J DM 11.06
4r Greek — (Nat Mort. Bank of Greece.) The interest due 1De40) was paid on that date in London on Sterling, Coupon 18 (Coupon 16 in case of Series 'B')
4t The amount payable by the purchaser is the bargain price plus an amount equal to the gross interest accrued to the settlement date for which the bargain was done.
5a Preference Share capital carrying rights to vote in all circumstances at general meetings of the company.
5c Redeemable at Government Option.
5d S.Rhodesia 4% 1972–74 (Last xd 8No65). See Council Notices No.96/65 and No.118/79 London Sterling, Coupon 18 (Coupon 16 in case of Series 'B')
5e S.Rhodesia 3.5% 61–66 & 6% 78–81 (Last xd 15De65) See Council Notices No.3/66 and No.118/79
5f S.Rhodesia 3% 71–73 (Last xd 11Je66). See Council Notices No.26/66 and No.118/79
5g S.Rhodesia 3.5% 67–69 4.25% 77–82 and 5% 75–80 (Last xd 15Fe66) See Council Notices No.43/66 and No.118/79
5h S.Rhodesia 2.5% 65–70 and 4.5% 58–68 (Last xd 1Mr66). See Council Notices No.50/66 and No.118/79
5j S.Rhodesia 6% 76–79 (Last xd 21Ap66). See Council Notices No.65/66 and No.118/79
5n Calcutta Elect.Supply Corp(India) Ld. Payment of dividends to non-resident holders to be made after necessary approval from Reserve Bank of India
5v Anglo-Indonesian Corp.PLC Flg.Rate Uns. Ln. Stk. 85/98 interest for period 7/4/86 to 6/10/86 at the rate of 11% p.a.
5w Mercantile House Hldgs PLC V.R. Uns. Ln. Stk. 84/89. Interest for period 16/6/86 to 15/12/86 at the rate of 9.4375% p.a.
5y U.K. Transfer Agent provided, see Council Notice 73/83. Special Shapes and Marking
Name requirements do not apply
6a Represented by Bonds – Notes/Debts to Bearer in denom of $1,000
6b Represented by Bonds – Notes to Bearer in denom of $5,000
6c Represented by Bonds – Notes to Bearer in denom of $10,000
6d Represented by Bonds – Notes to Bearer in denom of $1,000 and $5,000
6e Represented by Bonds – **Notes to Bearer in denom of $1,000 and 10,000**
6f Represented by Bonds – Notes to Bearer in denom of $1,000 and 100,000
6g Represented by Bonds – **Notes to Bearer in denom of $10,000 and 100,000**
6h Represented by Bonds – Notes to Bearer in denom of $1,000, 10,000 and 100,000
6i Represented by Bonds – Notes to Bearer in denom of $500
6j Represented by Bonds – Notes to Bearer in denom of £1,000
6l Represented by Bonds – Notes to Bearer in denom of £1,000 and £10,000
6m Represented by Bonds – **Notes/Debts to Bearer in denom of $C1,000**

Figure 5.2 *(c) The key to symbols*

shares, such as building society deposits or gilt-edged securities. This phenomenon of risky investments offering a higher yield than low-risk investments is sometimes called the *reverse yield gap*. It exists for two reasons:

(a) Investors expect the dividends from shares to grow each year with the company's profits. This provides not only a growing income but protection against increases in the cost of living. Low risk cash investments do not provide this protection.

(b) Although share prices go up and down in the short run, investors expect them in the long run to grow with the company and more than keep up with inflation. Without a yield greater than the rate of inflation, the real value of cash investments will fall.

9. Why do dividend yields vary between companies? Share prices reflect investors' expectations concerning the future rate of growth of the sales, profits and dividends of a company. The more optimistic their expectations, the higher the current share price will rise, and so the lower the current dividend yield will fall. Thus companies with low dividend yields are viewed as those with a prospect of rapid future growth of profits and dividends, while companies with high dividend yields are seen as offering either more modest or little growth potential.

When selecting shares to provide an income, an investor should be extremely wary of selecting those with the highest dividend yields. Some of these would be very risky investments, and the companies may cease to trade. The investor should seek out those companies whose income is securely based on a sound range of products, but where the yield is above average because the market does not expect dynamic growth.

10. Why do P/E ratios vary between companies? Again, the fact that the current share prices reflect investors' expectations concerning future rates of growth of profits is the key to understanding this ratio. The greater the expectations of investors, the higher the share price relative to current earnings per share, and hence the P/E ratio. There are two types of situation which give rise to a share having a high P/E ratio.

(a) Growth stocks – where the market expects rapid future rates of growth of profits and dividends.

(b) Recovery stocks – where earnings per share have been depressed by poor past performance, but the share price has risen in anticipation of the correction of the problems and the restoration of a higher level of earnings per share.

Thus the gross dividend yield and P/E ratio of a share convey similar information. Growth and recovery shares will have a high P/E ratio and a low dividend yield. Poor performers have a higher dividend yield and a lower P/E ratio. The symmetry between the two ratios is a consequence of them both using the current share price and the degree of stability in the relationship between dividends and earnings per share.

Using available information to assess a company's prospects

11. Reviewing prospects. When selecting shares, an investor should review the prospects of alternative companies by:

(a) Attempting to assess the strengths and weaknesses of each company. What is the quality of its management and leadership? What is the quality of its products or services? Do they meet a growing market need? What new products and ventures is it planning? Is it investing for the future to take advantage of opportunities? What threats are present either from other companies at home or from international competition?

(b) What has been the recent financial performance of the company? Does an analysis of the company's accounts show a good record of growth in sales, profits and dividends? Is it in a financially strong and secure position with adequate cash flow and interest and dividend cover?

Having evaluated alternative companies, the investor can then use the information provided by the 'London Share Service' to help select investments. Remember that the P/E ratio and dividend yield of a share reflect the market's rating of that share. The best investments will be those where the investor believes that the current share price does not fully reflect the company's prospects. A company may have excellent prospects, but if that is already fully reflected in the share prices, its shares may not prove to be the best investment.

Table 5B shows the information provided by the 'London Share Service' for the Burton group and some alternative 'Drapery and Stores' investments. Comparison of the P/E ratios shows that at that time, the market rated Next and Marks and Spencer slightly more highly than the Burton Group. If an investor believed that the prospects for the Burton Group were as good or better than the others, this would make the shares in the Burton Group a good investment. This analysis must be subject to an important word of caution. The P/E ratio and dividend yields shown in the *Financial Times* have been calculated using earnings per share and dividend figures from the last financial year. They are therefore called the *historical P/E ratio* and the *historical dividend yield*. What really matters is how the company will perform in the future. Analysts attempt to forecast future earnings per share and dividend figures to find the 'prospective P/E ratio' and the 'prospective dividend yield'.

Table 5B *Selected shares from the 'Drapery and Stores' sector*

1986 High	1986 Low	Stock	Price	+ or −	Div Net	Cvr	Y'ld Gr's	P/E
354	242	Burton Group 50p	296	+2	4.4	3.1	2.1	21.0
£15	880	Great Universal	£12½	−	18.0	3.4	2.0	19.4
227	167	Marks & Spencer	200xd	+2	3.9	2.1	2.7	23.9
294	188	Next 10p	248	−	3.75	2.3	2.1	28.6

12. The calculation of prospective ratios. To find a company's prospective P/E ratio and dividend yield requires an estimate of its likely earnings per share and dividend in the next set of annual accounts. To calculate these figures, an investor would need to make the following estimates:

(*a*) *Turnover*: the investor must take account of the state of the economy, the company's markets at home and abroad, the level of competition, changes in the product range, and the level of inflation and product price increases. If a company is divisionalized and operating simultaneously in several sectors of the economy, e.g. ICI, it would be more meaningful to forecast the turnover and profit for each activity and then to aggregate them. Any results announced recently by the company's competitors may provide a useful guide. Forecasting may be made easier if the investor can find a 'leading indicator' – a statistical series which always seems to change in the same direction as the company's turnover, but several months in advance. For example, the Index of Housing Starts may be a useful guide to carpet sales nine months later.

(b) *Trading profit before interest and tax*: this may be estimated by applying an estimate of the prospective trading profit margin to the turnover figure.

(c) *Profit after interest and tax*: interest can be estimated by adjusting the previous year's figure for anticipated repayments or increases in debt capital, and changes in the level of interest rates charged on overdrafts. The tax charge will become easier to forecast now that tax allowances on capital investment have been reduced and replaced by a lower rate of corporation tax.

(d) *Profit available to shareholders*: preference dividends, if any, can be easily calculated, and an allowance made for the share of profits due to minority shareholders in subsidiary companies. Prospective earnings per share are found by dividing the profit available to ordinary shareholders by the number of shares issued.

(e) *Dividends*: the investor should examine the past dividend record to see whether there is any policy to distribute a constant proportion of earnings per share or maintain a constant rate of growth of dividends.

Investment recommendations are made by stockbrokers and investment analysts after a comparison of the prospective P/E ratios, prospective dividend yields, and the longer-term outlook of different companies. Their selections would normally be those companies with the lowest prospective P/E ratios relative to their prospects.

The use of Extel cards

13. The information provided by Extel. A more detailed study of a company will require analysis of its accounts for several years previous to the latest financial year so that the investor can see how it came to be in its present position. The investor may be lucky to have access to a set of Extel cards, either through the place of employment, or through the public library. Extel cards are a set of information sheets, filed like the card index for books found in libraries, but instead of authors being in alphabetical order, it is the names of companies. In a full set of Extel cards, each company has three paper sheets or cards.

14. The Annual Card. The 'Annual Card', which is white, gives a wealth of data taken from the published accounts of the previous ten years. It includes the following details.

(*a*) Nature of the business, principal subsidiary companies, associated companies.

(*b*) Names of the company's directors, professional advisers, and Registrar.

(*c*) Details of the authorized and issued share capital, share options outstanding, and share option schemes.

(*d*) The directors' interests in the company.

(*e*) Dividend record and dates of announcement, ex div, and payment.

(*f*) Earnings per share record.

(*g*) A record of the prices of shares and warrants.

(*h*) Details of loan capital.

(*i*) Consolidated profit and loss account for the past ten years.

(*j*) Current cost profit and loss account.

(*k*) Consolidated priority percentages.

(*l*) Analysis of turnover and profit before tax by activity.

(*m*) Statement of source and application of funds for the ten past years.

(*n*) Historical cost balance sheet for the past ten years.

(*o*) Summary of the chairman's last annual statement.

15. The News Card. The 'News Card', which is yellow, gives details of the latest and preceding interim results that have been announced during the company's financial year. As the name of the card suggests, it also contains details of any important announcements since the previous annual report. This card should be studied carefully in conjunction with the Annual Card as it may contain more recent information if there has been a set of interim results since the last annual report. The interim results can be used with the annual results to construct six-monthly measures of turnover

5. The selection of shares 91

and profit before tax. These figures can then be used to calculate the percentage changes in turnover and profit before tax on a six-monthly basis. They also permit changes in the profit margin (profit before tax as a percentage of turnover) to be examined. When trying to forecast what the next set of annual turnover and profit figures will be, the risk is reduced if the results of the first six months of that year are already known and if, as a result of the analysis of preceding years' interim results, allowance can be made for any seasonal variations between the results of the two half-years.

16. The Analysts Card. The 'Analysts Card', which is blue, uses the information from the first two cards to present accounting ratios much used by investment analysts in a standardized form for each company. This is very useful if a rapid assessment of a company is necessary since changes in key accounting ratios over the past decade can be examined. The card starts by recasting the capital employed in the company's balance sheet in a standardized form to include bank loans and overdrafts and exclude intangible assets such as goodwill. This aids the calculation of the level of gearing discussed earlier, and allows a return on capital employed to be shown based on this definition of sources of capital. There are also measures of profit margin, working capital and liquidity similar to those explained in the Appendix to this chapter. The last part is devoted to an analysis of dividends, earnings per share, and yields on the share price. All this is very useful for rapid reference but, if unavailable, can be calculated from the published accounts.

Technical analysis

17. Definition. Technical analysis involves the charting and analysis of recent price movements as a guide to the prediction of future price movements.

18. Types of charts. Price movements are charted in one of three ways:

(*a*) *Line charts* plot the closing price each day on the vertical axis and time along the horizontal axis. The closing prices are then joined to form a continuous line.

(*b*) *Bar* (*range and close*) *charts* also plot prices on the vertical axis and time along the horizontal axis. Each day, a vertical line is recorded showing the maximum and minimum price, and a horizontal bar is drawn across the line to indicate the closing price.

(c) *Point and figure charts* plot closing prices on the vertical axis, but nothing along the horizontal axis. The chartist selects a minimum price interval or 'box' that is to be recorded, e.g. a price interval of 2 pence means that an increase in the share price from 100 pence to 104 pence will be recorded but not a further increase to 105 pence. Each increase in price of 2 pence on the scale is recorded by an 'X', while each decrease in price of 2 pence is recorded by an '0'. When a change in the direction of the price movement means that there is no space in the current column against the latest share price, a new column is started. To iron out minor price fluctuations, the chartist may decide not to record a change in direction of price unless it moves by more than, say, two boxes. This chart is then called a *two box reversal*.

An illustration of the methods of charting is shown in Figure 5.3.

19. The analysis of charts. Having plotted the charts, the main patterns that chartists look for are levels of support and resistance, and trend lines.

(a) *Levels of support and resistance.* A level of support is a price at which there has previously been buying support suggesting that the market is unwilling to allow the security to fall further as it would be under-valued.

Conversely, a level of resistance is a price which the security has previously failed to breach on at least one occasion, suggesting that the market is unwilling to pay a higher price as it would be over-valued.

Thus there is a tendency for securities to fluctuate between levels of support and resistance. This gives rise to the pattern referred to as the *rectangle* shown in Figure 5.4.

When the security price breaks through the level of resistance or the level of support, the change in security price is then expected to at least equal the width of the band. The longer the security has fluctuated within the band, the greater the expected strength of the break out.

(b) *Trend lines.* In the example of the rectangle, there was no

5. The selection of shares

Assumed sequence of prices (pence): 100, 106, 110, 106, 110, 116, 108

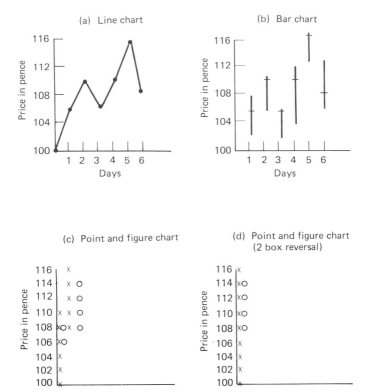

Figure 5.3 *Plotting security price movements*

underlying direction of change in the security price. However, the security may be experiencing either an upward or downward trend with short-term divergences from trend as shown in Figure 5.5. The sloping trend lines now become the levels of support and resistance. They may be fitted either by eye or by the use of a moving average calculation with parallels fitted to envelope the fluctuations about the trend as shown in Figure 5.6. The selection

94 Stocks and shares

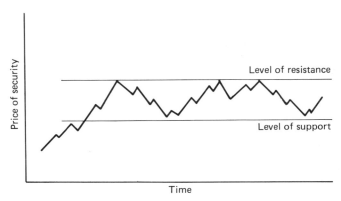

Figure 5.4 *The rectangle*

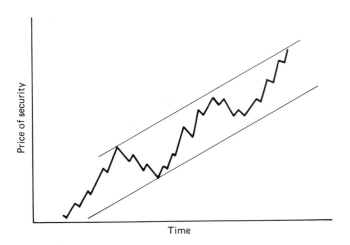

Figure 5.5 *Trend lines in a bull market*

5. The selection of shares 95

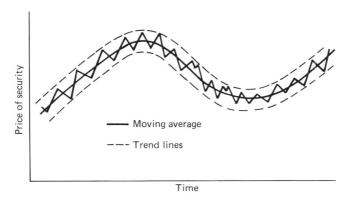

Figure 5.6 *The use of a moving average to plot trend lines*

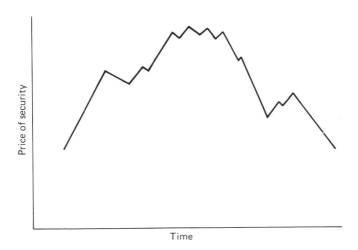

Figure 5.7 *A head and shoulders formation*

of the most appropriate moving average and the width of the bands either side are part of the skills of the individual analyst.

Having identified trends, chartists then concentrate upon identifying major turning points in the market which represent important buy or sell situations. A *bull market* is one where the underlying trend is a rising market while a *bear market* describes a market with an underlying downward trend. The end of a bull market is the time for investors to sell, and the end of a bear market is the ideal time to buy. One of the best-known formations at the peak of a security's rise in price is called the head and shoulders, shown in Figure 5.7.

The explanation for this formation is that profit-taking at the end of a long bull period creates the first shoulder. A further surge in price caused by those taking advantage of the cheaper price creates the head, but the buying enthusiasm wanes. The price falls and support is not reached until it has fallen below the level of the left shoulder. The third rally has less volume than either of the previous two, and peaks well below the level of the head. The share price has run out of steam and, thereafter, the security price heads down quite sharply.

The reverse of this formation may be found at the end of a bear market, in which case it is referred to as a triple bottom (*see* Figure 5.8).

20. Further indicators. Other important items of information frequently plotted by chartists for individual securities are:

(*a*) *Relative strength* – this shows how the security is performing relative to the market. The relative strength of a company's share is calculated by dividing its price by the *FTA* all-share index and plotting the result. This is used as a means of confirming the analyst's view of movements in the share price.

(*b*) *Rate of change or momentum* – this measures the speed at which the share price is changing. It can give an advance indication of a change in direction of share price and hence is used as an over-bought/over-sold indicator.

When charting the stock market indices, other information that is monitored by technical analysts include:

(*a*) *The volume of transactions* – the *Financial Times* gives figures for both the turnover and the number of bargains. Both of these are

5. The selection of shares 97

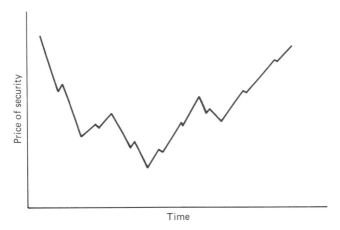

Figure 5.8 *Triple bottom formation*

important: the number of bargains indicates the number of investors active in the market and the volume statistic indicates whether or not the big financial institutions were active. Important changes in the direction of price movements are usually signalled by both large turnover and volume. Since the 'big bang' the *Financial Times* has published daily turnover figures for alpha stocks dealt through the SEAQ system.

(*b*) The *advance/decline line* is a measure of the number of share price increases relative to decreases. One way of presenting the information is to plot a running total of net advances by adding each day's net total to the previous day's figure. It is a useful measure of the strength or weakness of the market which may be used to confirm the movement of the market indices.

(*c*) *Moving average calculations* – one well-known example of moving average calculations for the world's major stock markets is the set of Coppock indicators published monthly in the *Investors Chronicle*. If the indicators are rising, the market is in a bull phase; if they are declining, the market is in a bear phase. The indicators are weighted ten month moving averages of the percentage changes of the index of each market over a one-year period. As with all moving average calculations, these indicators are unlikely to give a sell signal until after the peak of the market has passed, or a buy signal until after the low point has passed. Nevertheless, they have been found very helpful by investors.

21. Trading rules. Another type of technical analysis requires investors to follow certain mechanical trading rules. Some of them are very simple, such as 'the weekly rule'. This advises investors to buy if the highest price in the week is higher than the highest price in the previous four weeks and sell if the lowest price of the week is lower than in the previous four weeks. This rule can be modified in various ways, e.g. by altering the length of time of the reference period.

Another example is the use of filter rules designed to select shares with the prospects of a gain and to dispose of those which might create a serious loss. One example of a filter rule is 'buy the share if its price rises by more than x per cent from a low point, and sell if it falls by more than y per cent from its most recent peak'. This is sometimes referred to as the *hatch system*. The problem for the investor is finding the optimal values for x and y. If they are too large, then investors will lose out on most of the rises in share prices and suffer from most of the falls; if they are too small, the investors will lose most of their potential gains due to frequent transaction costs.

The efficient market hypothesis

22. Is it possible to pick winners? The last paragraph of the previous section highlighted the dilemma facing investors. Can they spot investment opportunities soon enough to make gains of a sufficient size to offset transaction costs? If so, then active investment management involving buying and selling of securities is justified. If not, investors would perform as well or better on average by selecting a diversified portfolio of securities and just holding it. The debate that has raged around this question has given rise to 'the efficient market hypothesis'.

23. What is the efficient market hypothesis? The 'efficient market hypothesis' (EMH) states that investors on average cannot beat a buy and hold strategy by active trading, both because of transaction costs and because the market is very efficient, and all known information that might affect future share prices is already discounted in

5. The selection of shares

present prices. The efficient market hypothesis has been debated in three forms.

24. The weak form of EMH. This argues that the market is efficient enough for all information that can be gained from studying share price movements to be already reflected in the share price. Hence technical analysis will not enable investors to beat a buy and hold strategy. Academic research has shown that the direction of change in share prices is random, i.e. they follow a random walk. This is because share prices already reflect all known news, and future good and bad news occur at random causing future share price changes to be random.

Although statistical tests have claimed that technical analysis is worthless, the demand for this type of investment research continues. Indeed, the larger the number of investors believing the forecasts of technical analysis, the more likely these forecasts are to occur. They become a self-fulfilling prophecy. For example, if most investors believe that the market has breached an important level of support, they will sell their shares, and the result will be further falls in the market index.

25. The semi-strong form of the EMH. This claims that since all known information is already fully discounted in security prices, it is a waste of effort to undertake fundamental analysis in the hope of identifying under-valued securities. It is ironic that it is only because there are so many investors and analysts undertaking fundamental analysis that the market is efficient. If they were all to cease, the market would no longer be efficient, and fundamental analysis would be able to identify exceptional investment opportunities.

Academic research to support this version of the efficient market hypothesis has shown that investors following the recommendations of research departments of stockbroking firms have not succeeded in consistently outperforming a buy and hold strategy. In some time periods they may have better results than the market index, but in other periods their results are worse. Hence on average, their returns are similar to that of the market index – adjusted for the level of risk of their portfolio.

26. The strong form of the EMH. This claims that not only is publicly available information fully reflected in share prices, but also all possible information about the company. This suggests that even the managers of a company with access to privileged information are unable to make extraordinary gains. Research published in the USA and the activities of insider traders dealing on privileged information have shown that this version of the efficient market hypothesis is incorrect.

Progress test 5

1. What are the risks associated with investment in shares? (**3**)
2. What is the difference between fundamental analysis and technical analysis? (**4, 5, 17–21**)
3. What is a prospective P/E ratio? Why is it important? (**11, 12**)
4. What are point and figure charts? (**18**)
5. What are momentum, the advance/decline line and Coppock indicators? (**20**)
6. What is the efficient market hypothesis? What is its validity? What is its relevance to investors? (**23–25**)

Appendix to Chapter 5

The analysis of a company's annual report and accounts

1. What to look for in a set of annual accounts. To illustrate the process of analysing a company's annual report and accounts, we shall use those produced by the Burton Group plc for 1986. They are reproduced as Tables 5C, 5D and 5E. To build up an accurate picture of the health of the company, the investor should inspect the following.

The chairman's statement

2. Content. This will give the investor a summary of the company's performance and comment upon the events that have influenced it. The chairman may also make some comments on the prospects for the future. It is quite helpful to have some idea about what has happened before attempting to analyse and interpret the company's accounts.

Points in the chairman's statement relevant for this analysis.

(*a*) In August 1985, the last month of the Burton Group's financial year 1984/85, the Group acquired Debenhams plc. Debenhams itself owned Harvey Nicols, Hamleys, Rayne, and Lotus shoes. These acquisitions, together with Collier Holdings plc in the same month, tripled the selling space of the Burton Group. The financial year 1985/86 saw the integration of the new acquisitions into the Group and some restructuring and rationalization including the disposal of Lotus and Hamleys. Capital investment increased by 50 per cent to £112.4 million and more than £200 million will be spent over the next three years on the revitalization of Debenhams.

(*b*) The acquisitions were largely financed by increases in bank loans and overdrafts. During the 1986 financial year, the Company was able greatly to reduce and restructure its debt capital. The profits generated by the integration of the new acquisitions into the Group produced some dramatic gains in performance which can be seen in the profits reported in the profit and loss account and the strengthening of the balance sheet.

Stocks and shares

Table 5C *The Burton Group plc – Consolidated profit and loss account for the fifty-two weeks ended 30 August 1986*

	1985 £ million	1986 £ million
Turnover	551.0	1,228.8
Cost of sales	(432.4)	(991.3)
Gross profit	118.6	237.5
Distribution costs	(12.7)	(26.4)
Administrative expenses	(24.3)	(53.4)
Income of related companies	—	22.2
Trading profit	81.6	179.9
Net interest	(2.4)	(31.7)
Other income	1.0	0.5
Profit on ordinary activities before taxation	80.2	148.7
Taxation	(28.7)	(51.8)
Profit on ordinary activities after taxation	51.5	96.9
Extraordinary credit	—	3.7
Profit for the financial year	51.5	100.6
Dividends	(21.5)	(31.4)
Retained earnings	30.0	69.2
Earnings per share	14.6p	17.8p

The profit and loss account and balance sheet

3. **Some important indicators.** The investor should calculate the following:

   (*a*) the increase in turnover: £551.0m to £1228.8m = +123 per cent
   (*b*) the increase in trading profit £81.6m to £179.9m = +120 per cent
   (*c*) the increase in profit before tax: £80.2m to £148.7m = +85 per cent
   (*d*) the increase in earnings per share: 14.6p to 17.8p = +22 per cent
   (*e*) the increase in dividends: £21.5m to £31.4m = +46 per cent

These are all large increases which reflect the growth in the size of the group. Now we shall calculate some measures of profitability.

Appendix to chapter 5

Table 5D *Consolidated balance sheet at 30 August 1986*

	1985 £ millions	1986 £ millions
Fixed assets		
Tangible assets	660.5	593.9
Investments	83.6	120.0
	744.1	713.9
Current assets		
Stocks	171.0	178.3
Debtors	79.9	94.6
Properties held for sale	44.5	14.9
Investments	14.4	0.4
Bank balances and cash	9.1	66.2
	318.9	354.4
Creditors (due within one year)	498.0	429.9
Net current liabilities	179.1	75.5
Total assets less current liabilities	565.0	638.4
Creditors (due after one year)	114.2	144.1
Provisions for liabilities and deferred tax	66.5	39.1
Minority interests	15.0	14.7
Net assets	369.3	440.5
Capital and reserves		
Called up share capital	135.1	274.4
Share premium account	1.9	0.9
Revaluation reserve	102.4	30.1
Other reserves	0.2	0.2
Retained earnings	129.7	134.9
	369.3	440.5

4. **Profit margin.**

$\dfrac{\text{Trading profit}}{\text{Turnover}}$ This ratio shows the proportion of each £ of sales that is profit before adjustment for the financing costs of the company, i.e. interest and dividends.

$$1985\ \frac{£81.6\text{m}}{£551.0\text{m}} = 14.8\%$$

$$1986\ \frac{£179.9\text{m}}{£1228.8\text{m}} = 14.6\%$$

104 Stocks and shares

The very slight easing in the profit margin resulted from a faster rate of growth in the cost of the goods sold (129%) than the increase in the revenue received.

5. Return on capital employed.

$$\frac{\text{Profit before interest and tax}}{\text{Total sources of finance} - \text{Intangibles}}$$

This ratio measures the rate of return earned on the total finance provided to the firm. Profit before interest and tax therefore includes income and interest received from investments and associated companies and is shown before the deduction of interest paid on bank loans and debt capital. Since the profit and loss account shows only the figure for net interest, i.e. the difference between interest received and interest paid, the investor needs to use the footnotes to the accounts to discover the figure for each. The total sources of finance used in this calculation should include all ordinary share capital and reserves, preference share capital, loan stocks, bank loans and overdrafts, deferred tax and provisions, and minorities. Intangibles such as goodwill should be subtracted.

The figures needed from the footnotes of the published accounts are:

Interest	£ millions
1985	1.2
1986	4.3

Bank loans and overdrafts due within one year (and therefore not included in the entry creditors due after one year):

	£ millions
1985	181.0
1986	83.2

Calculation of return on capital employed

$$1985 \ \frac{£83.8m}{£746.0m} = 11.2\%$$

£83.8m = trading profit + interest received + other income
      = £81.6m + £1.2m + £1.0m

£746.0m = capital + reserves + creditors due after one year + bank loans and overdrafts + provisions for liabilities and deferred tax + minorities
       = £369.3m + £114.2m + £181.0m + £66.5m + £15.0m

$$1986 \frac{£184.7m}{£721.6m} = 25.6\%$$

£184.7m = trading profit + interests received + other income
= £179.9m + £4.3m + £0.5m

£721.6m = capital and reserves + creditors due after one year + bank loans and overdrafts + provisions for liabilities and deferred tax + minorities
= £440.5m + £144.1m + £83.2m + £39.1m + £14.7m

The profits generated by the assets acquired at the end of the 1985 financial year have generated sufficient extra income to more than double the rate of return on capital employed. (The 1984 figure was 20.2% so the 1986 rate of return is an improvement upon the pre-acquisitions figure.)

6. Return on shareholders' capital and reserves. This measures how profitably the shareholders funds have been employed by the ratio:

$$\frac{\text{Profits available to shareholders}}{\text{Shareholders' capital and reserves} - \text{Intangibles}}$$

$$1985 \frac{£51.5m}{£369.3m} = 13.9\%$$

$$1986 \frac{£100.6m}{£440.5m} = 22.8\%$$

The rate of return earned on shareholders funds has risen very strongly due in part to the inclusion of the profits from the 1985 acquisitions, and in part to the way the acquisitions were financed. By using bank loans and debt capital rather than raising new share capital, the earnings available to the Company's shareholders have not been diluted.

> NOTE: Rate of return calculations can sometimes be misleadingly high. This can occur if fixed assets, e.g. freehold land and buildings, are undervalued in the balance sheet, or if the company has not been investing in new assets in recent years so that the net book values of their fixed assets are low.

7. Gearing. The investor should now measure the proportion that borrowings including bank loans, overdrafts, loan capital and leasing obligations contribute to long term sources of capital. The higher the proportion, the higher the level of gearing, and the greater the risk to the company's shareholders if profits and cash flow should fall.

106 Stocks and shares

$$\frac{\text{Bank loans and overdrafts + loan capital + lease obligations}}{\text{Total borrowings + shareholders capital and reserves +}}$$
$$\text{preference share capital + minorities} - \text{intangibles}$$

$$1985 \ \frac{£218.5\text{m} + £51.4\text{m} + £13.2\text{m}}{£283.1\text{m} + £369.3\text{m} + £0\text{m} + £15\text{m} - £0\text{m}}$$

$$= \frac{£283.1\text{m}}{£667.4\text{m}} = 42\%$$

$$1986 \ \frac{£84.2\text{m} + £112.5\text{m} + £15.6\text{m}}{£212.3\text{m} + £440.5\text{m} + £0\text{m} + £14.7\text{m} - £0\text{m}}$$

$$= \frac{£212.3\text{m}}{£667.5\text{m}} = 32\%$$

The repayment of bank loans, partly with other medium term borrowings, has significantly reduced the level of gearing.

8. Interest cover. One way of assessing the potential danger arising from the level of gearing is to calculate the level of interest cover. This is a measure of the number of times that interest can be paid out of profit before tax plus the interest payable.

$$\frac{\text{Profit before tax + interest payable}}{\text{Interest payable}}$$

$$1985 \ \frac{£80.2\text{m} + £3.7\text{m}}{£3.7\text{m}} = 22 \text{ times}$$

$$1986 \ \frac{£148.7\text{m} + £38.7\text{m}}{£38.7\text{m}} = 4.8 \text{ times}$$

The fall in interest cover in 1986 was due to the interest payable on the loans raised at the very end of the 1985 financial year to finance the acquisitions. We can expect a further reduction in borrowings during 1987 and hence some improvement in interest cover.

9. Dividend cover. The safety of the dividend can be measured in a similar way.

$$\frac{\text{Profit available to shareholders}}{\text{Dividends}}$$

$$1985 \ \frac{£51.6\text{m}}{£21.5\text{m}} = 2.4 \text{ times}$$

$$1986 \ \frac{£100.6\text{m}}{£31.4\text{m}} = 3.2 \text{ times}$$

Appendix to chapter 5

In spite of a 46% increase in dividends, the increase in earnings was sufficient to raise the dividend cover significantly.

10. Ratios commonly used to measure liquidity.

(*a*) *Current ratio.* The ratio of current assets to current liabilities gives an indication of the liquidity available to meet current commitments.

$$\frac{\text{Current assets}}{\text{Current liabilities}} \qquad 1985 \; \frac{£318.9\text{m}}{£498.0\text{m}} = 0.64$$

$$1986 \; \frac{£354.4\text{m}}{£429.9\text{m}} = 0.82$$

An improvement in the cash position and the reduction in bank overdrafts are the main factors accounting for the strengthening of the Company's position.

(*b*) *Quick ratio.* This is a similar formula to the current ratio except that it omits stocks from current assets since they can be a very illiquid asset if a company encounters a liquidity crisis. This calculation is sometimes called the *acid test*.

$$\frac{\text{Current assets} - \text{stocks}}{\text{Current liabilities}} \qquad 1985 \; \frac{£147.9\text{m}}{£498.0\text{m}} = 0.30$$

$$1986 \; \frac{£176.1\text{m}}{£429.9\text{m}} = 0.41$$

Source and application of funds statement

11. Measurement of cash flows. Now the investor should investigate the movement of cash into and out of the company by examining the source and application of funds statement (see Table 5E). It will be noticed that:

(*a*) 1985 was a year when the expenditure of over £250 million on properties, fixed assets and the acquisition of subsidiaries, was about two and a half times greater than the cash generated from both trading and the disposal of assets. The £170 million extra cash required during the year was funded by an increase in bank loans and overdrafts (£100 million) and the balance by an increase in trade and other creditors.

(*b*) 1986 was a year of dramatic financial retrenchment and progress. The inflow of cash quadrupled to over £450 million with the proceeds from trading nearly doubling at £160 milion, and the sale of assets and subsidiaries bringing in over £200 million. The Company also raised new debt capital of some £60 million. With all these funds the Company was able to maintain a high level of investment of over £150 million, reduce bank borrowings by nearly £100 million and increase cash holdings by over £50 million.

Other important measures

12. The stock turnover and debtor turnover ratios. The investor should also monitor the relationship between stocks and turnover and debtors and turnover. If either of these fall significantly, it could create liquidity problems for the company. The *stock turnover ratio* is an estimate of the number

Table 5E *Source and application of funds for the fifty-two weeks ended 30 August 1986*

	1985 £ million	1986 £ million
Sources of funds		
Funds generated from operations	95.4	161.8
Proceeds of disposal of subsidiaries	—	47.5
Disposal of tangible assets	10.4	138.7
Disposal of current asset investments	3.6	14.4
Disposal of properties held for sale	—	29.6
Shares issued for cash less expenses	2.1	2.4
Loan stock issues less expenses	—	59.9
	112.5	454.3
Application of funds		
Additions to properties and other tangible assets	75.1	112.4
Cost of property revaluation	0.1	—
Additions to fixed asset investments	1.1	44.2
Acquisition of subsidiaries	179.7	—
Disposals and rationalization	0.2	61.4
Taxation paid	13.6	28.8
Dividends paid	12.4	25.9
Minority interests	—	0.3
	282.4	273.0
Increase (decrease) in working capital	(169.7)	181.3
Increase (decrease) in stocks	13.9	7.3
Increase (decrease) in debtors	18.9	(3.8)
(Increase) decrease in creditors	(104.2)	13.6
Increase (decrease) in cash	2.2	57.1
(Increase) decrease in bank loans and overdrafts	(100.5)	97.8
Adjustment in respect of disposals of subsidiaries	—	9.3
	(169.7)	181.3

of times that stocks are traded in a year. It is sometimes calculated by dividing turnover by the amount of end of year stocks, but is shown here using the cost of sales figure to eliminate the effect of any change in the Company's policy concerning its profit margin.

$$\frac{\text{Cost of sales}}{\text{End of year stocks}} \qquad 1985 \frac{£432.4\text{m}}{£171.0\text{m}} = 2.5 \text{ times}$$

$$1986 \frac{£991.3\text{m}}{£178.3\text{m}} = 5.6 \text{ times}$$

The *debtor turnover ratio* is the number of times turnover exceeds the end of year debtors.

$$\frac{\text{Turnover}}{\text{End of year debtors}} \qquad 1985 \frac{£551.0\text{m}}{£79.9\text{m}} = 6.9 \text{ times}$$

$$1986 \frac{£1228.8\text{m}}{£94.6\text{m}} = 13.0 \text{ times}$$

The large increases in both indicate a better performance by the company and are a result of the large rise in turnover following the Company's acquisitions at the end of the 1985 financial year.

13. Net asset value. This measures the balance sheet value of shareholders' funds per share (net of any intangible assets).

$$1985 \frac{£369.3\text{m}}{270.2\text{m shares}} = 137 \text{ pence}$$

$$1986 \frac{£440.5\text{m}}{548.8\text{m shares}} = 80 \text{ pence}$$

The fall in net asset value of the share was mainly due to a capitalization issue which more than doubled the number of shares that had been issued at the end of 1985. Net asset value per share is frequently compared with the share's market price, but this may reveal little unless the assets of the company are both highly marketable and valued at market prices in the balance sheet, e.g. a property company. In this type of company, a fall in the share price below net asset value would signal that the company was very vulnerable to takeover bid and hence that the shares are possibly cheap.

14. What does this analysis of the accounts of the Burton Group plc for 1986 show? During 1986 the Company has rationalized its 1985 acquisitions. It has sold off companies not related to its mainstream businesses and other surplus assets, and integrated the remainder into the Group's activities. It has also greatly increased its level of investment expenditure to ensure that the enlarged Group is in the forefront of retailing nationally. It has strengthened its financial base by reducing its level of gearing, lengthening the period to maturity of its debt capital by new issues, reducing its bank overdrafts, and building up its cash holdings. Profit margins have been maintained and other measures of profitability and corporate performance improved.

Points for the investor to watch for are:

(*a*) The outlook for retailing in the UK.
(*b*) The progress of Burton management in maintaining the Company at the forefront of its sector.
(*c*) The level of interest rates which will affect the interest payable.

The calculation of ratios from the published accounts of a company can give valuable evidence concerning its progress. The actual figure for any ratio in isolation conveys little information. It is the direction of change of the values of these ratios and comparison with competitor companies which enable the analyst to use them to form investment advice. The investor should also recall that the accounts are a measure of past performance, and that successful investment depends upon predicting future performance. Hence the analyst's task is to predict the prospective profits and earnings per share so that the prospective P/E ratios and dividend yields of different companies can be compared.

Priority percentages

15. Method of calculation. There are two calculations of priority percentages which are designed to indicate the relative safety of investors in the company's different securities.

(*a*) *Capital priority percentages.* These show the percentage of the total long-term sources of capital of the company, less intangibles, that each issue of capital contributes. The ranking is the same as for repayment in the event of liquidation.

(*b*) *Income priority percentages.* These show the proportion of profits absorbed by all the interest and dividend claims upon them. Again, the ranking is in accordance with legal priorities.

An example of a hypothetical company is shown in Table 5F to illustrate their calculation.

Current cost accounting

16. Introduction. The accounts produced by companies are drawn up using historical costs, i.e. turnover and expenses are traceable by the firm's auditors to specific transactions that have taken place. In times of rapid inflation, using the historical costs at which transactions took place a long time before the end of the accounting period can result in distortions in the profit figure reported. For example, if the depreciation charge on fixed assets is a percentage of the cost paid several years ago, the amount of depreciation shown in the current profit and loss accounts will not reflect the fall in the value of these assets to the business. The replacement cost of these assets will be much greater than their historical cost, so the depreciation charge shown will be too small and hence the reported profit figure too large.

17. Description of current cost accounting. It was this argument which persuaded Sir Francis Sandilands and his committee investigating inflation accounting to recommend in their report to the government in 1975 that firms should produce current cost accounts. The basis of current cost accounts is that assets should be shown at their value to the business, not their historical cost. This requires three adjustments to historical cost profit in the profit and loss account to obtain current cost operating profit. These adjustments are:

Table 5F *Illustrative calculation of priority percentages*

Balance sheet

	£
Net assets	2,000,000
10% debentures 1995	200,000
5% unsecured convertible loan stock 1993	100,000
7.5% preference shares £1	300,000
Issued share capital (1 million ordinary shares 50p)	500,000
Reserves	900,000
Capital employed	2,000,000

Profit and loss account

Trading profit	125,000
Interest	25,000
Profit before tax	100,000
Corporation tax at 35%	35,000
Profit after tax	65,000
Preference dividends	22,500
Profits available to shareholders	42,500
Ordinary dividends	30,000
Retained profits	12,500

Capital priority percentages

		Priority percentage	Overall cover
£200,000	10% debentures 1995	0–10.0	$\dfrac{£2,000,000}{£200,000} = 10$ times
£100,000	5% unsecured convertible loan stock 1993	10.0–15.0	$\dfrac{£2,000,000}{£300,000} = 6.7$ times
£300,000	7.5% preference shares	15.0–30.0	$\dfrac{£2,000,000}{£600,000} = 3.3$ times
£1,400,000	1 million 50p ordinary	30.0–100.0	$\dfrac{£2,000,000}{£2,000,000} = 1$ time

The overall cover for a class of finance is calculated by dividing the net assets of the business by the amount of capital provided by that class plus the amounts provided by the other classes of long term capital ranking higher in the event of liquidation.

Income priority percentages

To calculate these percentages, the net of corporation tax cost of interest payments is added to the amount of profit after tax available to shareholders. The net of corporation tax interest payments are £25,000 × (1−0.35) = £16,250.

		Available profits £	Net of tax cost of interest or dividend £	Times covered	Priority %
£200,000	10% debentures 1995	81,250*	13,000**	6.25 times	16
£100,000	5% unsecured convertible loan stock 1993	68,250	3,250†	21 times	16–20
£300,000	7.5% preference shares £1	65,000	22,500	2.9 times	20–48
£1,000,000	Ordinary shares 50p	42,500	30,000	1.4 times	48–85
	Retained profit	12,500			85–100

* £81,250 = profit after tax + net of corporation tax interest payments = £65,000 + £16,250
** £13,000 = interest payable on 10% debentures × (1 − rate of corporation tax)
= £20,000 × 0.65

† £3,250 = interest payable on 5% unsecured convertible loan stock 1993 × (1 − rate of corporation tax)
= £5,000 × 0.65

114 Stocks and shares

(a) Depreciation of fixed assets adjustment: increases the historical cost depreciation charge to reflect the value to the business of the proportion of the assets consumed. The value of the assets used in the calculation is normally their replacement cost.

(b) Cost of sales adjustment: increases the cost of sales to take account of any difference between the replacement cost and the historical cost of stocks.

(c) Monetary working capital adjustment: reduces profit by the amount necessary to maintain the same real level of 'debtors minus creditors'.

18. Use of current cost statements. Since current cost accounting claims to present a truer picture of the operating profit of a manufacturing company, it is an additional useful set of information when provided by a company in its annual report and accounts. Some of the main uses that can be made of the current cost statements are:

(a) The calculation of the percentage increase or decrease in current cost operating profit.

(b) The calculation of the current cost operating profit margin, i.e. current cost operating profit divided by turnover.

(c) The change in the current cost earnings per share.

(d) The change in the rate of return on current cost capital employed, that is:

$$\frac{\text{Current cost operating profit}}{\text{Current cost capital employed}}$$

Current cost profit attributable to shareholders, from which earnings per share is calculated, is increased by a 'gearing adjustment'. This reduces the three adjustments to the historic cost profit listed above to the extent that the company is financed from other sources than the shareholders. The gearing adjustment is intended to reflect the benefit that shareholders gain in times of inflation from the fall in the real value of the company's borrowings or debt capital.

Current cost accounting is embodied in the *Statement of Standard Accounting Practice No. 16*. The production of current cost accounts is at present optional.

Progress test, Appendix 5

1. In what ways can (a) the profitability and (b) the liquidity of a company be assessed? (**3–11**)

2. What are capital and income priority percentages? (**14**)

3. Define (a) the acid test, (b) current cost operating profit, (c) stock turnover, (d) the monetary working capital adjustment, (e) profit margin. (**4, 10, 12, 17**)

6
Investment in gilt-edged and fixed-interest securities

In this chapter, the nature of gilt-edged and fixed-interest securities will be examined, and the influences affecting their prices and yields. The factors which potential investors should take into consideration are then discussed and details given on how they should select and buy them.

Gilt-edged and fixed-interest securities

1. Gilt-edged securities. A gilt-edged security is a fixed-interest loan to the UK government which will be redeemed at a time specified when the security was initially sold. If cash is required before the maturity date, the investor can arrange for the stocks to be sold on the Stock Exchange. These securities comprise a large part of the *National Debt*, which is the government's past and present borrowings to finance wars, nationalized industries and public expenditure. They are called gilt-edged because they are risk-free as there is virtually no possibility of the Treasury failing to meet its interest or redemption payments.

2. Details in the financial press. Some basic information concerning the gilt-edged stocks available to the investor is given in the daily financial press alongside the listing of company shares and their prices. In the *Financial Times*, for example, on the inside back page headed 'London Share Service', in the top-left-hand corner is

116 Stocks and shares

the heading 'British Funds'. This is the list of gilt-edged stocks, starting with those that will be redeemed first, with the year of redemption receding progressively into the future. This list of gilt-edged stocks is sub-divided under five headings:

(*a*) *Shorts (lives up to five years)*: gilts that will be redeemed in the next five years.

(*b*) *Five to fifteen years:* medium-term gilts to be redeemed between five and fifteen years from now.

(*c*) *Over fifteen years:* long-term gilts to be redeemed in more than fifteen years from now.

(*d*) *Undated:* gilts with no fixed redemption date.

(*e*) *Index-linked:* gilts whose interest payments and redemption value are linked to the Retail Price Index.

3. The titles of gilt-edged stock. Each issue of gilt-edged stock has its own title such as Treasury 11¾ per cent 1991 or Funding 5¾ per cent '87–'91. Whether it is called Exchequer, Treasury, Gas, Transport or War Loan etc. is of no consequence as all are guaranteed by the UK government. The percentage following the name and the year or years in the title are of great importance. The percentage is called the *coupon rate of interest* and specifies the annual fixed income that the investor will receive. All short, medium, and long-dated gilts will be redeemed at £100, irrespective of what their market price is today. The coupon interest rate is the annual income in £s per stock with a redemption value or *nominal value* of £100.

EXAMPLES:

Funding 5¾ per cent '87–'91	gross annual interest income = £5.75 per £100 nominal
Treasury 11¾ per cent 1991	gross annual interest income = £11.75 per £100 nominal

The year in the title is the year of redemption, and where there is a range of years, as in Funding 5¾ per cent '87–'91, the government has the option to choose the year in which to redeem the stock. In practice, if the market rate of interest required on the issue of new

6. Gilt-edged and fixed-interest securities

gilts is higher than the coupon interest rate, the stock will be redeemed at the latest date; if the required rate of interest is lower than the coupon interest rate on the stock, it will be redeemed at the earliest date. This is to minimize the cost to the taxpayer of funding the national debt.

4. Other fixed-interest bonds. Immediately below gilt-edged stocks listed in the *Financial Times* will be found 'International Bank and Overseas Government Issues'. These are fixed-interest sterling bonds issued by other governments and international agencies like the European Investment Bank. Sterling issues by foreign governments and international agencies are sometimes called *bulldog bonds*. Beneath these are some issues made by UK local authorities called *corporation loans*, issues by other public bodies such as the Metropolitan Waterworks, and one-year bonds issued by the Nationwide Building Society.

5. Fixed-interest securities of UK companies. UK companies also use the Stock Exchange to raise fixed-interest loans by issuing debentures, loan stock and preference shares. Once issued, there is rarely an active secondary market in these stocks. This is because they are mostly bought by financial institutions, such as insurance companies and pension funds, as long-term investments. The attraction of debentures and loan stocks is that they give a higher rate of return than gilts. However, to sell them before redemption would incur heavier transaction costs than gilts which is why they are normally held to maturity. The attraction of preference shares to financial institutions is that their dividends are franked income and hence carry a tax credit. This means that the dividends received have been paid out of profits that have already paid corporation tax and so are exempt from further payment of it when received by the financial institutions. (The advance corporation tax that has been deducted from dividends to make them qualify as franked income is the same rate as the basic rate of income tax which is a much lower rate than that of the corporation tax which financial institutions have to pay on their unfranked investment income.) Because the turnover of these securities is so low, few of them are listed in the pages of the *Financial Times* or other newspapers. To obtain details of this type of security, the investor should consult the *Stock Exchange Daily Official List*.

118 Stocks and shares

6. Fixed-interest bonds in foreign currencies. All the fixed-interest securities described above are denominated in sterling. However, the investor may want to invest in fixed interest bonds denominated in a foreign currency. Bonds issued by overseas governments, international agencies and multinational companies and denominated in a foreign currency are called *Eurobonds*. They are not bought and sold on the Stock Exchange, although some brokers will obtain them for clients. The main dealers have been the London offices of US brokers such as Bache Securities and E. F. Hutton. Details of the largest issues are given in the *Financial Times* on the page headed 'International Capital Markets' in a table headed 'FT International Bond Service'. Most Eurobonds are in US dollars, but there are numerous issues denominated in Deutschmarks, yen, Swiss francs, guilders, Canadian dollars, Australian dollars, sterling and ECUs (the European Currency Unit which is based on the value of a basket of European currencies). The investor should now look for this page in the *Financial Times* and examine the list of Eurobonds noting which have fixed rates of interest and which have floating rates.

Gilt prices and yields

7. Details of gilts in the financial press. The British funds section of the London Share Service on the penultimate pages of the *Financial Times* where all the gilts are listed give the following information about each stock:

(1) 1986		(2) Stock	(3) Price £	(4) + or −	(5) Yield Int%	(6) Yield Red%
High	Low	Exchequer				
$113\frac{1}{8}$	$101\frac{13}{16}$	$12\frac{1}{2}$pc 1990	$112\frac{1}{16}$	$+\frac{1}{8}$	11.15	8.70

Column (2): the name of the stock giving its coupon rate of interest which shows the annual interest income per £100 of nominal stock and the year or range of years within which the stock will be redeemed.

Column (1): the high and low price of the stock in £s during the current year. In the Monday edition, the dates on which interest payments are made are published in this column.

Column (3): the closing price of the stock on the previous day.

6. Gilt-edged and fixed-interest securities

Column (4): the change in price of the stock on the previous day. The system of quotation for gilts has not been decimalized and so the unit of measurement is £$^1/_{32}$. On Mondays, this column gives the date when the stock last went 'ex div' (*see* 5:**6**).

Column (5): the 'interest yield' measures the rate of return provided by the annual interest income as a percentage of the market price of the gilt. The interest yield shown is the gross interest yield.

Column (6): the 'redemption yield' measures the rate of return if the gilt is held until it is redeemed. It takes account not only of the interest income but also the capital gain or loss arising from the difference between the current market price and the redemption value of £100. (In the example above, there will be a capital loss of £12$^1/_{16}$ if the gilt is held until redemption. This is why the redemption yield is lower at 8.70 per cent than the interest yield of 11.15 per cent.) The redemption yield shown is the gross redemption yield.

8. Calculating the interest yield of gilts. The interest yield is calculated in the following way:

$$\text{Interest yield} = \frac{\text{Gross annual interest income}}{\text{Market price of gilt stock}}$$

EXAMPLE:

Exchequer 12½ per cent 1990: interest yield = $\frac{£12^1/_2}{£112^1/_{16}}$

= 11.15 per cent

9. Calculating the redemption yield. The redemption yield is the rate of interest which discounts all the future gross interest payments until redemption and the redemption value of £100 to the same value as the current market price. It is the value of r in the calculation:

$$\text{Market price of gilt} = \frac{I}{1+r} + \frac{I}{(1+r)^2} + \frac{I}{(1+r)^3} + \cdots \frac{I+£100}{(1+r)^n}$$

where I = interest payment per period
  n = number of periods until redemption
  r = semi-annual yield to redemption

This is an internal rate of return type of calculation. Since practically all gilts pay interest at six-monthly intervals, the period used in the calculation is six months and the discount rate calculated is the semi-annual redemption yield. The figure shown in the *Financial Times* is double the semi-annual redemption yield.

An estimate of the redemption yield can be made without using present value tables to perform this type of calculation by undertaking the following steps:

(*a*) Calculate the difference between the current gilt price and the nominal value of £100 and divide it by the number of years to redemption.

(*b*) Add this capital profit/loss per year to the interest yield.

EXAMPLE:
Exchequer 12½ per cent 1990   Price £112¹/₁₆
Prospective capital loss = £12¹/₁₆
Number of years to redemption = 5
Average annual capital loss = £2.4 per annum
Average annual capital loss as percentage of market price = £2.4 ÷ £112¹/₁₆ = 2.15%
Interest yield = 11.15%
Estimated yield to redemption = 11.15% − 2.15% = 9.00%
Actual yield to redemption = 8.70%

These estimates are only approximate and can be quite inaccurate when the market price is very different from the nominal value, as the calculation makes no allowance for the effects of compound interest.

10. Main features of investing in gilt-edged stock. One of the major differences between holding gilt-edged stock and investing in a building society or high-interest bank account is that the income from gilts is fixed, while that from deposits with savings institutions varies with the general level of interest rates. On the other hand, the capital value of the initial investment in a bank or building society is secure, while the market price of a gilt will rise and fall with the level of interest rates. To be precise, there is an inverse relationship between interest rates and the prices of gilt-edged stock.

When interest rates rise, an increase in the interest and redemption yields will be accomplished by a fall in the market price of gilt-edged stocks. Conversely, falling interest rates implies a rise in fixed-interest stock prices.

6. Gilt-edged and fixed-interest securities

EXAMPLE:
Exchequer 12½ per cent 1990: Interest yield = 11.15%   Price = £112 1/16
If the interest yield rises to 12½ per cent, the gilt price will fall to £100.

$$\frac{\text{Coupon interest income}}{\text{Market price}} = \text{Interest yield} \quad \frac{£12½}{£100} = 12½\%$$

If the interest yield falls to 10 per cent, the gilt price will rise to £125.

$$\frac{\text{Coupon interest income}}{\text{Market price}} = \text{Interest yield} \quad \frac{£12½}{£125} = 10\%$$

Interest payments are made twice a year (with the exception of Consols 2½ per cent which pays quarterly) on the dates shown in the Monday issue of the *Financial Times*. The interest payments for Exchequer 12½ per cent 1990 are on 22 March and 22 September. When an investor buys gilts, the price paid is the market price plus accrued interest (calculated on the number of days since the last interest payment (excluding payment day) up to and including settlement day which is the day after purchase. The amount of accrued interest is the proportion of the semi-annual interest payment represented by the number of days just calculated divided by the total number of days between the last and the next interest payments).

EXAMPLE:
Purchase Exchequer 12½ per cent 1990 on 1 June. Settlement day is 2 June.
(72 days after last interest payment on 22 March; 23 March to 22 Sept = 184 days)

$$\text{Accrued interest} = \frac{72}{184} \times £6.25 = £2.446$$

The stock went 'ex div' (*see* 5:**6**) on 13 February for the interest payment on 22 March. If the stock is bought between 13 February and 22 March, interest due will have to be subtracted from the price paid. For example, stock purchased on 1 March will forgo 20 days' interest (3–22 March incl.) to which the purchaser is entitled. Hence this amount is subtracted from the purchase price:

$$\frac{20}{181} \times £6.25 = 69 \text{ pence}$$

11. Factors influencing prices and yields of gilt-edged stock. A rise in gilt prices is usually a response to good news in the financial markets. A number of examples of the type of situation which will cause gilt-edged stock prices to rise are shown below.

(*a*) *Monetary policy*: an increase in confidence in the City and international investment community that the money supply is under control and that prudent monetary and government borrowing targets are being followed.

(*b*) *Inflation*: a decline or expectation of a decline in the rate of inflation which increases the stability of the value of money.

(*c*) *Balance of payments*: an improvement in the volume of exports or the current account surplus. Since oil is of particular importance to the UK balance of payments, an increase in the world demand for oil or a decrease in the world supply causing a rise in its price, will strengthen gilt prices.

(*d*) *Exchange rate*: increased stability or a strengthening of the value of the pound.

(*e*) *Interest rates*: a downward trend of interest rates resulting from the good news of any of the events already listed or the need by the government to provide some stimulation to the level of economic activity in the economy. UK interest rates may be high to compete with US interest rates, so a fall in US interest rates would normally boost gilt prices.

(*f*) *Political and other events*: any news which strengthens confidence in the prospects for non-inflationary growth in the UK economy is good news for the gilt market.

Of course, the opposite of any of the examples described above would result in a fall in gilt prices and an increase in their yields.

Main considerations when investing in gilts

12. Main considerations. The main factors an investor should consider when deciding whether to invest in gilt-edged stock are:

6. Gilt-edged and fixed-interest securities

(*a*) What are the main investment objectives – income or capital growth?

(*b*) How much risk are the investors prepared to take?

(*c*) What is the investment outlook for equities and fixed interest stocks?

13. Considerations for investors requiring income. If investors require income, they will receive a higher yield from gilts than equities in the first few years as the interest yield on gilts exceeds the dividend yield on most equities. In the longer run, gilts are less attractive as dividends can be expected to increase in line with profitability while the interest payments on gilts are fixed.

Investors seeking income should select from the gilts with high coupon interest rates which give the highest interest yield. The interest and redemption yields are quoted gross in the financial press (i.e. before the deduction of income tax). Interest payments on gilts are paid net of the basic rate of income tax if purchased through the Stock Exchange (except Treasury 3 per cent, one of the undated stocks), but gross if purchased through the Post Office. The investors' net interest yield can be calculated by multiplying the gross yield by (one minus their marginal rate of income tax). Thus income-seeking investors should select gilts offering the highest net income yield calculated for their own marginal rate of income tax. However, the gilts offering the highest interest yield are priced above their redemption value of £100 and so investors should also consider the effect upon their finances of a capital loss if they are held until redemption.

14. Considerations for investors requiring capital growth. For capital growth, the selection of gilts with a low coupon interest rate where the market price is below the redemption price guarantees a minimum rate of growth. However, unless index-linked gilts are selected, the investors are not protected against a fall in the value of money. Furthermore, in the longer term, equities may provide a better growth performance, depending upon the rate of growth of company profits.

For investors seeking capital growth, the net yields to redemption of different gilts should be compared. The calculation of the net redemption yield takes account of the capital gain or loss from holding the gilt until redemption. Since 1 July 1986, all capital gains obtained from investment in gilts have been exempt from capital gains tax. Until this date, only gilts held for more than a year and a day were exempt. Table 6A(a) shows the calculation of the net redemption yields for Exchequer 12½ per cent 1990, the stock that was used as an example earlier in the chapter. It shows the calculation of the net interest yields and net redemption yields for non-taxpayers, basic rate and 60 per cent taxpayers. Having calculated the net interest yield, the net redemption yield is found by adjusting for the capital gain or loss by adding any positive annual return or subtracting any negative annual return. This annual return is found by subtracting the gross interest yield from the gross redemption yield.

Table 6A *Calculation of net interest and net redemption yields*

(a) *Exchequer 12½ per cent 1990:* Gilt price £112$\frac{1}{16}$; gross interest yield 11.15%; gross redemption yield 8.70%.

	0% Taxpayer	29% Taxpayer	60% Taxpayer
Gross interest yield	11.15%	11.15%	11.15%
Tax	—	3.23%	6.69%
Net interest yield	11.15%	7.92%	4.46%
Subtract capital loss (8.70% − 11.15%)	2.45%	2.45%	2.45%
Net redemption yield	8.70%	5.47%	2.01%

(b) *Treasury 3 per cent 1990:* Gilt price £89½; gross interest yield 3.35%; gross redemption yield 6.01%.

	0% Taxpayer	29% Taxpayer	60% Taxpayer
Gross interest yield	3.35%	3.35%	3.35%
Tax	—	0.97%	2.01%
Net interest yield	3.35%	2.38%	1.34%
Add capital gain (6.01% − 3.35%)	2.66%	2.66%	2.66%
Net redemption yield	6.01%	5.04%	4.00%

Table 6A(b) shows another example: Treasury 3 per cent 1990. Examination of the figures in the table show that if investors are either non-taxpayers or pay income tax at the standard rate and are prepared to hold the gilt to maturity, they would obtain a higher return by investing in Exchequer 12½ per cent 1990. Investors with a marginal rate of tax of 60 per cent would be better off investing in the Treasury 3 per cent 1990. Lower coupon gilts will usually provide a higher net yield to redemption for higher rate taxpayers as most of the total return is earned in the form of the tax-free capital gain as the price rises to redemption.

15. The yield curve. The yield curve shows the redemption yield for securities with differing lengths of time to their maturity, as shown in Figure 6.1.

The two main uses of the yield curve to investors are anomaly spotting, and the identification of market expectations concerning the future level of interest rates.

Once the yields on all the stocks have been plotted, a curve can be drawn through the points, and those with yields significantly above or below the yield curve identified (*see* curve A in Figure 6.1). The first task is to identify whether the anomaly is normal or temporary. It would be normal, for example, for low coupon gilts to be below the yield curve since their tax efficiency for higher rate taxpayers forces their gross yield down relative to other stocks. If there is no

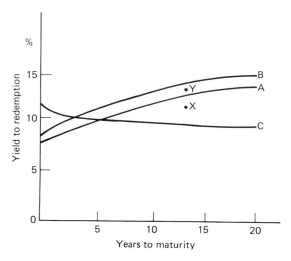

Figure 6.1 *Yield curves for gilt-edged stocks*

explanation for a stock being either below or above the yield curve, then a stock with a yield below the curve such as X should be sold, and one with a yield above such as Y bought.

A yield curve can be produced for gross yields, or the net yields for each marginal rate of income tax. For investors seeking anomalies, it is the net yield curve calculated using their own marginal rate of income tax that will be the most useful.

The normal slope of the yield curve is upwards, as in curve A, showing a higher yield on the longer-dated maturities. The higher yield is the reward to the investor for holding a less liquid and more risky asset than a short-dated gilt. A general rise in interest rates will cause the yield curve to shift upwards, say from position A to position B.

An 'inverse yield curve' is one which shows lower yields at the long end of the market than the short, as in yield curve C. This situation can arise when the market expects interest rates to fall in the near future, and investors are therefore switching into the longer-dated stocks to obtain the larger rises in price available from these.

16. Risks involved in investing in gilts. One of the attractions of gilt-edged stocks is that investors are exposed to a lower level of risk than if they invest in equities. Three types of risk are associated with investment in a fixed-interest stock.

(*a*) *Risk of default.* This risk does not apply to gilt-edged stocks. The interest and redemption payments are made by the Bank of England on behalf of the Treasury.

(*b*) *Price volatility.* If investors know how long they wish to hold their investments in gilt-edged stocks, they can make their investment risk-free by selecting from stocks which match their maturity requirements. This will eliminate any capital gains or losses caused by interest rate fluctuations as they will be locked into the net redemption yield applying at the time of their purchase.

The prices that can be obtained from the sale of gilts at any time before their redemption is uncertain as they fluctuate with the economic and political influences listed previously. These price fluctuations can only impose a loss on investors if they sell before redemption. They also provide opportunities for investors to make capital gains by selling before their prices fall, and buying back before their prices rise.

6. Gilt-edged and fixed-interest securities

A change in interest rates does not cause all gilt prices to change by the same amount. The factors that determine the volatility of the prices of gilt-edged stocks are the length of the period to their redemption and the size of their coupon interest rate.

(*a*) *Period to redemption*: the shorter the period to redemption, the less volatile the gilt price. This is because it is known with certainty that the stock will be redeemed at £100 and so its price will neither rise nor fall far from its redemption value.

(*b*) *Coupon interest rate*: the lower the coupon interest rate, the greater the change in gilt price for a given change in interest rates. This is because a low coupon rate gilt will be substantially below its redemption value of £100, and so a change in interest rates makes its price react like a long-dated stock.

Thus investors who want to minimize the fluctuations in value of their stocks should buy gilts with a coupon rate close to the current average yield to redemption. The shorter the period to redemption, the more stable their value.

(*c*) *Inflation risk*: except in the case of index-linked gilts, the interest and redemption payments for gilts are fixed at the time of issue. This means that inflation will erode the real purchasing power of the returns that can be made from investment in them. However, investment in index-linked gilts (described in 22 below) can eliminate this risk.

17. Direction of change in long-term interest rates. If interest rates are expected to rise, investors should invest their money in a building society or high-interest bank deposit until they believe interest rates have peaked. This is then the ideal time to purchase gilts as interest yields will be at their maximum and there will be opportunities to take capital gains before redemption as interest rates fall.

18. The effect of inflation. If the rate of inflation exceeds both the interest yield and yield to redemption on a gilt, as occurred for much of the 1970s, then the real rate of return is negative. A quick way of estimating the real rate of return is to subtract the rate of inflation from the interest yield or the yield to redemption earned on the gilt. A more accurate calculation is to use the formula:

128 Stocks and shares

$$\text{Real rate of return \%} = \left(\frac{1 + \text{Interest yield \%}}{1 + \text{Rate of inflation \%}} \right) - 1$$

EXAMPLE: If the interest yield is 10.5 per cent and the rate of inflation 4.5 per cent, the real rate of return is:

$$\left(\frac{1.105}{1.045} \right) - 1 = 5.74\%$$

19. Comparative prospects for investment in equities. If falling interest rates coincide with economic growth, soaring company profits and a bull equity market, then the capital gains to be made from investment in shares will outstrip the gains available in the gilt market. However, if the reduction in interest rates is a consequence of the slide of the economy into recession, gilt prices will be rising at a time when equity prices may be falling.

20. Other factors. There are numerous other factors as indicated in **11** above which should also affect investors' choice between investment in equities or gilts. A weakening of the pound on the foreign exchange market tends to cause a fall in gilt prices as yields have to rise to prevent an outflow of capital. However, the investor can expect a rise in the share price of those companies with large overseas earnings which will increase in sterling terms. A loss of confidence in the economic policies of the government or the prospect of a change of government to one which is likely to pursue policies that will adversely affect the profitability of industry will cause both gilt and equity prices to fall.

Special types of gilt investments

21. Undated gilts. There are six undated gilts listed in the *Financial Times*. Since they are undated, they obviously have no redemption yield. The prices are low in order to give a competitive interest yield against other gilts. Investors who have held these stocks for thirty years or more have seen their capital eroded as higher interest rates have forced down their prices. Since these gilts are both low coupon and undated, they are among the most risky or volatile available. Two additional points of interest are that Consols 2½ per cent are the only gilts to pay interest quarterly rather than half-

6. Gilt-edged and fixed-interest securities

yearly, and Conversion 3½ per cent after 1961 are slowly being redeemed by the Bank of England. The redemptions are met from a *sinking fund* – a sum of money set aside annually to meet redemptions. This extra attraction makes this gilt sell at a small premium to the other undated stocks, giving it a marginally lower interest yield.

22. Index-linked gilts. An index-linked gilt has both its semi-annual interest payment and its redemption value linked to the Retail Price Index (RPI) to give a guaranteed real rate of return. It therefore overcomes one of the risks associated with conventional gilts – that of inflation reducing the purchasing power of both the income provided and the capital invested in the security. The coupon interest rate is expressed as a real rate of interest, and in consequence at 2 or 2½ per cent appears lower than the coupon rates on conventional gilts which vary between 2½ and 15½ per cent but are unprotected against inflation.

The indexing operates as follows. The RPI used in the calculation of interest payments and the final redemption value is always lagged eight months behind the current RPI value. Thus when an index-linked gilt is redeemed, the redemption value is calculated as:

$$\text{Redemption value} = \frac{\text{RPI 8 months before redemption}}{\text{RPI 8 months before issue}} \times £100$$

The RPI eight months before issue is shown daily for each gilt-edged stock in the *Financial Times*. The semi-annual interest payment is calculated in a similar manner.

$$\text{Semi-annual interest payment} = \frac{\text{RPI 8 months before interest payment}}{\text{RPI 8 months before issue}} \times \frac{\text{Real coupon rate}}{2}$$

EXAMPLE:
Index Linked Treasury 2½ per cent 2001: Interest payable 24 March and 24 September
Interest payable on 24 September 1986 =

$$\frac{\text{RPI January 1986}}{\text{RPI base date}} \times \frac{£2.5}{2}$$

Stocks and shares

$$\frac{379.7}{308.8} \times \frac{£2.5}{2} = 153.7p$$

The reason for the eight month time lag in RPI data is so that the next interest payment will always be known and hence the accrued interest which has to be added to the market price to obtain the full purchase price can be calculated.

Although index-linked stocks attempt to provide protection against inflation, there is no protection against an upsurge during the final eight months before redemption. To obtain protection for this period, investors should sell the stock before the final eight months are reached and purchase another longer-dated index-linked stock.

Since future rates of inflation and hence the redemption price and future interest payments are unknown, it is impossible to calculate an index-linked gilt's yield to redemption. However, the *Financial Times* shows the results of two yield to redemption calculations assuming, first, 10 per cent per annum and, secondly, 5 per cent per annum inflation rates until redemption. These calculations are gross yields and relevant only to non-taxpayers. The calculations for higher-rate taxpayers is quite complicated and advice should be taken from a stockbroker concerning which gilts would best suit the investors' needs. (For the enthusiast, the method of calculating real yields to redemption can be found in *The Investment Analyst*, July 1983.)

The investor can compare the yields on index-linked gilts with conventional gilts by converting the yields on conventional gilts into real yields as follows:

Real redemption yield =

$$\left(\frac{1 + \text{Nominal redemption yield on conventional gilt}}{1 + \text{Rate of inflation}}\right) - 1$$

EXAMPLE:
Exchequer 12½ per cent 1990. The *Financial Times* calculated the nominal yield to redemption to be 8.70 per cent
With assumed 5 per cent rate of inflation:

$$\text{Real redemption yield} = \left(\frac{1.087}{1.05}\right) - 1 = 3.52\%$$

6. Gilt-edged and fixed-interest securities

With assumed 10 per cent rate of inflation:

Real redemption yield $= \left(\dfrac{1.087}{1.1}\right) - 1 = -1.18\%$

The *Financial Times* on the same day showed:

Treasury 2 per cent Index Linked 1990
Yield to redemption with 5% inflation: 2.45%
Yield to redemption with 10% inflation: 3.33%

In this example, it can be seen that with an inflation rate of 5 per cent, non-taxpayers would be better off purchasing the conventional gilt; while with an inflation rate of 10 per cent, they would earn a higher real yield with the index-linked gilt. Stockbrokers with a large gilt department calculate break-even rates of inflation for different marginal rates of income tax. Above the break-even rate, investors are better off with index-linked stock; below it, conventional gilts are preferable. The higher the marginal rate of income tax, the lower the break-even rate of inflation and hence the greater the attraction of index-linked gilts. This is because in the case of index-linked stocks, more of the return is in the form of a tax-free capital gain and less in the form of taxable interest income.

23. Convertible gilts. A convertible gilt gives investors the option to convert the stock on specified dates into another gilt with a longer maturity, e.g. Treasury 10 per cent 1990 is convertible into Conversion 9½ per cent 2004. The attraction of this type of gilt is that it has the advantages of a long-dated gilt without the risk. It has already been stated that long-dated gilts are more risky as a change in the general level of redemption yields in the gilt market has the biggest effect on their prices. By purchasing a convertible with a redemption date within five years, it behaves as any other short-dated gilt and is less risky than long-dated stock, but if investors believe that the outlook for interest rates has improved and expect gilt prices to rise, they can convert into the long-dated stock to increase the size of their capital gain as interest rates fall.

How to buy and sell gilts

24. Ways of buying and selling gilts. There are three ways of buying and two ways of selling gilts. They can be bought by filling out an invitation to subscribe for a new issue advertised in the press, or through a stockbroker or through the Post Office. If gilts are purchased through the Post Office, they can only be sold via the Post Office. If investors acquired their gilts through a stockbroker or an advertisement in the press, they must sell them through a stockbroker.

25. Purchasing through the press. If investors purchase a new issue through the press, it may require payment in full on application or only part-payment with the remainder due by instalments (like the British Telecom share issue). If it is issued in partly-paid form, it provides an opportunity to benefit from the implicit personal gearing. For example, if a gilt had been issued at £100 (fully paid) and as a result of a fall in market interest rates rises to £101, this represents a gain of 1 per cent. If the gilt had been issued in partly-paid form at £25, the market price would rise to £26, giving a gain of 4 per cent if sold before the second instalment is due.

26. Purchasing through a stockbroker or the Post Office. The advantage of buying gilts through a stockbroker is that the investors can ask for advice upon which particular one to purchase. A broker can also carry out purchase instructions within a minute or two. The Post Office not only is unable to provide any advice on which gilts are appropriate to the investors' requirements, but the instructions have to be given by completing a special application form GS1 obtainable from the Post Office and posted to the Bonds and Stock Office in Blackpool. They are, therefore, unable to undertake to buy or sell bonds at any particular price other than that ruling at the time of the receipt of the investors' instructions.

27. The Bonds and Stock Office. The Bonds and Stock Office has a restricted list of gilt-edged stocks, currently fifty-one in total, which are available on the National Savings Stock Register for purchase and sale through them. They are, however, a representative cross-section of the gilts available. The maximum purchase of any one stock is restricted to £10,000 on any one day. There are two advantages of purchasing gilts this way. First, interest is paid gross so that if the investors are non-taxpayers, they do not have to reclaim it from the Inland Revenue. If they are taxpayers, receiving the interest gross gives them the chance to use the tax payable until it is due. Secondly, the commission charges are lower on small transactions than the charges of a stockbroker, e.g. on a purchase of £1,000 of stock the Post Office charge would be £4, less than half that likely to be charged by a stockbroker.

28. Specifying how much to invest. There are two ways of specifying the quantity of stock which investors wish to purchase. They can either specify the amount of money they wish to invest or the amount of the nominal value of stock they wish to purchase. In the latter case, they will not know the cost of the investment until the required stock has been purchased on their behalf.

Investment in other fixed-interest securities

29. Common features. The common features of all fixed-interest securities are:

(*a*) greater security than equities;
(*b*) lower variability of price than equities;
(*c*) an inverse relationship between price and market interest rates.

These characteristics make fixed-interest securities the ideal investment when interest rates are falling, especially during the downswing of the trade/investment cycle when equities can be expected to perform badly.

30. Bonds issued by foreign governments and international organizations. The attractions of these sterling-denominated securities are the higher yields than those obtainable on gilts and the fact that interest is paid gross. In the case of countries with serious economic problems, the yield is significantly higher, e.g. Mexico 16½ per cent 2008.

If the bonds are denominated in a foreign currency, their attraction is the protection they give against a fall in the value of sterling against the particular currency in which the bond is denominated. The risk assumed by investors is greater in the case of bonds denominated in foreign currency for, in addition to the three types of risk described above, they will now also have exchange rate risk. Since this type of investment is a specialist area, investors may prefer to invest in a managed bond fund as described in Chapter 8.

A rather special type of bond is the zero coupon bond, sometimes called a *Zebra*. They pay no interest and so, like low coupon securities, will be particularly sensitive to interest rate changes. However, the Inland Revenue consider that part of the gains of this type of bond are income and hence liable to income tax.

31. Corporation stocks. These are issued by British local authorities and are the least risky fixed-interest stocks after gilts as they are a charge on the rates income received by the issuing authority. Some have specified redemption dates, others are irredeemable, but because the size of their issues is relatively small, there is not a very active market in them.

32. Local authority bonds – 'yearlings'. Yearling bonds issued by local authorities carry a fixed rate of interest and are redeemable at the end of one year. Although they are not guaranteed by the government, they are as safe as gilts and make a very suitable investment when interest rates are falling. They are allotted in denominations of £1,000 and, while there is a secondary market for resale, should be viewed as an investment to be held to redemption. They are obtained through a stockbroker who enters the name of the investors on the placing list. The interest rate offered is not known in advance, but the investors can instruct the broker concerning the minimum that they are prepared to accept. New issues take place on Tuesday mornings.

33. Building society bonds. The Nationwide Building Society also issues one-year bonds every third Friday. These are quoted on the Stock Exchange and so a secondary market does exist if resale is necessary. The fixed coupon on these bonds is fractionally above that obtainable on local authority yearlings.

34. Fixed-interest securities issued by companies. These are called *loan stock* or *debentures* and may be secured against specific assets of the company. Mortgage or fixed debentures are a safer investment than unsecured loan stock, but in either case the investors' first concern must be to evaluate the financial health of the company that has issued the securities. Apart from analysing the nature and prospects for the business of the company, an examin-

6. Gilt-edged and fixed-interest securities

ation of its accounts will reveal the amount by which profit exceeded its interest obligations – called *interest cover*.

$$\text{Interest cover} = \frac{\text{Profit before interest and tax}}{\text{Interest payable}}$$

Investors should also examine the capital and income priority percentages (*see* Appendix 5:**13**).

Profitability is only one of the conditions necessary to guarantee payment of interest – the other being liquidity. An analysis of the funds flow statement will reveal whether the company's liquidity is steady, increasing or decreasing.

The market for most debentures and loan stock is not very active since most are held from issue until redemption. Hence there are few listed in the daily press and investors need to consult the *Stock Exchange Daily Official List* which gives the latest available prices for all securities. The yield is larger than on gilts and increases with the risk as perceived by the market and its marketability. Some companies provide for the redemption of their loan stocks by creating a 'sinking fund'. Part of each year's profits are set aside and either:

(*a*) invested to provide income until the redemption year; or

(*b*) used to purchase some of the outstanding stocks in the market; or

(*c*) used to redeem stocks selected by ballot.

35. Preference shares. These are an investment showing some of the characteristics of both fixed-interest stocks and shares. They resemble bonds in that their dividends are fixed, but they resemble shares in that the dividend can be passed if the company is experiencing financial problems and the directors consider that the dividends cannot be afforded. Cumulative preference shares are a type where the holders have a right to the payment of any past dividends as well as the current dividend as soon as the company recovers and before the ordinary shareholders receive a dividend.

The yield on a preference share is expressed as a percentage of its nominal value. For example, the ICI 5 per cent Preference £1 share pays an annual dividend of 5 pence gross per share. Since interest yields on gilts, at the time of writing, are in the range 8.5/9 per cent, the price of the ICI preference share is below its par value and at 53.5 pence is giving a yield of 9.3 per cent.

136 Stocks and shares

36. Comparison of preference shares and gilts. When comparing investment in preference shares with gilts, the following points are relevant:

(*a*) Capital gains on preference shares are not exempt from capital gains tax.

(*b*) The yield is much higher than on ordinary equities, but being fixed provides no protection against inflation. Compared to gilts, the yields are not significantly higher. This is because they are attractive to investing institutions like investment trusts and insurance companies for their dividends carry a tax credit (i.e. are exempt from corporation tax in their hands since they have already had advance corporation tax at a rate equal to the basic rate of income tax deducted at source). Interest from debentures and gilts are subject to the higher rate of corporation tax.

(*c*) There is a narrow market in preference shares which can affect the time it takes to purchase or sell stock and the size of the bid offer spread.

(*d*) New issues of preference shares are fairly rare as it is cheaper for a company to raise capital by issuing loan stock. This is because interest is payable by the company out of their profits before tax while dividends are paid out of post-tax profits.

(*e*) Gilts are risk-free while the purchase of preference shares requires that investors undertake an analysis of the current and prospective profitability and liquidity of the company. As with debentures, dividend cover is a useful guide to the amount of profit currently earned to cover the preference dividends. It is calculated as follows:

$$\frac{\text{Preference}}{\text{dividend cover}} = \frac{\text{Total profit available to shareholders}}{\text{Preference dividends}}$$

The capital and income priority percentages also give an indication as to the security of an investment in a company's preference shares (*see* Appendix 5:**13**).

37. Convertible loan stock. Another fixed-interest investment which has some of the characteristics of both loan stock and shares is the convertible loan stock. It is a loan stock with the right to convert into a specified number of ordinary shares at a price specified at the time of issue.

6. Gilt-edged and fixed-interest securities

EXAMPLE:
Racal Electronics 7 per cent Convertible Loanstock 2009–14

This stock is redeemable by the company if conversion has not taken place any time between 30 September 2009 and 31 October 2014 at three months' notice. Conversion may take place on any 30 September between 1988 and 2008, on the basis of one share per 260 pence of stock (i.e. each £100 nominal can be converted into 38.46 shares).

The ordinary share price of Racal Electronics at the time of writing is 210 pence and the price of the convertible loan stock £110. The dividend yield on the ordinary share is 2.03 per cent and the interest yield on the convertible loan stock 6.36 per cent. From this information it can be seen that:

(*a*) If conversion took place at these prices, the conversion price per share would be:

$$\frac{\text{Conversion}}{\text{price per share}} = \frac{\text{Price of convertible}}{\text{No. of shares received}} = \frac{£110}{38.46} = 286\text{p}$$

(*b*) The conversion premium measures the amount by which the conversion price exceeds the market price of the ordinary share. If the conversion price is less than the market price of the share, it is called a conversion discount.

$$\frac{\text{Conversion premium}}{\text{(or discount)}} = \left(\frac{\text{Conversion price}}{\text{Market share price}}\right) - 1 = \frac{286\text{p}}{210\text{p}} - 1 = 36\%$$

(*c*) Thus conversion will not be considered by investors before the ordinary share price has risen by at least 36 per cent. Even when the conversion premium has fallen to zero, it may still not be in the investors' interest to convert. It then becomes necessary to compare the income obtainable from each investment. The shares are currently yielding only 2.03 per cent, less than one-third of the yield obtainable from the convertible loan stock. Once the income from the shares exceeds that from the convertible and the conversion premium is zero, investors should convert.

(*d*) As the ordinary share price rises, the price of the convertible will follow, increasing the conversion price but lowering the interest yield. This will occur in response to the increased attractiveness of the convertible loan stock which will be viewed by investors as a cheap way into the ordinary shares. At the prices quoted, the convertible loan stock offers the chance to acquire ordinary shares at 286 pence up until the year 2008 and, in the meantime, to earn a yield of 6.36 per cent. If conversion has not taken place by the last conversion date, 30 September 2008, the stock will be valued thereafter as an ordinary loan stock. This will result in a large fall in price when this date passes if the convertible's price is at a premium to that of an equivalent loanstock.

Investors should now update these calculations by finding the latest prices of the convertible loan stock and the ordinary share in the *Financial Times*.

38. Advantages of convertibles. The attractions of convertibles to investors can be summarized as:

(*a*) A fixed interest rate of return which is higher than the dividend yield on the ordinary shares. If the company performs badly, the stock will be redeemed at par. If the company fails, the stock will be redeemed before preference or ordinary shares.

(*b*) If the ordinary share price rises strongly, there is the opportunity to convert into shares. Hence investors have the opportunity to participate in the growth of the company if it is successful.

These characteristics make convertibles very attractive to investors seeking income as well as capital growth, and provide some protection against inflation not given by ordinary loan stock or gilts.

39. Considerations when investing in convertibles.

(*a*) If investors want capital growth, they should look for companies with good growth prospects and hence a high chance of conversion.

(*b*) If investors want income, some convertibles offer higher yields than can be obtained from gilts if there is little prospect of conversion. However, investors must investigate the financial soundness of the company.

(*c*) The ideal characteristics of a convertible are a high yield compared to that on the ordinary share, and a low premium over the price of the ordinary share.

(*d*) Part of the risk associated with investing in a convertible is the variability of the premium. Some analysts measure this and compare the risk of different convertibles. A high yield and low

6. Gilt-edged and fixed-interest securities

premium should ideally be combined with low risk.

(*e*) The length of the conversion term remaining and the number of occasions when conversions can take place. The longer the period available for conversion and the more frequent the opportunity to convert, the more attractive the convertible.

(*f*) Investors should remember that gains made on the sale of a convertible loan stock are liable to capital gains tax, unlike debentures and loan stock of UK companies purchased since 13 March 1984 or gilts.

Progress test 6

1. What are Eurobonds and bulldog bonds? (**4, 6**)
2. What are the differences between the coupon interest rate, gross interest yield, gross yield to redemption, net interest yield, net yield to redemption and real interest yield? (**7, 14, 18**)
3. Why do yields and bond prices change in opposite directions? (**10**)
4. What are the risks involved when investing in bonds? (**16**)
5. How does an index-linked gilt differ from a conventional gilt? (**22**)
6. Why is a convertible gilt less risky than a long-dated gilt? (**23**)
7. Which gilts pay interest gross and which pay interest net of tax? (**27**)
8. What is the difference between a local authority yearling and a corporation stock? (**31, 32**)
9. What are the attractions of investment in (*a*) preference shares and (*b*) convertible loan stocks? (**35–39**)

7
Warrants, traded options and futures

Some investors will want risk-free or low-risk investments, others might want to take a greater risk in the expectation of earning a higher rate of return. This chapter will examine how investors can use investment in warrants, traded options and futures to either increase or decrease the risk of their investments.

Investment in warrants

1. What is a warrant? A warrant is an investment certificate which gives the holder the right to buy a specific number of stocks or shares from the company at a price fixed at the time the warrant was issued. They are usually attached by the company to a new issue of loan stock or shares as a 'sweetener' to make the issue more attractive to investors. Once issued, the warrants can be traded separately from the stocks or shares with which they were issued.

> EXAMPLE: A United Biscuits warrant gives the holder the right to purchase one share from the company for 149 pence any time up to 31 March 1989.

Until this date, the warrant will be a tradeable security with a value determined by the market price of United Biscuits' ordinary shares. The higher the price of the ordinary share, the greater the value of the warrant. If the option to buy the share has not been exercised by 31 March 1989, the warrant will become worthless after this date.

7. Warrants, traded options and futures

2. The volatility of warrant prices. Investment in warrants can increase investors' risk because their price is more volatile than that of the ordinary share.

EXAMPLE:

	Time A	Time B	Increase
Price of United Biscuits' ordinary share	176 pence	245 pence	+39%
Price of United Biscuits' warrant	59 pence	108 pence	+100%

The prices shown in column B were exactly eight months later than those shown in column A. If investors had bought warrants at time A, they would have lost money if they had immediately exercised their right to buy shares. The cost of each share would have been 59 + 149 = 208 pence, a loss of 32 pence compared with the market price. However, by holding the warrants for eight months, they would have made a gain of 100 per cent while investment in the ordinary shares would have produced a gain of only 39 per cent.

The *intrinsic value* of a warrant is the difference between the ordinary share price and the price at which a new share can be bought from the company. At time A, it was 176 − 149 = 27 pence; at time B, it was 245 − 149 = 96 pence. This represents a floor value for the warrant. If the price were to fall below this, holders could exercise their option to purchase a new share which they could then sell at a profit.

It should be noted that the intrinsic value of a warrant is less than its market price. The premium over the intrinsic value is the extra that investors are prepared to pay in the hope of making a larger percentage return than if they invested directly in the ordinary shares. The magnitude of the premium has decreased over the eight months from 54 per cent of the warrant's price to 11 per cent. This reduced the gain that investors in warrants made, for while the intrinsic value of the warrant rose from 27 pence to 96 pence, an increase of 256 per cent, the market price of the warrant increased by 100 per cent. What determines the size of the premium on warrants? The following factors are influential:

(*a*) The expectations of investors concerning the prospects for a rise in the ordinary share price. The more optimistic their expectations, the higher the premium they are prepared to pay.

(b) The length of time until the warrant's right to buy shares expires. The longer the period, the higher the premium investors are prepared to pay. Here the premium is sometimes referred to as the *time value* of the security.

(c) The intrinsic value of the warrant. The higher the intrinsic value, the higher the price of the warrant, and the smaller the potential extra percentage gain compared with direct investment in the ordinary shares. You should also note that warrants, unlike shares, do not provide their holders with any income. Thus the higher the intrinsic value, the lower the premium investors are prepared to pay.

The example given shows the effect of an increase in the price of the ordinary share upon the price of a warrant. If the share price were now to fall, the percentage loss in value of the warrant would be greater than the percentage fall in price of the ordinary share. It is these greater fluctuations in price which make warrants a more risky investment than the ordinary shares themselves.

3. Investment strategies using warrants.

(a) *To increase risk*. Since the price of warrants is below that of the company's shares, a given sum available for investment can purchase more warrants than ordinary shares. At time period A in the case of United Biscuits, three times as many warrants could have been purchased as ordinary shares. If the share and warrant prices rise, investors' gains will be much greater if they have invested in warrants. Conversely, if the share and warrant prices fall, their losses will be greater.

(b) *To reduce risk*. A low-risk strategy is for investors to buy the same number of warrants as the number of shares they would otherwise have purchased. The balance is then put on deposit in a bank or building society to earn a risk-free return. If the price of the warrant is already fairly low, as in the case of the United Biscuits' warrant at time A, a fall in share price will not impose a large loss provided there is still some time left until its expiry. Two-thirds of the investor's capital would have been on deposit earning interest. If the share price rises, the value of the warrant rises more rapidly so

7. Warrants, traded options, futures

that investors participate in the benefits.

You will now see that by varying the proportion of their capital invested in warrants, and the proportion they place safely on deposit, investors can obtain a wide variety of different levels of risk.

Investment in traded options

4. What is a traded option? An investor purchasing a traded option has the right either to buy or sell a fixed number of shares at a fixed price up to a specified date of expiry. The significance of the word *traded* lies in the existence of a market on the floor of the Stock Exchange where they can be bought and sold up to expiry. The list of traded options and their closing prices are shown daily in the *Financial Times* and the *Daily Telegraph*. In the *Financial Times*, you can find them under the heading 'London Traded Options', usually on the page headed 'London Stock Exchange' which contains the 'Market Report'.

It is from this table in the *Financial Times* that the following details of traded options in Marks and Spencer shares were taken:

(1)	(2)	(3) CALLS			(4) PUTS		
		JAN	APR	JULY	JAN	APR	JULY
Marks and	140	46	51	–	1	2	–
Spencer	160	26	32	37	2	4	6
(185)	180	10½	17	21	7	9	10
	200	4	9	14½	20	21	23

Column (1): this gives the name of the share in which traded options are available. Underneath is the market price of the share at the close of trading on the previous day.

Column (2): this shows the *exercise price* – the price at which the purchaser of a traded option has the right to buy or sell shares in Marks and Spencer. There will usually be at least one exercise price above and below the market price of the share.

Column (3): this shows the prices or *premiums* of call options at the close of business on the previous day. There are two types of traded options: *call options* and *put options*. Calls give the purchaser of the traded option the right to buy 1,000 shares at the exercise price at any time up to expiry. The seller or *writer* of call options has the

144 Stocks and shares

obligation to supply 1,000 shares at the exercise price if called upon to do so before expiry.

Traded options are bought and sold in *contracts* which are units of 1,000 shares. The prices shown in each column are the price in pence per share. Each column, January, April and July, is a different expiry date. Thus the price of one call option contract in Marks and Spencer giving the right to buy 1,000 shares at 200 pence was £40 for any time up to the end of January, £90 up to the end of April and £145 up to the end of July. (Price per share in pence × 1,000.) These prices exclude dealing costs.

Column (4): this gives the prices of premiums of put options at the close of business on the previous day. The purchaser of a put option acquires the right to sell 1,000 shares at the exercise price at any time up to expiry. The writer or seller of a put option has the obligation to purchase 1,000 shares at the exercise price if called upon to do so before expiry.

The price of one put option contract in Marks and Spencer giving the right to sell 1,000 shares at 200 pence was £200 for any time up to the end of January, £210 up to the end of April and £230 up to the end of July. These prices exclude dealing costs.

5. Buying and selling traded options. In order for investors to purchase a call or put option, there must be a seller. The seller may be either a previous purchaser who now wishes to sell, or an investor writing a new option. Thus if an investor wishes to buy a Marks and Spencer call option of the 200 pence series that expires in January, the quotation given by the broker might be '4/2' – that is 4 pence per share to buy, 2 pence per share to sell. If the demand exceeds supply at this quotation, the prices will rise, and at the higher prices either some existing holders will decide to sell, or investors holding Marks and Spencer shares will write new options. The motive of the writer of the new option is to obtain the premium in return for writing the option. The writer will consider it unlikely that the share price will rise to 200 pence so that the premium can be retained, but will be happy to sell at a price of 200 pence plus the premium received if it does. Thus, the reader will have noted that:

(*a*) There is no limit to the number of traded options. They can be created by new options being written and eliminated by existing

7. Warrants, traded options, futures

ones being bought back.

(b) The bid offer spread fluctuates to bring demand into equilibrium with supply.

(c) The buyer of a traded option pays the premium which the seller or writer receives.

When investors purchase or sell a trade option, their contract is not with another investor, but with the London Options Clearing House which acts as an intermediary guaranteeing all contracts. This has two advantages. First, the value of an investor's contract is not dependent upon the solvency of the opposite party to it. Secondly, investors can sell an option they have bought or buy back an option they have sold before expiry without affecting the opposite party in the original transaction.

Traded option contracts become worthless if they are not exercised by the end of the last day of trading in the expiring month. The expiry date for call and put share options is two days before the end of the last complete Stock Exchange Account of the expiry month. At any time up to expiry, investors holding a traded option contract can take their profits or cut their losses by either:

(a) Selling an option they have previously bought, or buying back an option they have previously sold.

(b) If they have bought an option, instruct their stockbroker to arrange for it to be 'exercised'. Since the traded option contract is with the London Options Clearing House and not a specific investor, the Clearing House would then use a computerized random selection process to call upon a writer of an option of the same series to deliver the shares in the case of a call option, or purchase the shares in the case of a put option.

Up until the time when the traded option is about to expire, the first of these two alternatives will usually be used. This is because the traded option price normally exceeds its intrinsic value. Like a warrant, the price of a traded option is made up of its intrinsic value (market price per share minus exercise price) and a premium over intrinsic value called *time value*. The size of the time value element in the traded option price, as in the case of the warrant, depends upon:

(a) The expectations of investors concerning the prospects for a favourable change in the ordinary share price (a rise in price for a call option, and a fall in price for a put option).

(b) The length of time until the traded option expires.

(c) The intrinsic value of the traded option. The higher the intrinsic value and the greater the outlay required, the smaller the time value element in the price.

Thus it can be seen that a call option is very similar to a warrant with a short life. Other points that should be noted about the table of premiums for traded options in Marks and Spencer shares are:

(a) With call options, the higher the exercise price, the lower the price of the traded option contract. If the exercise price is above the market price of the share, the option is said to be 'out of the money' and all of the premium for the contract is time value. If the share price fails to rise, the value of the contract will fall as time passes and expire worthless. If the exercise price is below the market price of the share, the option is said to be 'in the money' as it will have some intrinsic value. If the exercise price is equal to the market price of the share, the option is said to be 'at the money'. As the expiry date approaches, the price of in the money options will converge upon their intrinsic value.

(b) For put options, the same principles apply in reverse. Since the purchase of a put option gives investors the right to sell shares at the exercise price, the lower the exercise price, the less valuable the contract. The 200 series of Marks and Spencer put options are in the money and the other three are out of the money.

(c) The longer the period to expiry, the higher the premium or price per share of the traded option. This extra value is 'time value', the extra price investors are prepared to pay since there is a greater chance that share price movements will increase the intrinsic value of their investment.

(d) At any one time, there are always three expiry dates available at three-monthly intervals for each traded option. When the January Marks and Spencer options expire, a new class of October options will be made available. The maximum period to expiry is therefore nine months. It should be noticed in the table of 'Traded Option Prices' in newspapers that there are three separate cycles, e.g. January/April/July/October, with some 12/15 different securities on each cycle. The Stock Exchange periodically creates a market for

7. Warrants, traded options, futures

additional securities and adds them to one of the cycles.

6. What traded options are available? An examination of the table of traded option prices reveals that options are available in some 40 UK companies, Vaal Reefs, a South African gold mining company, De Beers, a South African diamond mining and trading company, two gilt contracts and an index option related to the *FT* SE index.

(*a*) *The gilt contracts.* The Treasury 11¾% 1991 is a short-dated gilt while the Treasury 11¾% 03/07 is a long-dated gilt.

The call option gives investors the right to buy £50,000 nominal of the particular gilt at the exercise price up to the date of expiry. Conversely, each put option gives investors the right to sell £50,000 nominal of the particular gilt at the exercise price up to the date of expiry. The price of each contract is quoted in points and 32nds of a point where each point represents 1 per cent of the nominal value of the contract which is £50,000. Thus each point is worth £500 and each 32nd of a point £15.625.

(*b*) *The FT SE index contracts.* If investors purchase and exercise a *FT* SE index call option, what would be delivered? Since it is unrealistic for settlement to take place in the form of the shares comprising the index, there is a cash settlement of £10 for every point of intrinsic value. The prices quoted in the newspaper are the closing offer prices on the previous day, and have to be multiplied by £10 to obtain the price per contract.

(*c*) *Foreign currency contracts: US$/£ and US$/DM.* In the *Financial Times*, these are not listed with the other traded options, but on the page with the heading 'Currency, Money and Capital Markets'. The exercise price and premiums are quoted in US dollars for delivery of £12,500 and DM62,500 respectively. A US$/£ call option contract gives the investor the right at any time up to expiry to require delivery of £12,500 for payment in dollars using the exercise exchange rate. Conversely, a put option gives the investor the right at any time up to expiry to sell £12,500 for the number of dollars calculated using the exercise price exchange rate. Premiums quoted are US cents per £ or per DM.

The reader should now examine the current tables of prices carefully.

7. Using call options to increase risk.

(a) Like a warrant, call option prices change by a larger percentage than the share price.

EXAMPLE:

	Starting price	New price	Increase
Marks and Spencer ordinary share price	185	210	13.5%
Call Option 160 series expiry January	26	50	92%

Investors can greatly increase their risk by holding some call options in place of shares, e.g. £1,850 would have purchased 1,000 shares or 7 contracts. If the share price rises to 210 pence, the investors' gain will be nearly 7 times greater if they had invested all their money in traded options rather than shares. However, if the share price dropped to 160 pence and remained there until the expiry of the options, the loss incurred by investors would be 100 per cent of their capital, but only 13.5 per cent if they had invested in the shares. Investors should note that the transaction costs when dealing in traded options are a much larger percentage of the sum invested and that the time value of a contract is being constantly eroded. Thus, even if the share price is constant, the value of a call option gradually falls.

(b) Investors' risk can also be increased by 'writing' or selling call options against shares they do not possess. If the share price were to rise dramatically, the option would be exercised and investors would be forced to buy the shares in the market and make a large loss by selling them at the lower exercise price. The Stock Exchange rules relating to writing options require the writer to supply the broker with either the shares or 'margin' in the case of an investor who does not own the shares writing an uncovered or 'naked' option. Margin is the deposit required in the form of cash and is 20 per cent of the market price of the security plus the amount by which the option is in the money, or less the amount by which it is out of the money. As the margin requirements are recalculated daily, the broker will require a larger deposit than the minimum figure.

7. Warrants, traded options, futures

The attraction of writing uncovered options is a much greater rate of return if the option is not exercised. If the option is exercised because the share price has risen rapidly, there is no limit in theory to investors' potential losses. In practice, they would try to limit their losses by making a closing purchase of the same number and type of options that they have written as soon as they realize that their investment has gone wrong.

8. Using put options to increase risk. Put options can be purchased to make money in a bear market. If investors believe that the prices of their investments are going to fall by much more than the transaction costs incurred in selling them and buying them back again later after their prices have fallen, they should go liquid and place the proceeds on deposit. They can then make profits in a falling market by selling shares short (same account trading) or buying put options. We will use a *FT* SE index put option as an example.

EXAMPLE:

	14 May	*16 May*	*Change*
FT SE index	1,626	1,576	−3.0%
FT SE index put option 1575	10	27	+170%

9. Using call options to reduce risk. It must not be thought that traded options are only for speculative investors. They can be used to reduce an investor's risk. This transfer or reduction of risk is sometimes called *hedging*. Two examples will now show this.

(*a*) If investors are uncertain whether to take their profits and sell their investments or to hold on and remain invested, they could combine going liquid with the purchase of call options. If no traded options are available in the particular shares in which they have invested, then they could purchase the call options of either another company in the same sector or the *FT* SE index options. If their fears are confirmed and the share prices then fall, the fact that investors have gone liquid means that their maximum loss is limited to the price paid for the call options. If, contrary to their expectations, the share prices rise, they can either sell the call options at a profit or exercise their right to buy the shares. Thus having taken their profits, the purchase of call options acts as an insurance against missing out on a further upsurge in share prices.

(b) Instead of selling the shares and buying call options, investors could keep their shares and sell or write the appropriate number of call options. If the share prices then fall as expected, the income investors have received from writing the options will at least partially offset the loss from not selling their shares. If the fall in share price is small, the premium they receive may exceed the fall in value of their shares. However, if the share price rises above the exercise price of the options, they will be required to sell their shares at the exercise price unless they close their hedging position first by buying back the same number of call options. This strategy requires that investors write 'at the money' or 'out of the money' options. At the money options provide larger premiums, but there is a greater chance of the option being exercised. Out of the money options provide lower premiums but there is also less risk of the option being exercised. Investors must decide on the balance they wish to strike between the size of the premium received and the amount of risk they assume.

10. Using put options to reduce risk. Put options can be used like an insurance policy to protect investments against a fall in market prices. If share prices rise, a put option will expire worthless. If share prices fall, investors can either sell their investments at the exercise price of the options or sell their put options at a profit.

Investment in conventional options

11. What is a 'conventional' or 'traditional' option? The investor in a *conventional* call option pays a premium called *option money* for the right to buy a specified number of shares at a *striking price* which is specified in the contract and is usually a little above the current offer price on the market. For a put option, the striking price will be a little below the current bid price in the market. Investors can also buy a *double option* which gives them the right to buy or sell. These options can be negotiated through a stockbroker on most shares or stocks except gilts. The opportunity to buy *conventional* or *traditional* call or put options predates the London Traded Option

7. Warrants, traded options, futures

Market, and this earlier type of option cannot be sold.

These negotiated options are usually for three months. While they may be written on any business day, they may only be exercised on any 'declaration day' in the Stock Exchange account up to expiry. The dates for option declarations are shown at the top of the 'Market Report' daily in the *Financial Times* on the page headed 'London Stock Exchange'. They are normally the last Thursday in the Stock Exchange account. On the same page the business conducted on the previous day is described under the heading 'Traditional Options'. The price or option money is usually around 5 to 15 per cent of the share price, and a list of three-month call rates is given at the end of the section on 'Insurance, Overseas and Money Funds'.

EXAMPLE:
The Burton Group ordinary share price 302 pence
Option money 32 pence i.e. 10.6 per cent of share price (excluding brokers' commission).

Since they may not be sold, a profit can only be taken by exercising the option and, in the case of the call option, buying the shares to resell them.

12. Taxation and conventional options. The tax treatment is different from traded options. In the eyes of the Inland Revenue, a conventional option is a 'wasting asset' which means that the amount that can be set off against tax decreases to zero at a constant rate over its life. If the option is abandoned, the loss is not allowable for capital gains tax purposes, unlike traded options. If the option is exercised, the gain for tax purposes is not based on the cost of the option, but the proportion of the cost unexpired.

Similarly, a tax loss can be established to be set off against other gains by exercising the option, but it is the unexpired cost that is used in the calculation, not the purchase cost.

Investment in futures

13. The London International Financial Futures Exchange (LIFFE). When LIFFE opened in the Royal Exchange building in the City of London in September 1982 it offered only futures contracts. However, it has now ventured into the area of traded options as well as futures with its Eurodollar, long-gilt, US Treasury bond and £/$ call and put options. The size of the unit of trading for these traded options is likely to render them of little interest to most private investors. The £/$ contract is £25,000, twice the size of the Stock Exchange contract, and the Eurodollar call option gives the holder the right to buy a Eurodollar interest rate futures contract which has a unit value of $1 million! Already it can be seen that LIFFE is aiming primarily at commercial organizations rather than the private investor. However, the differences between a futures contract and a traded option will now be examined and illustrated by means of the *FT* SE 100 index futures contract which is probably the one likely to be of most interest to the private investor.

14. What is a futures contract? A futures contract requires the purchaser to take delivery of a specified quantity of a particular asset at the price agreed and on the date specified when the contract is purchased. The seller is similarly required to supply the specified quantity of the particular asset at the price agreed and on the date specified. The price at which delivery must take place is the *quotation* at the time the contract was agreed. As with traded options, the contract is not considered to be with a specified individual investor but with the clearing house of the Futures Exchange. Similarly, investors are not required to hold the contract to the delivery date but can close out their commitment by purchasing a futures contract if they originally sold one, or vice versa. The size of their profit or loss will depend upon the difference between the quotations at the time of opening and closing their position.

The London International Financial Futures Exchange offers futures contracts in five interest rates (a twenty-year gilt, a short gilt, a US Treasury bond, a three-month sterling deposit, and a three-month Eurodollar deposit), four currencies (sterling, Deutschmark, Swiss franc and Japanese yen, all denominated in terms of dollars), and the *FT* SE 100 index. It is the last of these that we shall now consider.

15. Futures quotations in the financial press. The quotations for futures are shown in the *Financial Times* on the page headed

7. Warrants, traded options, futures

'Currencies, Money and Capital Markets'. Assume the *FT* SE index closed yesterday at 1,624.8 and the entry for the *FT* SE 100 index future in this morning's paper is:

(1)	(2) CLOSE	(3) HIGH	(4) LOW	(5) PREVIOUS
June	163.70	164.50	162.40	161.40
September	166.00	167.00	164.70	163.75
December	168.50	–	–	165.75

(6) Estimated volume 734 (181)
(7) Previous days open interest 2599 (2591)

Column (1): this shows the delivery month for the futures contract. All the futures on LIFFE are on a March, June, September and December cycle. The delivery day for the *FT* SE index future is the first business day after the last trading day of the delivery month.

Column (2): this gives the quotation at the close of business. The quotation for the *FT* SE index future is the index divided by ten. Thus the quotation 163.70 is equivalent to a value of the index of 1,637.0. Each full index point is valued at £25 (compared with £10 for the Stock Exchange traded option). The quotation of 163.70 is therefore equivalent to an investment of $1,637.0 \times £25 = £40,925$ in a portfolio of shares identical in composition to the *FT* SE 100 index. Settlement is in cash if the future is not closed out by equal and opposite futures transactions. The size of the cash settlement will depend on the difference between the value of the index on the last trading day and the quotation at the time of purchase/sale of the futures contract.

EXAMPLE:
Purchase futures contract at	163.70
Sell futures contract at	166.90
Gain	3.20

Investor's gain = 32 points × £25 = £800

Columns (3) and (4): these show yesterday's high and low values of the quotation.

Column (5): this gives the quotation at the close of business on the previous trading day.

Row (6): this shows the estimated number of futures contracts made during yesterday's trading. The figure in brackets is the number of futures contracts made during the previous trading day.

154 Stocks and shares

Row (7): this gives the number of outstanding open futures contracts with the previous day's number in brackets.

When investors buy or sell a future, there is no premium to pay or receive as in the traded option market. Instead, a futures market operates on the principle of collateral or margin. The initial margin that has to be deposited with the clearing house when a *FT* SE index futures contract is opened is £1,500. Thereafter, variation margin must be deposited to offset the extent to which the futures contract moves against the investor, i.e. £25 for every full index point. For example, if an investor bought one index future when the quotation was 163.70 and the quotation fell to 162.50, this is a fall of twelve points on the index which would require the investor to deposit additional variation margin of $12 \times £25 = £300$.

16. How investors can use index futures to increase or reduce risk.

Purchasing one *FT* SE index future at a quotation of, say, 160.00 is equivalent to buying a portfolio of shares with a market value of $1,600 \times £25 = £40,000$ for an initial outlay of £1,500. Thus, if investors do not have £40,000 to invest, they would be increasing their exposure to risk. If they do have £40,000 to invest in a portfolio of UK equities, to purchase a *FT* SE index future and place the remainder on deposit with a bank or building society involves no extra risk. In fact, it has the advantage of much lower transaction costs and it is much easier to move into and out of the market with no actual shares to buy or sell.

If investors want to increase their risk, they can use the futures market acting as a 'trader', buying a future if they expect the index to rise, and selling one if they expect it to fall. For example, if the quotation is 160.00 when they sell an index future and the quotation falls to 155.00 when they buy it back to close out their position, their gain will be $50 \times £25 = £1,250$.

To reduce risk, they can use the futures market as a 'hedger', doing the opposite in the futures market to what they are doing in the stock market. For example, if they have a diversified portfolio of equities worth approximately £40,000 when the index quotation is 160.00, they can effectively insure themselves against any loss from a fall in share prices without having to sell their shares by selling one index future.

7. Warrants, traded options, futures

This is how it works:

(a) Opening position

Value of portfolio of shares £40,000
Sell one *FT* SE index future at quotation 160.00

(b) All share prices fall 10 per cent

Value of portfolio of shares £36,000: loss £4,000
Buy one *FT* SE index future at quotation 144.0:
$$\text{Gain} = 160 \times £25 = £4,000$$
$$\text{Net gain} = \text{zero}$$

Conversely, if share prices had risen by 10 per cent, the gain of £4,000 in the market value of their portfolio of shares would be offset by their loss of £4,000 in the futures market. Thus by using the futures market to hedge, wealthy investors can dramatically reduce the risk of investment.

It should be noted that the hedging achieved by investors is unlikely to be as perfect as the simple illustration above suggests, as the stock market index and futures market quotation do not always change at the same rate or by the same amount. This fact is one of the explanations for the extreme volatility in share prices that has been experienced on Wall Street. It has caused a high volume of 'program trading' as large investors and financial institutions have used computers to calculate how they can exploit differences between the Stock Exchange index and the futures market quotation to make profits.

To illustrate how this occurs, assume that some financial institutions which are nervous about the prospects for the US economy decide to hedge the value of their equity portfolio by selling index futures. (If the stock market falls, the losses can be offset in the futures market by purchasing index futures contracts to close their position at a lower quotation.) The sale of the futures will tend to reduce the quotation of the index futures relative to the Stock Exchange index itself. This divergence may then cause other financial institutions to enter the market to make a quick profit from arbitrage. (Arbitrage is the making of a risk-free profit by exploiting price differentials between two markets.) The arbitrageurs will sell shares in the Stock Exchange and effectively buy them back more cheaply by buying index futures on the futures market at a lower quotation. This process causes a fall in share prices on the Stock Exchange which can spark off another round of falls on the futures and stock markets if the investing institutions are very nervous.

17. A comparison between index options and index futures. Both index options and futures can be used to increase or decrease risk. However, while the purchase of a future confers the *obligation* to purchase at a fixed price, an option only confers the *right* to purchase at that price. Thus an option limits investors' exposure to risk, so that the maximum they can lose is the premium they have paid if they choose not to exercise their option. With a future, their risk is much greater and in theory can be without limit.

The underlying values of the contracts also differ considerably. One point on the *FT* SE 100 index is worth £25 for a futures contract but only £10 for a Stock Exchange traded option. Thus the implicit investment when the index is at a value of 1,600 is £40,000 for the index future and £16,000 for the traded option. These differences in risk and the implicit scale of investment will make the use of traded options more appropriate for all but the fairly wealthy private investor.

The traded option market has two disadvantages compared with the futures market. First, the commission and transaction costs are much higher. Secondly, the premium paid for a traded option involves a large element of time value. This means that the value of the option decreases if the index remains constant. It also means that changes in the *FT* SE index will be followed more closely by the quotation of the futures contract than the premium of the traded option.

Finally, the gains obtained from both futures and traded options are liable to capital gains tax, and realized losses can be offset against other gains in the same period or carried forward.

Progress test 7

1. What are the differences between a warrant, a traded option and a conventional option? (**1, 4, 11**)
2. What is the difference between a call and a put? (**4**)
3. What is the difference between using the traded option market as a trader and as a hedger? (**7–10**)

7. Warrants, traded options, futures

4. What determines the size of the premium of a traded option? (**5**)

5. Explain the difference between a futures contract and an option. (**4, 14, 17**)

6. What is an index contract? What types are available? (**6, 15, 17**)

Part three
Investment in professionally managed funds

In the next three chapters, we shall look at investments in funds where the securities included in that fund are chosen by professional investment managers. This has the advantage for investors that it relieves them of the day-to-day investment responsibilities such as deciding when to sell securities already held and replace them with others, and how to reinvest the dividends received. It also gives them the greater security of investment in a large diversified portfolio at a much lower cost than they could obtain the same level of diversification themselves.

8
Investment in unit trusts

The nature of unit trusts

1. Definition of unit trusts. A unit trust is a portfolio of securities selected and managed by a professional fund management company from whom shares or units in the portfolio can be purchased. The price of these units is directly related to the value of the securities in the portfolio and the number of units issued. The higher the value of the portfolio, the higher the price of the units.

2. Authorized and offshore unit trusts. There are two types of unit trust available: authorized unit trusts and others located offshore, i.e. outside mainland UK. Authorization is by the Department of Trade and Industry which under the Prevention of Fraud (Investments) Act 1958 is required to vet all proposed new unit trusts to ensure that the interests of the prospective investors are adequately protected (*see* NOTE at the end of this chapter). Only authorized unit trusts can advertise in the press and promote their investments directly to the public without dealing with prospective clients via professional advisers like a stockbroker or bank. Some offshore unit trusts do advertise in the UK press, but they too must satisfy legal conditions designed to protect investors. Their funds must be quoted on a recognized stock exchange and they are not permitted in their advertisements to invite the public to subscribe for units, only to apply for the prospectus of the fund which gives all the legal details of its structure.

162 Professionally managed funds

3. Rules governing authorized unit trusts. An authorized unit trust must conform to the following rules:

(*a*) It must be run in accordance with a trust deed that has been approved by the Department of Trade and Industry. The trust deed specifies the investment objective of the fund including any limits on the geographical area or the type of securities that can be purchased. The responsibility for the unit trust is divided between the management company and the trustee. The management company is responsible for the selection of the investments and the decision on when to buy and sell. The trustee, which is usually a bank, is responsible for ensuring that the register of unit holders is kept properly and that all income and expenditure is recorded. The trustee also keeps all the cash and securities belonging to the trust fund.

The trust deed specifies the management charges which may be levied. The management may include a front end charge at the time of purchase (usually 5 per cent but it varies between 1–6 per cent), and this is included in the offer price paid by investors. There is also provision for an annual management charge which varies between ¼ and 3 per cent but is typically ¾ or 1 per cent of the assets under management. The management company must meet all their own advertising and commission expenses from these charges. Only dealing expenses may be charged to the fund.

(*b*) No more than 5 per cent of the value of the fund at the time of purchase may be invested in any one company. This means that a unit trust's portfolio is likely to have investments in a minimum of 25 companies and usually considerably more. This gives investors the safety of a reasonable spread of investments.

(*c*) A unit trust must not acquire more than 10 per cent of the shares of a company. This is to prevent the trust from acquiring an unmarketable holding in any company.

(*d*) A unit trust is allowed to invest only in securities quoted on a recognized stock exchange although they may hold up to 25 per cent of their funds in companies traded on the London USM, the Tokyo OTC, the United States OTC, and the French Second Market. This facility applies only to relevant funds, e.g. a UK smaller companies unit trust could not invest in the Japanese OTC. Unit trusts are not permitted to invest directly in property or commodities, only in the shares of companies involved in this type of business.

8. Investment in unit trusts

(*e*) The method of calculation of the offer and bid prices must also be approved by the Department of Trade and Industry.

(*i*) The *offer price* is the price at which the management are prepared to sell units to investors. In principle, it should reflect the cost of replacing the existing portfolio of shares.

(*ii*) The *bid price* is the price at which the management are prepared to buy back the units from investors. In principle, it should not be less than the portfolio's break-up value.

Because of the dealers' spread between buying and selling prices for shares on stock exchanges, commissions, stamp duty, etc., the spread between bid and offer prices could be as much as 14 per cent without infringing the Department of Trade and Industry formula. Such a large spread would act as a serious disincentive to invest in unit trusts for their prices would have to rise by at least 14 per cent before investors could make a profit. So, in practice, the fund managers value their units either on an offer basis or a bid basis.

(*i*) *Offer basis* – when the demand for units in a fund exceeds those being offered back to the managers, they need to create new units to satisfy demand and so price them on an offer basis. With the money received from their sale, they invest in new securities thereby increasing the size of the trust's portfolio. The bid price at this time will not be 14 per cent below the offer price, but typically some 6–7.5 per cent.

(*ii*) *Bid basis* – when the encashment of units exceeds the demand for new units by investors, the management may have to sell some of the portfolio's investments to obtain the cash to buy back the units. In this situation, the managers will fix the bid price of the units at the break-up value of the portfolio and the offer price some 6–7.5 per cent above it.

Thus, if investors are buying units when they are priced on a bid basis and selling them later when they are priced on the offer basis, their gains will be enhanced.

Unfortunately, there is no way of telling whether units are currently priced on the underlying bid or offer basis short of ringing up the fund managers and asking.

4. The taxation of investment in authorized unit trusts.

(*a*) *The taxation of the authorized unit trust fund.* All dividend

164 Professionally managed funds

income received from companies in the UK is paid out of profits that have already been subjected to UK corporation tax and is therefore exempt from further corporation tax. This income is called *franked income*. However, interest payments and dividends received from overseas are subject to corporation tax, although the tax liability of the trust is reduced by management charges and dealing expenses. The levying of corporation tax on interest renders unit trusts investing in fixed-interest securities rather tax inefficient since corporation tax is higher than the basic rate income tax paid by most investors, and this explains why, apart from gilt funds, there are so few fixed-interest unit trust funds available.

Unit trust funds are exempt from capital gains tax. This allows the value of the trust's portfolio of investments to grow more rapidly.

(*b*) *The taxation of investors in an authorized unit trust.* All income received by unit trusts after tax and expenses have been deducted is paid in dividends. These may be distributed or, upon the instruction of the investor, reinvested in additional units. Some unit trusts are called *accumulator trusts* because they pay no dividends and so the value of the units grow more rapidly since they are retained. However, all dividends, whether distributed or not, and whether in an accumulator trust or not, are subject to the investor's marginal rate of income tax. Dividends are paid net of the standard rate of income tax, so only investors who pay higher rate tax will have further tax payments to make, while non-taxpaying investors can reclaim the tax deducted. Investors will be liable for capital gains tax on the increase in capital value of any units they sell if the gain is greater than that permitted by the indexation allowance and the annual exemption. You should note that switching between trusts, even when managed by the same fund managers, counts as a disposal for capital gains tax purposes.

5. The taxation of investment in offshore unit trusts.

(*a*) *The taxation of the offshore unit trust fund.* Being located outside the area of UK tax jurisdiction, offshore unit trusts are not subject to UK corporation tax or capital gains tax. They are, however, subject to the taxes of the country in which the funds are located. Hence offshore funds are located in financial centres with low taxes such as the Channel Islands, Luxembourg, Bermuda and the Isle of Man.

This exemption from UK tax makes offshore unit trusts highly tax efficient and, as already discussed in the case of onshore funds, gives them a distinct advantage in funds investing in fixed-interest securities.

(*b*) *The taxation of investors in an offshore unit trust.* In the early 1980s, UK residents were able to use offshore funds in the Channel Islands to convert income which would have been liable to higher rates of income tax into capital gains which would be taxed at only 30 per cent. This was achieved by accumulator funds which 'rolled up' the interest income in the price of the units rather than paying it out as dividends – hence the name *roll up* funds. Since January 1984, all gains received by UK residents from investment in offshore funds are taxed as income unless the fund in question has applied to the Inland Revenue and obtained *distributor status*. To qualify for distributor status, the fund must distribure at least 85 per cent of its income and not invest in other funds that do not have this status.

The taxation postition of the investor can be summarized as follows.

(*i*) If the fund has not obtained distributor status, all dividends and capital gains will be taxed as income. This type of fund is appropriate for investors who either are already non-resident in the UK or intend to obtain non-resident tax status before they sell their units.

(*ii*) If the fund has obtained distributor status, investors will pay income tax on dividends paid by the fund and capital gains tax on taxable gains when they sell the units.

The range of unit trusts

6. How many unit trusts are available? There are about 1000 authorized unit trusts offered by some 150 fund managers for investors to choose between.

7. Sources of information. The main sources of information available are:

(*a*) The daily press – the *Financial Times*, the *Daily Telegraph* and *The Times* contain details of the bid and offer prices of unit trusts listed under their fund managers. Investors should look in these papers and familiarize themselves with the information available there. Brochures can be obtained from the management companies giving details of all the funds for which they are responsible.

(*b*) The daily and weekend press also contain advertisements for unit trust funds, articles and information on their recent relative performance, and the background to the launch of new funds. League tables of performance are particularly useful for indicating which sectors are doing well and badly, and the relative performance of different fund managers in these sectors. The *Sunday Times* publishes weekly a unit trust index showing the performance over one, two and five years and, since the previous Sunday, of the average UK, international, North American, European, Japanese, Australian and Far Eastern unit trusts. It also shows the average bid/offer spread for each area.

The *Investors Chronicle*, published weekly, gives news relating to unit trusts and periodically performance tables for different types of trust.

(*c*) More specialized magazines such as *Planned Savings*, *Money Management*, *Money Magazine*, *Money Observer*, *Unit Trust Management* and *What Investment* not only give detailed performance statistics on each unit trust, but articles on fund management companies, new unit trusts, and other matters of interest to unit trust investors.

(*d*) The Unit Trust Association can provide general information and up-to-date performance figures.

Information on offshore unit trusts is included in the *Financial Times* in the section headed 'Offshore and Overseas' which is found after 'Authorized Unit Trusts' and 'Insurances' at the back of the newspaper. Performance tables of offshore funds are included in the monthly magazine *Money Management*, also showing whether each fund is a distributor or an accumulator fund.

8. The range of funds. Examination of the financial press will quickly reveal that the range of funds offered by different fund managers varies from a single fund to more than 30 with some of the larger selections offered by Henderson, MIM Britannia, M&G, and

8. Investment in unit trusts

Save and Prosper. The main types of funds have been classified by the Unit Trust Association as below (for details of the performance of funds in each category, see *Money Management* or *Unit Trust Management*, published monthly).

9. UK funds.

(*a*) *UK general funds* – aim to achieve a balance between income and growth, and a yield in the range of 25 per cent either side of the *FTA* all-share index by investing at least 75 per cent of the portfolio in UK equities.

(*b*) *UK growth funds* – aim for capital appreciation and, in consequence, the yield may be less than 75 per cent of the *FTA* all-share index. Again, at least 75 per cent of the portfolio is invested in UK equities. Within this classification are special situation, recovery and smaller company funds which managers believe provide the opportunities for above average growth. Examples of the type of special situations that fund managers seek are companies likely to be takeover victims and those where the share price has fallen as a result of a set of problems which the managers believe will soon be resolved. Smaller companies are a more risky investment, but have shown a faster rate of growth of profits.

(*c*) *UK equity income funds* – aim to provide income by investing at least 85 per cent of the portfolio in high-yielding equities or convertibles. The expected yield is at least 25 per cent above that of the *FTA* all-share index and at least 75 per cent of the portfolio is invested in UK shares. In recent years, the average equity income fund has not only provided a higher income than the average growth and general fund, but a higher rate of growth as well!

(*d*) *UK mixed income funds* – aim for a higher income than the equity income funds with a target yield exceeding that of the *FTA* all-share index by at least 33 per cent. The higher yield is achieved by investing between 15 and 85 per cent in preference and fixed-interest securities. Investors seeking the highest yields should look in the next section on gilt and fixed-interest funds.

10. Gilt and fixed-interest funds.

(*a*) *Gilt and fixed-interest growth funds* – aim at capital appreciation with at least 85 per cent of the portfolio invested in UK gilts and other fixed-interest securities.

(b) *Gilt and fixed-interest income funds* – aim at providing a high income with at least 85 per cent of the portfolio invested in UK gilts and other fixed-interest securities. Included in this category are some preference share trusts which frequently top the yield table.

The attraction of gilt and fixed-interest funds has declined recently because of changes in the tax regulations which affect investors in both types.

(a) Growth funds used to enhance their returns by a technique known as *bond washing*. This involved the fund managers purchasing gilts 'ex div' (i.e. after entitlement to the next dividend had lapsed so that the price of the gilts was lower) and selling them later just before they went 'ex div' with their dividends included in the price. Since February 1986, the sale price of gilts has to be divided into accrued income, upon which the fund managers must pay corporation tax, and the underlying gilt price. This has stopped fund managers obtaining capital growth by this means. However, these new rules do not apply to preference shares.

(b) Both types of fund have also been affected by the abolition of capital gains tax on gilts and certain corporate bonds since July 1986, for this has not been extended to investors in unit trusts which invest in these securities. Thus, if investors are likely to utilize their annual capital gains tax exemption fully, they should invest directly in gilts and corporate bonds to avoid payment when they sell their units. If investors' capital gains from their gilt and fixed-interest units are covered by their annual exemption, there is no problem.

The attraction of these funds to investors now relies upon the convenience of a managed portfolio and the skill of the managers to spot anomalies and impending market movements to obtain a higher rate of return.

There is no separate category for funds investing in foreign bonds. There are only a few authorized unit trusts specializing in international bonds, such as those managed by Abbey, Save and Prosper, and Sun Alliance. Compared to offshore bond funds, they have the disadvantage that the fund's interest income is subject to corporation tax. However, they do provide investors with a currency hedge against a fall in the value of sterling and also against a

8. Investment in unit trusts

widespread fall in equity prices.

11. Special sector funds.

(*a*) *Investment trust funds* – aim for capital growth by investing at least 85 per cent of their portfolio in the shares of investment trusts.

(*b*) *Financial and property funds* – unit trusts are not allowed to invest directly in property, so these trusts seek capital growth by investing in the shares of property companies. Some trusts invest just in property, some just in financial institutions such as banks and insurance companies, while others invest in both.

(*c*) *Commodity, gold and energy funds* – again, unit trusts are not permitted to invest directly in commodities or gold bullion, only the shares of companies trading in them. A commodity fund will include an international selection of shares in oil companies, mines, metal-processing companies, and plantations producing tea, rubber and palm oil. Trusts investing in gold shares and energy companies may also invest world-wide or, as in the case of Waverley's Australasian Gold Trust, just in one of the world's markets.

(*d*) *Technology funds* – these are classified with international funds as growth funds specializing in companies world-wide that are involved in the application of high technology.

12. International funds.
These provide a portfolio of internationally diversified companies selected to achieve economic growth. This type of fund is lower risk because of its diversification and is an alternative for investors to the diversified investment trusts discussed in the next chapter. Now that the rate of corporation tax has been reduced, there is a current trend among fund managers to launch international income funds which offer investors a modest yield with growth prospects that is fairly well protected against a fall in the value of sterling.

13. Geographically based funds.
Apart from UK funds, there are many unit trusts available investing just in North America, Europe, Japan, the Far East or Australia. Within each of these areas, their are more specialist funds concentrating on, say, smaller companies, high technology or single countries. The investor should note that the more specialist the fund, the greater are the constraints imposed

on the fund managers and hence the greater the risk. For example, selection of a fund investing in Japanese high-technology companies rather than one investing in Japan would prevent the fund managers from diversifying into, say, building and property companies, public utilities and banks if they thought these had better prospects than high-technology companies that are dependent upon exports.

The specialist funds such as those concentrating in Hong Kong, Singapore and Malaysia, Germany, Pacific Basin energy, or global health care are of interest to investors who will be actively managing their investments. Otherwise, investors should select a less specialized fund.

Investors' considerations when selecting unit trusts

14. Main considerations. The major factors investors should consider are as follows:

(a) Are they looking primarily for income or growth?
(b) How much risk are they prepared to take?
(c) Do they want to manage the future switching of investments between trust funds or do they want to have this task undertaken for them by professional investment managers?
(d) The range of different funds offered by managers.
(e) A comparison of charges.
(f) The reputation of the fund managers.
(g) Does the investor require a monthly saving scheme?
(h) Does the investor require a monthly income scheme?

15. Income or growth? If investors are seeking income, they should invest in one of the UK equity income, mixed income, gilt and fixed-interest income, or overseas income funds described above. The greater the proportion of fixed-interest and preference shares in the fund, the higher the yield, but the lower the potential future growth in capital value and protection against inflation. On the other hand, at a time of dull or falling equity prices, fixed-interest securities provide better protection. Overseas income funds stand to gain if the pound should fall against other currencies.

The dividend yield of each unit trust is given daily in the *Financial*

8. Investment in unit trusts

Times and monthly in *Money Management*. The comparative performance of different trusts is tabulated in *Money Management*, *Planned Savings*, *Unit Trust Management* and *What Investment*.

As explained in **4** above, all income received by the trusts is paid out as dividends, net of the standard rate of tax, except for the income of accumulator trusts. For investors seeking capital growth, the advantage of accumulation units in an accumulator trust is that there is no front end management charge on the reinvestment of dividends for they are simply 'rolled up' in the price of the units. Remember that these dividends are still subject to income tax and hence are ineffective as a means of reducing an investor's tax liability.

16. How much risk? The price of units can go down as well as up, and even though their price may have risen steadily for several years, this is no guarantee that they will continue to do so. However, the risk to which investors are exposed when investing in unit trusts is the risk of the particular market in which the trust is invested and, if this is overseas, the risk that the sterling exchange rate will alter. By investing in a unit trust, investors are automatically investing in a diversified portfolio which protects them from the misfortunes which might befall a single company, and the fund is managed professionally to a high standard within safeguards imposed by the Department of Trade and Industry.

However, not all markets and trusts are equally risky. A diversified international portfolio is less risky than investing in a single country or a single sector. Some markets are more volatile than others. Hence the fluctuations in price of the units of a gilt and fixed-interest fund will be less than the fluctuations of units in a Hong Kong or gold share trust.

Selecting a trust which invests in an overseas stock market will also expose investors to currency risk. For example, the average Australian unit trust fell by 20.7 per cent in 1985 because the currency halved in value against sterling. Fund managers can protect their investors against such currency losses in advance by *hedging*. There are various ways of currency hedging including selling foreign currency forward, using currency futures and options, and back-to-back loans. Authorized unit trusts are only allowed to use back-to-back loans. (Offshore unit trusts and investment trusts can use all these methods of hedging.) Hedging by a back-to-back loan involves borrowing from a bank the same foreign currency as the one in which the fund's investments are priced. The bank loan is then converted into sterling and placed on deposit to earn interest. Sometimes the interest earned is greater than the interest paid on the foreign currency borrowed, thereby making a profit. Sometimes a loss is made. If sterling then appreciates against the foreign currency, the foreign exchange loss made on the fund's investments in overseas securities is offset by the gains made when the loan is repaid. (The fund's managers will have to pay less sterling to obtain the foreign currency on the foreign exchange market to repay the loan.)

Most fund managers are cautious about hedging against a rise in sterling against foreign currency. Although hedging against the dollar paid off in 1985 when the dollar fell, earlier hedging in 1983 and 1984 had lost money. If investors have strong views that sterling is likely to rise against a foreign currency, then if they want to invest in that country's securities, they should find a fund where the management have hedged their currency exposure. There are two fully-hedged funds investing in North America: Gartmore's Hedged American Trust is an authorized unit trust and Fidelity's Sterling American Fund is an offshore fund based in Jersey which is managed to qualify for distributor status.

17. Do the investors wish to manage their own investments?
While investing in a unit trust hands over the responsibility for the selection of the particular securities included in the portfolio, investors still have to decide if and when they wish to switch from one unit trust portfolio to another, or whether they also want this decision to be taken by professional investment managers.

(*a*) If investors wish to retain this responsibility for their own switching, then their initial choice of unit trusts in which to invest must be influenced by the range of trust funds offered by the fund management company, their management charges including the cost of switching from one fund to another, and the investment performance of the fund management company (*see* **18–20** below).

(*b*) If investors wish to hand over the responsibility for switching between unit trusts, there are a number of alternatives open to them.

8. Investment in unit trusts

(*i*) Use the unit trust management services offered by many members of FIMBRA and stockbrokers. These are advertised in the financial press and there is a regional directory of names at the back of each month's issue of *Money Management* and *What Investment*. If investors select a firm that has no in-house unit trusts, their advice can be impartial. Management charges should be compared carefully.

(*ii*) Use the unit trust management services offered by fund management companies (e.g. Oppenheimer) which will invest part of investors' funds in their own trusts and part in those of other management companies which they judge to have the best prospects. Again the investor should watch for charges, the size of the minimum investment, and whether the fund managers can go liquid if they consider it appropriate.

(*iii*) Use one of the new 'fund of funds' offered by unit trust management companies which are managed portfolios comprising not less than four of their own unit trusts with no more than 50% in any one of them. The fund managers undertake to switch between their different trust funds as they consider the investment prospects require.

(*iv*) Buy units in an international trust fund where the fund's managers will spread the portfolio of investments in the stock markets which they consider have the best prospects. Their disadvantage is that the portfolio cannot be switched between world markets or go liquid in a bear market as rapidly as the other three alternatives.

18. The range of funds offered by the managers. Investors who wish to manage their own selection and switching between trust funds should examine the range offered by different management companies. While discounts are available for switching between funds managed by the same company, it is very unusual to obtain any discount for switching between funds managed by different companies. Not only is the range of funds on offer important, but also the facilities available to go liquid in a bear market. If no provision is made, investors would lose the full bid offer spread of approximately 6.5 per cent of their capital when they decide to reinvest.

The only authorized unit trust to offer a deposit fund is the Royal

Trust Prestige Portfolio Trust. However, several fund management companies (e.g. Oppenheimer, M & G, and MIM Britannia) have made provision for investors selling their units to place their funds in a high-interest deposit account and then qualify for a switching discount when they choose to reinvest in one of their unit trust funds. Investors in Fidelity unit trusts have the opportunity to switch the proceeds from the sale of their units into any of the sixteen currency funds of the Old Court Currency Fund run by Rothschild Asset Management in Guernsey. This provides investors with the opportunity to protect their capital against a fall in the value of sterling. The fund qualifies for distributor status. When investors want to reinvest in Fidelity's unit trust funds they benefit from a 4 per cent discount on the offer price.

Of particular interest to investors are the type of offshore unit trusts available in the Channel Islands and Luxembourg which are referred to as *umbrella funds*. These offer a number of sub-funds from which the investor can choose. The advantages of these funds are:

(*a*) They are managed to qualify for distributor status which makes them tax efficient for UK investors.

(*b*) They offer a wide range of equity, fixed-interest and foreign currency deposit funds. In particular, they have an advantage over authorized unit trusts since they offer foreign bond funds (e.g. denominated in yen, Deutschmarks and dollars) and foreign currency funds which allow investors to protect their investments against a fall in sterling.

(*c*) Being located offshore, the interest received by the funds from investment in bonds is not subject to UK corporation tax.

(*b*) Investors can switch between the various sub-funds without incurring liability to capital gains tax. (This allows investments to continue to grow free of tax until withdrawn from the fund.) This benefit does not apply to authorized unit trusts.

(*e*) Offshore unit trusts can use the forward currency markets to hedge their portfolios, a technique of hedging denied to authorized unit trusts.

Examples of these funds are the Gartmore Capital Strategy Fund, the Guinness Mahon Global Strategy Fund, and the Schroder Portfolio Selection Fund. These funds should be found in the

8. Investment in unit trusts

Financial Times on the page with the heading 'Insurance, Overseas, and Money Funds'.

19. A comparison of charges. Most unit trust funds include a 5 per cent management charge in the offer price of their units and have a bid offer spread of about 6.5 per cent. The size of the spread can be calculated from the prices shown daily in the *Financial Times*, *Daily Telegraph* and *The Times*. The monthly magazine *Unit Trust Management* tabulates the initial charge, annual charge and the bid offer spread for all authorized unit trusts.

The differences between fund managers are not usually very large except in the case of gilt and fixed-interest funds where most, but not all, have a lower bid offer spread. Two gilt funds, Mercury Gilt and Abbey Capital Reserve, make no initial charge.

Of particular interest is the Royal Trust Prestige Portfolio Trust which offers nine equity sub-funds and a deposit fund between which investors can switch free of charge. The initial charge and bid offer spread at 3.5 per cent are lower than for all other comparable unit trust funds, but the annual management fee is higher at 1.9 per cent. Switching can be undertaken by giving instructions over the telephone. As with all authorized unit trusts, the proceeds of a switch are liable to capital gains tax.

Another fund management company of note is West Avon which has reduced its front end management charge from 5 per cent to 2 per cent by ceasing to pay commission to financial advisers who introduce business to them.

Also important to active investors is the size of the discount on the offer price available for switching between 'in-house' funds. The largest discounts available are given by Oppenheimer (5 per cent), Fidelity (4 per cent), Perpetual (4 per cent) and Target (4 per cent). This reduces the loss of investors' capital when switching from 1.5–2.5 per cent. The average discount is about 2.5 per cent.

Some offshore unit trusts have lower charges than authorized unit trusts. The Gartmore Capital Strategy Fund has no bid offer spread, and no initial charge. Switches are permitted free of charge, but the minimum initial investment is $25,000. The Guinness Mahon Global Strategy Fund has a very low bid offer spread, an initial charge of 3.5 per cent waived for investments over £50,000, and a switching fee of £25. The foreign currency bond funds of

176 **Professionally managed funds**

Foreign and Colonial Management also have a very low bid offer spread.

20. The reputation of the fund managers. The investment performance of the different fund management companies is a really important consideration as differences between the management charges and switching discounts of funds can easily be outweighed by the differences between their investment performance. While past performance can be no guarantee of future performance, investors should examine carefully:

(*a*) The comparative performance over six months, one, two, three, five and seven years shown in *Money Management* or the similar tables shown in *Unit Trust Management*, *Planned Savings* or *What Investment*.

(*b*) The fund manager's report, looking particularly at the fund's investment objectives, the composition of its portfolio, and the fund manager's views on the investment outlook and their hedging policy.

21. Funds with monthly savings schemes? A majority of unit trusts have a savings scheme with a monthly minimum contribution of from £10 to £50. To see which funds offer a scheme and the size of the minimum monthly investment, investors should consult the pink pages of statistics in *Unit Trust Management*. The advantages for investors of a savings scheme linked with unit trusts rather than life assurance (discussed in Chapter 10) is that the savings can be halted or withdrawn without any financial penalty. Some unit trust management groups offer a discount on the price of units to regular savers, e.g. Brown Shipley (3 per cent), Oppenheimer (2 per cent).

A regular monthly subscription buys more units when their price is low than when it is high. Thus when the price of units fluctuates, their average price will be higher than the average price paid by the investor. This situation is referred to as *pound cost averaging*.

EXAMPLE: Investor's monthly saving is £50

Month	Price of unit	Number of units purchased
1	£2.00	25
2	£1.00	50
3	£1.25	40

Average price of unit: (£2.00 + £1.00 + £1.25) ÷ 3 = £1.42
Average price paid per unit = £150 ÷ 115 = £1.30

22. Funds with monthly income schemes? Those investors who are fairly dependent upon the income from their investments may prefer to invest in one of the monthly income schemes offered by some twenty of the different fund managers. The yield is lower than that obtainable from investing in National Savings income bonds or high-yielding building society or bank accounts. This is because the unit trusts are investing primarily in equities which should offer a rising income and hence some protection against inflation. The schemes with the highest yields will include gilts and fixed-interest investments in their funds.

Buying and selling

23. Methods of buying unit trusts. There are four methods of purchasing units.

(*a*) By writing to the fund manager at the address shown in the *Financial Times* or other newspaper or magazine, enclosing a cheque for the amount to be invested and specifying the fund or funds. The system is very flexible. Investors can either buy £x worth of units (remember there is a minimum amount which varies between fund management companies) or they can buy y units at whatever is the prevailing price on the day the application is received. With this method, it is simpler to buy £x worth of units as the number of units purchased does not have to be a whole number. The fund management company then send investors a contract note detailing the number of units purchased.

(*b*) By filling out the applicaiton form on an advertisement in a newspaper or magazine and enclosing a cheque. When a new fund is launched, the newspapers contain several advertisements, and the price of the units is usually held constant for an introductory period during which some discount is often offered as well.

(*c*) By telephoning the management company (the telephone number is given in the daily financial press at the top of the list of the prices of units in each of their funds). The dealing room will take the order for £x worth of units or y units, and post a contract note

178 Professionally managed funds

giving details of the purchase to the investors. Upon receipt of the contract note, the investors just complete the form giving the name and address of the owner of the units and return it with a cheque in payment.

(*d*) By purchasing units through financial advisers such as a bank, an insurance broker, accountant, solicitor, etc. The adviser receives a commission from the fund management company, but this does not affect the price paid by investors or the number of units received.

Whichever of the four methods used by investors, they receive a contract note specifying the number of units purchased and the price paid for them. About one month later, they will receive a certificate from the trustee to the fund which must be stored carefully until they wish to sell the units.

24. Methods of selling unit trusts. Selling the units is just as easy.

(*a*) *By post:* investors simply sign the certificate on the back stating the number of units they wish to sell and return it to the fund managers.

(*b*) *By telephone:* investors telephone the fund managers and they will send a contract note specifying the number of units they have bought back and the price. When this is received, it is returned with the certificate duly signed on the back, and a cheque is normally received within seven working days.

For active investors, the use of the telephone avoids delays in the purchase or sale of units. Investors do not have to wait for the certificate to arrive from the trustee before selling units they have bought. The fund managers' bid and offer prices on any day are not necessarily the same as in that morning's paper. In the *Financial Times*, the letter (*b*) against the name of a fund management company, e.g. Henderson and Tyndall, means that the prices in the paper are today's prices at which they are prepared to deal. The letter (*g*) means that the prices are the opening prices at which they are prepared to deal, e.g. Barclays, Gartmore, MIM Britannia, Target. The letter (*z*) means that the prices are yesterday's prices and that today's dealing prices are calculated later, e.g. Fidelity, Save and Prosper.

8. Investment in unit trusts

The Personal Equity Plan (PEP)

25. The nature of the scheme. This scheme was announced in the 1986 budget and came into effect on 1 January 1987. It provides for UK residents over the age of 18 to invest up to £2,400 per annum into a PEP which must be managed by a dealer in securities recognized by the Financial Services Act who has registered as a plan manager with the Inland Revenue. Investors are not allowed to carry forward unused allowances into later years, but married couples will be treated as separate individuals. The plan managers may either select the portfolio for their clients, or act on their clients' instructions. However, only certain types of investments are eligible. Investments in shares must be in companies incorporated in the UK and which are listed on the Stock Exchange. Shares in foreign companies, preference shares, convertibles, options, and futures are ineligible. Investments of the larger of £420 per annum or 25 per cent of the amount subscribed to the PEP may be used to purchase unit trust or investment trust shares. These investments are not restricted to UK funds and so are a useful way to gain exposure to overseas markets.

26. The advantages of the scheme. The attraction of the scheme to investors is that the dividends received on the investments in the plan will be free of income tax and any gains will be exempt from capital gains tax. The plan managers will reclaim the advance corporation tax paid by companies from the Inland Revenue. However, the tax relief is automatically lost if the plan becomes void. This happens if it is not maintained throughout the year following that in which contributions have been made. Thus payments into a plan made during 1987 must not be liquidated before January 1989. During the year in which a plan is started, there are no restrictions on the amount of the PEP investment that can be held in a cash deposit account accumulating interest tax free. In subsequent years, it is only possible to keep up to 10 per cent or £240, whichever is greater, as a cash deposit.

27. The drawbacks of the scheme. As a means of attracting the small investor to take the plunge into equities, the PEP is not as generous as schemes in other countries. Given that the average

180 Professionally managed funds

small investor does not have capital gains in excess of the annual exemption allowance, this exemption provided by the scheme will only benefit more wealthy investors. The exemption from income tax on the dividends is also going to amount to very little in the early years. With a dividend yield on the *FTA* all-share-index of 4 to 5 per cent, the maximum dividend income will be about £100 and the tax saving about £30. However, if the plan is maintained for a number of years, the value of these tax concessions to investors will increase with the value of the investments.

An important disadvantage of the PEP is that investors can only go 10 per cent liquid after the first year if they wish to qualify for the tax relief. This means that if they believe that equity prices will fall, investors must decide whether the loss of the tax relief would be greater than the anticipated fall in the value of their investments.

Progress test 8

1. What are bid prices, offer prices and the management charges for unit trusts? (**3**)

2. What are the tax implications of investing in unit trusts? (**4, 5**)

3. What criteria should be used in the selection of unit trusts? (**14**)

4. What are the advantages and disadvantages of investment in offshore unit trusts? (**18, 19**)

5. How can investors purchase unit trusts? (**23**)

6. What are the attractions of investment in a Personal Equity Plan? (**25, 26**)

NOTE to section 2. This will be superseded by the implementation of the Financial Services Act 1986 which requires that unit trusts are regulated by Self-Regulating Organizations (SROs) approved by the Securities and Investments Board. The investment management companies must be approved by the Investment Management Regulatory Organization (IMRO) while the marketing and sale of unit trusts will be supervised by the Life Assurance and Unit Trust Regulatory Organization (LAUTRO) and the Financial Intermediaries, Managers and Brokers Regulatory Association (FIMBRA) (*see* Chapter 13).

9
Investment in investment trusts

This chapter aims to explain what an investment trust is and to examine its relative advantages and disadvantages for investors compared with unit trusts.

The nature of investment trusts

1. Definition. An investment trust is a public company which has used its capital and retained profits to invest in the shares of other companies and other financial securities to obtain income and/or capital growth for its own shareholders. Its status as a public company with its shares quoted on the Stock Exchange renders the trust subject to company law and the Stock Exchange regulations which provides its shareholders with protection against managerial malpractices.

2. Obtaining Inland Revenue approval. An investment trust that is approved by the Inland Revenue gains the advantage of exemption from capital gains tax, like unit trusts. To obtain this approved status, the investment trust must satisfy the following conditions.

(*a*) Be listed on the London Stock Exchange.
(*b*) Be legally resident in the UK.
(*c*) Derive its income wholly or mainly from shares and securities (normally over 70 per cent).
(*d*) Not invest more than 15 per cent of its assets in any one company unless it is another investment trust (the 15 per cent limit

182 Professionally managed funds

applies at the time of purchase so that increases in the value of an investment do not necessitate the run down of the holding).

(*e*) Not retain more than 15 per cent of its income from shares and securities. The rest must be paid to shareholders as dividends.

3. Additional restrictions for Stock Exchange listing. Since 1972, new investment companies have had to satisfy additional investment restrictions imposed by the Stock Exchange to qualify for listing as an investment trust. These restrictions do not apply to the investment companies in existence at that date and already recognised by the Stock Exchange as investment trusts. These new tighter rules of the Stock Exchange require that a new investment trust must not:

(*a*) lend or invest more than 10 per cent of its assets in any one company unless it is another investment trust;

(*b*) invest more than 25 per cent of its assets in unlisted securities and the shares of companies which hold 20 per cent or more of the equity of any other company except another investment trust. (Shares traded on the USM are treated as unlisted, while those quoted in the NASDAQ system in the USA are treated as listed.)

If a new company does not satisfy these criteria, it may still obtain a listing on the Stock Exchange as an *investment company*. To qualify as an investment company, it must maintain a reasonable spread of investments, not invest more than 20 per cent of the fund in a single company at the time of investment, pay dividends only out of dividends received, and not assume management or legal control over any of its investments. Thus it is possible for a new company which does not satisfy the criteria for a Stock Exchange listing as an investment trust to obtain a listing as an investment company and still satisfy the Inland Revenue criteria as an investment trust. One example is First Charlotte Assets which has some 60 per cent of its assets in unlisted investments but is approved by the Inland Revenue as an investment trust and is a member of the Association of Investment Trust Companies.

4. Range of investment trusts. There are about 200 investment trusts and together they make up the fourth largest sector of the stock market, accounting for some 5.5 per cent of the London Stock

Market's capitalization. Together they control some £17 billion of assets and the largest trust, the Globe, manages over £800 million of assets. Some are independent of other management companies and all their investment decisions are taken by their own management. However, the majority of trusts employ specialist investment management companies such as merchant banks, stockbrokers and investment management companies (most of which also manage unit trusts). Hence the same investment management company may be responsible for several investment trusts and there has been a trend for each trust in a management company's stable to specialize in a particular geographical market or industrial sector and to cater for the income or capital growth needs of different types of investors.

5. The marketing of investment trusts. Investment trusts are therefore an extremely important part of the investment scene and yet awareness of the opportunities they offer is generally not as widely spread as for unit trusts. This is partly because of the very high profile marketing of unit trusts whose fund managers are allowed to advertise their units as well as to pay commissions to investment advisers who arrange for their purchase. In contrast, investment trusts are not permitted by law either to advertise their own shares or to pay commissions to investment advisers.

However, investment trust management companies are attempting to overcome their disadvantage by advertising their annual results and investment performance in the press together with the range and objective of the trusts that they manage. They have also improved the presentation and amount of information available in their annual reports. The Association of Investment Trust Companies also advertises in the newspapers on behalf of all its members and collects valuable information which it makes available to investors.

6. Split capital trusts. There are a small number of split capital trusts which have two types of shares available: income shares and capital shares. The trust company is set up with provisions made for its winding up at a future date. Until this time, the income shares are entitled to all or nearly all the income received by the trust, and the capital shares receive either none of the income or a small share.

184 Professionally managed funds

On winding up, the income shares are redeemed at par or are entitled to a small share of any capital growth, while the capital shares are entitled to all the net assets after the payment of the income shareholders.

> EXAMPLE: The River and Mercantile Geared Capital and Income Trust 1999 was launched in the spring of 1986. The Trust will be liquidated in 1999 and, until then, the income shares will be entitled to all the dividend income. Upon liquidation, the income shares will receive one-third of the increase in asset value while the capital shares will be entitled to the remaining two-thirds.

The income shares will be particularly attractive to investors who seek a high income while the capital shares are a highly suitable investment for higher rate taxpayers seeking growth rather than income. There are a few split capital trusts that have been designed so that the income shares are held by charities, e.g. the British Kidney Patient Association Investment Trust.

7. The main features of investment trusts. These can be shown best by means of a comparison with unit trusts.

(*a*) The units of a unit trust are purchased from its fund managers either directly or through intermediaries. The shares of an investment trust are bought through a stockbroker as they are quoted on the Stock Exchange. This is why the fund managers of unit trusts can pay commission while those of investment trusts are in no position to do so.

(*b*) The total number of units held by investors in a unit trust is not fixed. If there are more purchasers than sellers of units, the fund managers create more units and expand the size of the fund under their management. For this reason it is sometimes referred to as an *open-ended fund*. The number of shares of an investment trust is fixed and they can only be bought from other holders via a transaction on the Stock Exchange. It is therefore sometimes referred to as a *closed-end fund*.

(*c*) The investment restrictions imposed upon an investment trust are not so severe as for a unit trust. An investment trust can hold larger stakes in a company, invest a larger proportion of its

9. Investment in investment trusts

assets in one company, and invest a larger proportion of its assets in unquoted companies. Unlike unit trusts, investment trusts can invest directly in property and commodities, but must observe the rule that their income must come mainly from shares and securities.

(*d*) Like unit trusts, investment trusts provide a choice between general trusts investing world-wide where the fund's management consider the best investment prospects exist or more specialist trusts investing in a particular geographical area or industrial sector. However, there are no investment trusts specializing in fixed-interest securities since the income received by the trust from its investments will not carry a tax credit as in the case of dividends from UK company shares, and will therefore be liable to corporation tax.

(*e*) The transaction costs and management charges associated with investment trusts are usually lower than for unit trusts. Most unit trusts make an initial charge of 5 per cent which is part of the average bid offer spread of 6.5 per cent. This means that less than 95 per cent of investors' initial investment in unit trusts is actually an investment in the assets held by the trust. With investment trusts, there are no initial management charges, only the same transaction costs as would be involved in purchasing any shares on the Stock Exchange. The larger the purchase, the lower the percentage of the investor's capital that is swallowed in transaction costs. While the transaction costs on selling the shares could make the total bid offer spread for investment trust shares equal to 5–6 per cent, slightly lower than for unit trusts, more of the investor's capital is invested initially to grow and earn dividends.

The annual management charges for investment trusts vary, but average 0.4–0.5 per cent of total assets, which is much lower than the 0.75 or 1.0 per cent charged by most unit trusts.

(*f*) Not only is a larger proportion of the investors' savings invested in the underlying assets in the case of an investment trust, but the purchase price of investment trust shares is usually at a discount to its net asset value. (The *net asset value per share* is defined as the value of the total assets or investments of the company, less its liabilities such as any debentures or preference shares issued by the company, divided by the number of issued ordinary shares – *see* Appendix to Chapter 5:**14**.) Since 1973, the average discount has fluctuated between 20 and 40 per cent, mostly in the range 25–30

186 Professionally managed funds

per cent. The prices of units in a unit trust are strictly related to net asset value and calculated by a formula approved by the Department of Trade and Industry.

The size of the discounts to net asset value in the case of investment trust shares is determined by the level of market demand relative to supply of its shares on the Stock Exchange. If the shares of the trust are much in demand because the area of its investment is currently in fashion, the size of the discount will fall and has on occasion even risen to a premium over net asset value. In a few cases, the size of the discount to net asset value has been reduced by a takeover of the investment trust by a pension fund, or conversion into a unit trust.

Discount or premium to net asset value is calculated as follows:

$$\frac{\text{Market price per share} - \text{Net asset value per share}}{\text{Net asset value per share}} \times 100$$

(g) Finally, investment trusts are permitted to borrow money and gear up while unit trusts are not. An investment trust, being a public company, can issue preference shares, convertible loan stock, loan stock, warrants and negotiate bank loans both in sterling and foreign currency. The effect of gearing on investments is to increase their risk.

In a bull market when security prices are rising in value, shareholders in a geared company experience faster gains in the net asset value of their shares and their earnings per share than in an ungeared company. Conversely, in a falling or bear market, their losses are greater. This is illustrated in Table 9A.

Table 9A *Example of the benefit of gearing to shareholders in a bull market. Faster rate of growth in net asset value per share.*

Before the bull market

	£m		£m
Issued 10 per cent loan stock	1	Value of investments	6
Issued ordinary share capital (4 million 25p shares)	1		
Reserves attributable to shareholders	4		
	6		

9. Investment in investment trusts

$$\text{Net asset value per share} = \frac{\text{Value of investments} - \text{Liabilities}}{\text{Number of issued shares}}$$

$$\frac{£6m - £1m}{4m} = £1.25 \text{ per share}$$

After the bull market

	£m		£m
Issued 10 per cent loan stock	1	Value of investments	9
Issued ordinary share capital	1		
Reserves attributable to shareholders	7		
	9		

$$\text{Net asset value per share} = \frac{£9m - £1m}{4m} = £2.00 \text{ per share}$$

Increase in the value of investments = 50 per cent
Increase in the net asset value per share = 60 per cent

Similarly, shareholders in a geared company experience faster gains in earnings per share than an ungeared company in a bull market, but greater falls in a bear market. Table 9B, which is a continuation of Table 9A, shows this.

Table 9B *Example of the benefit of gearing to shareholders in a bull market. Faster rate of growth in earnings per share.*

Before the bull market

	£
Income from investments	300,000
Less interest on 10 per cent loan stock (issued loan stock = £1 million)	100,000
Earnings available to shareholders	200,000

Earnings per share (4m shares) = 5.0 pence

After the bull market

	£
Income from investments	450,000
Less interest on 10 per cent loan stock	100,000
Earnings available to shareholders	350,000

Earnings per share = 8.75 pence
Increase in income from investments = 50 per cent
Increase in earnings per share = 75 per cent

188 Professionally managed funds

If the direction of change is reversed in these two examples, it can be seen how in a bear market the investor in a geared trust loses more than an investor in an ungeared trust. When the fund managers expect a bear market, there are several actions they can take to protect their shareholders.

(*i*) Reduce their liabilities by repaying bank loans and buying in their outstanding loan stock and debentures.

(*ii*) Increase their liquidity of the trust's investments by selling equities and increasing its holdings of cash and fixed-interest stocks.

The advantages and disadvantages of investment trusts

8. Advantages of investment trusts.

(*a*) The share price is usually lower than its net asset value giving investors a higher yield if they are seeking income. There is also the potential of a capital gain if the discount should narrow as a result of an improvement in market sentiment concerning the markets where the management have invested or an increased prospect of a takeover bid for the trust.

(*b*) Split capital trusts are available for investors who seek either high income or economic growth rather than a combination of the two.

(*c*) Investment trusts have concentrated on diversified international portfolios. While there are specialist trusts investing in a particular geographical area like Japan or an industrial sector like energy, there is not the same range of choice that is offered by unit trusts. The trend has been to make more specialist investment trusts available so investors should be able to meet most of their needs whether they seek a well diversified portfolio or specialization.

(*d*) Investment trusts can invest directly in property as well as in property shares.

(*e*) The investment *forte* of investment trusts is small emerging companies, particularly unquoted companies and those specializing in new technology. Unit trusts are allowed to invest only in securities quoted on a recognized stock exchange although they may hold up to 25 per cent of their funds in companies traded on the London USM, the Tokyo OTC, the United States OTC and the French

9. Investment in investment trusts

Second Market.

(*f*) Because there are no initial management charges when investing in investment trust shares, a larger proportion of investors' savings is invested in the assets of the trust than with unit trusts. Annual management charges are also lower for investment trusts.

(*g*) Investment trusts can gear up by borrowing and issuing fixed-interest securities and preference shares. Unit trusts are not permitted to do so.

(*h*) The managers of investment trusts do not have to keep a margin of liquidity or sell their investments before they think appropriate to meet redemptions.

(*i*) Investment trusts offer a range of securities to investors. At one end of the spectrum are the low-risk loan stocks and preference shares, then convertible loan stocks, ordinary shares and, providing the highest level of risk, warrants.

(*j*) The fund managers of investment trusts have more flexibility than unit trust managers in currency hedging. Unit trusts are restricted to back-to-back loans while investment trusts are also permitted to buy and sell currency forward and use currency futures and options.

9. Disadvantages of investment trusts.

(*a*) The ability of investment trusts to gear up by borrowing, invest in unquoted securities, buy and sell currency forward, and trade in currency futures and options increases investors' exposure to risk. When the fund managers make the right decisions, the gains will be greater than in unit trusts, but when the wrong decisions are made, the losses will also be greater.

(*b*) Similarly, the existence of a premium or discount to net asset value also exposes investors to a higher level of risk. With a unit trust, the main influence affecting the price of its units is net asset value, but in the case of the shares of an investment trust, the discount or premium can vary independently of this.

Sources of information on investment trusts

10. Books. Probably the best starting place is the book *How to*

190 Professionally managed funds

Make IT. Your 1987/88 Guide to Investment Trusts obtainable from the Association of Investment Trust Companies. This not only gives basic details of individual trusts with their investment objectives, portfolio distribution and principal investments, but also a ten-year record of each trust's earnings, dividends, net asset value and share price.

More detail is provided in the *Investment Trust Year Book and Who's Who* published annually and obtainable from the AITC.

The AITC produce a short explanatory booklet called *More for your Money* which is available free of charge.

11. Journals and newspapers. The AITC publish 'The Investment Trust Table' on the fourth Saturday of each month in the *Financial Times* and the *Daily Telegraph* giving details of the share price, net asset value, yield, geographical spread, gearing and five-year return on net asset value for each trust.

Day-to-day information on prices and yields together with news and commentary can be obtained from newspapers such as the *Financial Times*, the *Daily Telegraph*, *The Times* and the *Guardian*. The *Financial Times* provides share price data daily for some 250 investment trust shares, convertibles and warrants. The Sunday press reports on any issues of particular interest to investors.

The *Investors Chronicle* has a weekly column that discusses news relating to specific trusts and an annual feature in December. Other magazines such as *Money Observer* and *What Investment* also contain a regular commentary.

12. Other sources. Stockbrokers are also an important source of information. The AITC compiles a 'Private Investor's Stockbroker List' which is obtainable free from them and gives the names of the brokers throughout the country which have told the Association that they will deal on behalf of individual investors, and who should be contacted in each firm. It also gives details of the minimum size of the transactions they will handle, their commission and whether they provide an advisory service.

Investors can obtain a copy of the annual report and accounts of any of the trusts in which they are interested from the trust's managers.

Investors' considerations when selecting investment trusts

13. Main considerations. As in the previous chapter on unit trusts, the main factors to take into consideration are:

(*a*) Do investors primarily want income, growth or a combination of the two?

(*b*) How much risk are they prepared to take?

(*c*) In which geographical area or market sector do they wish to invest?

(*d*) The reputation of the trust's management and its past performance.

(*e*) Do investors want a savings scheme?

Without repeating all the points made in the previous chapter, considerations of particular relevance to investment trusts will now be discussed.

14. Capital growth or income? The AITC classifies the different trusts by investment objective in their *Year Book*, their book *How to Make IT*, and in their monthly *Investment Trust Table*. These are further subdivided between trusts investing just in the UK, or in a particular geographical area, or world-wide. These tables of information will help investors narrow down the choices available.

15. Risk. The most risky investment trusts are those concentrating their investments in a single investment area, e.g. oil and energy-related companies. If investors want to minimize risk, they should select a trust that has its investments spread between the UK, North America, Europe and Japan, and that does not concentrate in any particular sector.

Another factor increasing risk is the level of gearing. The AITC measures gearing in its monthly *Investment Trust Table* by showing the effect upon net asset value per share if the value of its equity assets increases by 100 per cent. There are two factors which will affect the change in the trust's net asset value per share.

(*a*) The proportion of the total capital of the company provided by shareholders. The higher the level of debt capital and hence

192 Professionally managed funds

gearing, the greater will be the impact on net asset value per share. Thus a 100 per cent increase in the value of an all-equity investment portfolio would cause a greater than 100 per cent increase in net asset value per share in a geared trust.

(b) The proportion of the investment portfolio that is equity capital. The effects of gearing can be offset by holding some of the trust's assets in cash or fixed-interest securities. Thus for an all-equity financed trust, the effect of a 100 per cent rise in the value of its equity investments will produce a less than 100 per cent rise in its net asset value per share if the portfolio is not fully invested in equities.

The gearing factor in the AITC table shows the net effect of these two factors.

Convertible loan stocks issued by investment trusts provide a less risky investment than the ordinary shares, while investors seeking a higher level of risk should consider investment trust warrants.

16. Which geographical area or industrial sector? The areas of specialism of investment trusts differ slightly from those of unit trusts.

(a) There is a larger proportion of investment trusts investing world-wide. This is part of their historical tradition for investment trusts were formed to provide a spread of investments for the small investor in foreign and colonial stocks. There are investment trusts which concentrate their investments in a particular geographical area, but fewer of them now. (The number of trusts with more than 85 per cent of their funds invested in the area specified: North America 4 Japan 6, Far East 4, Australia 2, Europe 2.) There are also more specialized trusts investing in a particular sector such as oil and energy companies, property, plantations, and precious metals.

(b) Investment trusts provide better opportunities than unit trusts to invest in small companies. They can invest in unlisted companies and venture capital projects so providing the opportunity to obtain a stake at an early stage in some of the growth companies of the future.

17. The reputation of the trust's management and its past perfor-

9. Investment in investment trusts

mance. The performance tables provided in the AITC's publications and the *Investors Chronicle* may be some guide to future performance, but can be no guarantee. The investor must evaluate the prospects of several investment trusts and for this their annual reports and accounts are an indispensable source of information. From these, the investor can compare the managements' objectives and the philosophies underlying their selections of shares and the distributions of their investments.

18. Do investors want a saving scheme? The first saving scheme was made available by the Foreign and Colonial Investment Trust in October 1984. Regular monthly purchases of stock worth a minimum of £25 and occasional purchases of a minimum of £25 for existing shareholders and £250 for new shareholders can be undertaken via the Royal Bank of Scotland, the registrars of the Investment Trust. These purchases are not made directly from the management but, like all shares, on the Stock Exchange. The bank aggregates all the small orders from investors into a single purchase at least once a month to keep purchasing costs down.

Other schemes have since been made available by the Globe Investment Trust, Robert Fleming Investment Management which manage ten trusts, and Touche Remnant which manage nine.

19. Investment in investment trusts via pension schemes, life assurance and unit trusts.

(*a*) Pensions – since 1984 it has been possible for an investor's personal pension plan with an insurance company to be invested in either one or a portfolio of investment trusts. This enables investors to benefit both from tax-subsidized contributions to their pension scheme, and the reinvestment of their dividends gross in further investment trust shares since pension funds are exempt from tax on dividends received (*see* 10:**27**).

(*b*) *Life assurance* – there are also regular premium life assurance policies and single premium bonds (*see* 10:**15, 18**) where investors' savings are invested in a portfolio of investment trust shares. There are six insurance companies providing this facility.

(*c*) *Unit trusts* – there are eight unit trusts investing in investment trusts including the second largest, the Save and Prosper Investment Trust Fund with a staggering £300 million under management, making it one of the largest single shareholders of investment trust shares.

Other investment trust securities

20. Debenture and loan stocks. Debenture and loan stocks are a safe fixed-interest investment since they are backed by the assets of the trust. Some debentures are redeemable, others perpetual.

21. Preference and cumulative preference shares. Preference and cumulative preference shares are nearly as safe as loan stocks, and carry a higher yield. If a dividend were to be passed in any year, it would be carried forward in the case of cumulative preference shares and paid before the payment of ordinary dividends was resumed.

22. Convertible loan stocks. Convertible loan stocks receive a fixed-interest payment up to the date of redemption unless they are first converted into ordinary shares. The number of shares per £100 nominal of loan stocks and the dates on which the conversion can take place are details that are fixed at the time of the issue of the stocks.

> EXAMPLE: The Fleming American Trust 7 per cent convertible unsecured loan stock 1999. This stock is convertible into 21.19 ordinary shares for every £100 nominal of stock on each 31 May from 1985 to 1999, and if not converted will be redeemed at par for £100 on 31 December 1999.

The attractions of this type of investment are:

(*a*) If the ordinary share price does not rise, the convertible will be traded on the Stock Exchange as a loan stock. It has a coupon interest rate of 7 per cent and will be redeemed in 1999, making it a safe investment. (The current price is £137 giving an interest yield of £7 ÷ £137 = 5.1 per cent. The high premium over its redemption value as a straight loan stock at £100 shows that the market expects the share price to rise considerably before 1999 and for conversion

9. Investment in investment trusts

to take place. Investors should look in the *Financial Times* for its latest price and recalculate its interest yield.)

(*b*) If the ordinary share price rises, it will become possible to convert into the ordinary shares at a profit. This will raise the market price of the convertible. Conversion can be expected to take place when both:

(*i*) the value of the shares into which the stock can be converted equals the market price of the stock;

(*ii*) the income from the shares exceeds the income from the stock.

(The current price of the ordinary share is 535 pence, so 21.19 shares are worth £113.36. Thus if investors were to convert at the present share price and the £137 price of the convertible loan stock, they would experience a fall in the value of their investments. The income per share is currently 7.394 pence gross so for 21.19 shares only £1.56 compared with £7 for the convertible. Again conversion is not yet worthwhile. Investors should look in the *Financial Times* for the latest prices and dividends and recalculate the latest position.)

This type of investment is attractive to investors seeking a higher yield than that available from direct investment in equities but also wishing to enjoy some of the capital growth that can be expected from equities. If the share price performs well, the investor participates in the capital gain, but if not, the investor receives a worthwhile yield from a safe investment and ultimately redemption at par.

23. Warrants. There are also some 30 issues of warrants by investment trust companies. Warrants give the holder the right to buy shares at a specified price on specified dates. They are sometimes given with shares when new trusts are launched as a 'sweetener'. This is because the new shares will in the short term almost certainly fall to a discount to net asset value. The attachment of warrants to the shares purchased, which may be sold separately from the shares, adds value to an investment in the new trust. Warrants may also be issued by existing trusts as a way of raising new share capital cheaply in the future if the trust is performing well and the share price has risen by the expiry date.

EXAMPLE: Drayton Far Eastern Trust. Each warrant entitles the holder to buy 1 ordinary share for 101 pence on 30 April each year

196 Professionally managed funds

from 1982 to 1991. Thereafter the warrant expires worthless.

The attraction of this type of investment is that it provides the investor with the same benefits as gearing. If the ordinary share price rises, the price of the warrant will rise even faster in percentage terms. Conversely, if the share price falls, the percentage fall in the warrant will be greater. (A warrant is like a traded call option with a long time until expiry – *see* Chapter 7.) This volatility in price of the warrant makes it a riskier investment than the ordinary share, but not as risky as a traded option.

The current price of the warrant is 92 pence and of the share 190 pence. Note that if these prices remain unchanged by the next 30 April, it would not pay investors to exercise the warrant as the purchase price of a share via the warrant would be 193 pence (92 pence for the warrant plus 101 pence for the share). The following hypothetical changes in price illustrate the gearing effect of warrants.

	Now	*Next 30 April*	*% change*
Ordinary share	190	380	+100%
Warrant	92	279	+203%

The share price has doubled to 380p. The intrinsic value of the warrant is now 380p − 101p = 279p, and so its increase in price would be at least 279p − 92p = 187p, roughly the same as for the ordinary share. However, the gain in price of the warrant has been achieved for half the outlay, giving the investor double the gain in percentage terms.

The investor with £1,900 can therefore choose between 1,000 ordinary shares or more than 2,000 warrants. If the share price rises, the investor in the warrants will make double the gain of the investor in the ordinary shares. Conversely, if the share price falls, the investor in the warrants will make double the loss. An alternative would be to buy 1,000 warrants and invest the remainder in a building society or bank. Such an investor would make the same capital gain or loss as the investor in the shares, but receive a higher yield (n.b. warrants pay no dividends).

Warrants are attractive investments for investors who are prepared to take higher risks to obtain greater prospective capital growth. Investors must remember to exercise their right to purchase the shares before the expiry date of the option if it has intrinsic value.

Progress test 9

1. Why are investors less aware of investment trusts than unit trusts? What advantages do they have over unit trusts? (**5, 7, 8**)

2. When an investment trust share is at a discount to net asset value, is this good or bad for investors? (**7, 9**)

3. What is the significance of the ability of investment trusts to undertake gearing? Is this good or bad for investors? (**7–9**)

4. What are the attractions to investors of the convertible loan stocks of investment trusts. (**22**)

5. How can investors benefit from personal gearing by investing in warrants? (**23**)

10
Life assurance linked investments

The link between life assurance and investment

1. The historical background. Savings and life assurance have frequently been part of an investment package in the past because of the tax concessions that were available. Until the 1984 budget, the whole of the premiums on certain life assurance policies, called *qualifying policies*, were eligible for income tax relief. The tax relief was 15 per cent of the gross premiums meaning that investors paying, say, £85 per month on qualifying policies had their premiums increased by £15 from the Inland Revenue so that the insurance companies in effect received £100. This tax subsidy resulted in insurance companies marketing life assurance schemes linked with saving since they could then show savers that more was invested than the amount of the premium paid and life assurance was included as well. The removal of life assurance premium relief (LAPR) in the 1984 budget has greatly weakened the case for linking saving and life assurance. However, the proceeds of qualifying policies upon redemption are still free of all income and capital gains tax.

2. Obtaining the status of 'qualifying' policy. The main criteria that have to be fulfilled to obtain this status as a qualifying policy are:

(*a*) The term of the policy must be at least ten years.
(*b*) The policy must not be surrendered nor made paid up (i.e.

10. Life assurance linked investments

the premiums must not be halted) during the first three-quarters of the term or ten years, whichever is the shorter.

(*c*) Premiums must be paid at least annually. This provision excludes single-premium life assurance policies.

(*d*) The sum assured must be at least 75 per cent of the total premiums payable.

This chapter reviews the different types of life assurance policy available and, where they are linked with saving and investment, evaluates their advantages and disadvantages for different types of investors.

What are the main types of life assurance?

3. Classification. Life assurance policies can be classified into the following types.

(*a*) term assurance;
(*b*) endowment assurance
   (*i*) without profits
   (*ii*) with profits;
(*c*) whole-life assurance;
(*d*) low-cost assurance;
(*e*) unit-linked life assurance
   (*i*) regular premium
   (*ii*) single premium

4. Term assurance. Term assurance is pure life assurance and has nothing to do with investment. The person's life is assured for an amount of money and a period of time determined at the commencement of the policy. If the person dies during the period of the policy, the predetermined amount is paid by the life assurance company to the trustees of the deceased's estate. Hopefully the person will outlive the period of the policy in which case there will be no refund or payment by the company to the person. The sum assured may be fixed throughout the period of the policy (called level-term assurance) or may decrease at a predetermined rate (reducing-term assurance). This second type is used in mortgage protection and family income policies. The premiums on term-assurance policies are lower per £1,000 assured than the other types of policy to be considered as there is no element of saving and investment.

5. Endowment assurance. This is also a fixed period of life assurance, but the premiums are larger than for term assurance as the policy combines life assurance with saving. An endowment policy with a term of at least ten years is a qualifying policy and benefits from tax relief on its premiums if commenced before the March 1984 budget. There are two types of endowment policy: 'without profits' and 'with profits'. The *without profits* policy provides the investor with life assurance cover of a fixed sum which would be paid out upon death or the expiry of the policy, whichever event is the earlier. These policies are not used much these days as a form of saving as they afford no protection against inflation and the fall in the value of the real sum assured. The *with profits* policy involves the payment of a higher premium per £1,000 assured than for a 'without profits' policy, but the investor will be entitled to a share of the life company's investment profits. The sum assured rises during the life of the policy by the annual share of the profits, called *reversionary bonuses*, which are added to the policy. Once a reversionary bonus has been added to the policy, it will not be removed. They are therefore a conservative distribution of profits to guard against a dramatic fall in the investment markets in the final year of the policy. When the policy matures, a *terminal bonus* is also added which because of the string of years of bull equity markets has been contributing 25–50 per cent of the pay out. The life assurance companies' investment funds are spread between equities, fixed-interest securities and property and are cautiously managed to provide security and a reasonable degree of protection against inflation. The investment performance of the different life assurance companies is frequently reviewed in the monthly magazines *Money Management* and *Planned Savings*.

6. Whole-life assurance. This type of policy also combines savings and life assurance, but the pay out does not occur until death. It can be cashed before this event but, in its earlier years, the surrender value is likely to be disappointing as it would suffer a penalty for early encashment. This type of policy can be used as a means of making provision for the investor's heirs.

10. Life assurance linked investments

7. Low-cost endowment assurance. This type of policy has become popular with house purchasers as part of their mortgage repayment and insurance protection scheme. It is a combination of a reducing-term assurance policy with an endowment policy which requires lower monthly premium payments than an endowment policy on its own. This is possible because the premiums on an all-endowment mortage have to be sufficiently large to provide life assurance cover for the whole mortgage since in the initial stages there will be no reversionary bonuses to add to the value of the policy. With a low-cost endowment policy, the initial sum assured under the endowment component is less than the amount of the mortgage outstanding. The insurance cover is topped up by a reducing-term assurance policy. The scheme works on the principle that the reversionary bonuses added to the endowment policy each year are more than sufficient to offset the reduction in the sum assured under the term-assurance component. In the event of death, the sum assured is always sufficient to repay the whole of the outstanding mortgage and, when the policy matures, there should be a surplus cash sum available to the investor after the mortgage has been redeemed.

8. Unit-linked life assurance. While unit-linked assurance schemes also combine life assurance and investment, their major attraction is that they provide investors with a choice between the *unitized funds* offered by the life assurance company. The unitized funds of a life assurance company are their portfolios of investments which may be specialized (e.g. Far East fund, North America fund or property fund) or diversified (e.g. international fund or managed fund). These funds are then divided into shares or units like a unit trust. With an endowment policy, investors have no control over which markets are selected for the investment of their premiums. If investors choose the managed fund from the unitized funds available, the investment performance will be similar to an endowment policy as the fund will be invested in a spread of equities, fixed-interest securities and property. If they choose one of the other funds, their risk will be greater as they are more specialized. Investors can also choose to switch their investment between the funds offered either at nil or fairly low cost.

Unit-linked life assurance funds are either managed by life assurance companies which have created unitized funds to compete with unit trusts, or by fund management companies which also run unit trusts and have created unitized life assurance funds to compete with the life companies.

The investor should examine the names of the managers and the types of fund they offer by looking under the heading 'Insurances' in the *Financial Times* on the page headed 'Authorized Unit Trusts and Insurances'. Similar information is also available in the *Daily Telegraph* and the Saturday edition of *The Times*. Comparative performance statistics are given monthly in *Money Management* and *Planned Savings*.

The basic principle of unit-linked life assurance is that a deduction is made from the investors's premiums for insurance and administration, and the remainder is invested in the purchase of units of one of the life company's funds. There are three types of unit-linked assurance policies:

(*a*) *Qualifying policies* with a life of ten or more years.

(*b*) *Shorter policies*, e.g. five years. The level of life assurance cover may be very low, e.g. 101 per cent of the value of the units at the time of death.

(*c*) *Single-premium policies*. Again, life assurance cover is minimal, typically 101 per cent of the value of the units at the time of death. These are usually called *insurance bonds*.

The taxation of life assurance linked investments

9. The taxation of the funds managed by the life company. Franked income from investments received by the investment fund is tax-free, i.e. dividends from a UK company paid from profits which have already borne corporation tax. Unfranked income (i.e. dividends from overseas companies and interest payments) is subject to corporation tax. These rules are the same as for unit trusts and investment trusts.

Capital gains made on investments within the insurance fund are subject to capital gains tax. The payment of this tax when a gain is realized reduces the size of the investment fund and is an important difference between life assurance investments and both unit trusts

10. Life assurance linked investments

and investment trusts where such gains are not liable to capital gains tax. The fund managers have to make provision from their unrealized profits for future payments of this tax.

10. The taxation of investors in life assurance linked investments. No dividends are paid out on life assurance linked investments. This allows all the income received by the fund to be reinvested without further payment of tax. This is another difference between this type of investment and either unit trusts or investment trusts. All income received by unit trusts, after expenses, is subject to the investor's marginal rate of income tax whether distributed or not. In the case of investment trusts, at least 85 per cent of income must be distributed as dividends and hence will be subject to income tax. This rule makes life assurance linked investments attractive to investors who are higher-rate taxpayers and those who seek capital growth rather than income.

The proceeds from encashment of a life assurance linked investment are free of capital gains tax as the investment fund has already been liable for this tax. This contrasts again with unit trusts and investment trust shares where the investors are liable for capital gains tax on the increase in value of their units or shares. However, the capital gains tax liability of investors in either unit or investment trusts is reduced by the effects of applying the indexation rules and by the size of the annual exemption limit.

These rules make investment in life assurance linked investments less attractive than investment in either unit trusts or investment trusts unless investors are already fully utilizing their annual capital gains tax exemption allowance.

The liability of investors for income tax upon the proceeds they receive upon the redemption of their life assurance policy varies with the type of policy, as shown below.

(*a*) The redemption proceeds from qualifying policies are exempt from all income tax. This makes them particularly attractive to investors paying high marginal rates of income tax. The proceeds can also be left with the life assurance company to yield a tax-free income.

(*b*) The redemption proceeds from regular-premium policies which do not satisfy the conditions of a qualifying policy are exempt

Professionally managed funds

from all income tax for investors whose marginal rate is the standard rate. Higher-rate taxpayers will be liable for some higher-rate tax, calculated using the *top slicing rule*, which is explained below.

(c) In the case of a single-premium bond, 5 per cent of the initial investment may be withdrawn without the payment of any tax in any tax year. If the annual allowance is not used, it may be carried forward on a cumulative basis and withdrawn in later years subject to the overall limit of 100 per cent of the initial investment. If more than the permitted amount is withdrawn it is subject to higher rates of income tax, although the excess is free of the basic rate of income tax. When the bond is cashed in, the proceeds are free of the standard rate of income tax, but higher rates are calculated using the top slicing rule. This rule involves the following four stages of calculation on termination of the policy:

(*i*) Calculate the total gain from the policy, i.e. proceeds from encashment plus early withdrawals minus initial premium.

(*ii*) Divide the total gain by the number of years since the policy was taken out to obtain the average annual gain.

(iii) Calculate the tax liability on the average annual gain by multiplying by the investor's marginal rate of income tax less the basic rate.

(*iv*) Calculate the total tax liability by multiplying the tax liability on the average annual gain by the number of years the bond was held.

EXAMPLE:

		£
Year 0	invest	10,000
Year 5	withdraw 5 × 5% of initial investment	2,500
Year 8	withdraw 5% of initial investment	500
Year 9	withdraw 5% of initial investment	500
Year 15	surrender bond	27,500

(1) Total gain = £27,500 + £2,500 + (2 × £500) − £10,000
       = £21,000

(2) Average annual gain = £21,000 ÷ 15 ÷ £1,400 p.a.

10. Life assurance linked investments

(3) Tax liability of an investor with a marginal rate of tax of 50 per cent on the average annual gain = £1,400 × (50% − 29%) = £294

(4) Total tax liability = £294 × 15 years = £4,410

By delaying encashment of the bond until a year when their marginal rate of income tax has fallen to the standard rate, e.g. by retirement, investors can avoid paying higher-rate tax.

A word of warning investors should note concerning the partial surrender of single premium bonds: if the amount received from the *partial* surrender of the bond exceeds the cumulative 5 per cent per annum allowance, the extra withdrawn is counted by the Inland Revenue as taxable income. There is no problem when the total of this extra amount and the rest of the investor's income is low enough for the investor to remain within the standard rate of tax band. No income tax will be payable on the higher amount withdrawn. However, if the extra amount is sufficient to push the investor's taxable income plus the extra amount withdrawn into a higher tax bracket, higher rate tax will be payable.

EXAMPLE:

Band of taxable income £	Marginal rate of income tax %
0–17,200	29
17,201–20,200	40
20,201–25,400	45

Investor's taxable income from employment is £17,000
Initial investment in a single-premium insurance bond 4 years ago was £50,000.
Investor withdraws £20,000 (a partial surrender)
Tax-free allowance = 4 × 5% = 20% of £50,000 = £10,000
Partial surrender value taxable as income = £20,000 − £10,000 = £10,000
Value of slice for top slicing calculation = £10,000 ÷ 4 = £2,500

Tax rate on slice	Amount of slice	Tax payable
29%	£200	£58
40%	£2300	£920
	£2500	£978

Average rate of tax on slice $= \dfrac{£978}{£2500} \times 100\% = 39.12\%$

Rate applied to gain = average rate of tax on slice − standard rate
= 39.12% − 29% = 10.12%
Tax payable = £10,000 × 10.12% = £1012.

When the bond is finally cashed, the investor who is a higher rate taxpayer can obtain a credit for the amount of tax paid. However, as this credit can only be used to reduce higher rate tax liabilities, the standard rate taxpayer has permanently lost the tax paid. The moral of this is that investors should not buy large single premium bonds, but a 'cluster' of bonds which add up to the same amount. Capital can then be withdrawn by the total surrender of some of the bonds (which will not be liable to the partial surrender rules), while leaving the other bonds intact (although the 5 per cent per annum withdrawal allowance can be utilized).

The merits of life assurance investments for different investors

11. Term assurance. While this has already been described as having no investment content, it is important to investors for two reasons.

(*a*) It is the cheapest form of life assurance.
(*b*) Investors will have to consider whether a combination of term assurance and other investments such as unit trusts or investment trusts would be a better investment than the other life assurance linked investments available.

12. Investment in a with-profits endowment policy. This is a suitable investment if investors want to play it safe. The investment fund of life assurance companies is well diversified between

10. Life assurance linked investments

equities, mostly UK companies, property, and a large slice of fixed-interest securities, mostly gilts. The sum assured is guaranteed and, once reversionary bonuses have been added to the sum assured, they too are safe. However, some 25–50 per cent of the payout on maturity has been made up of the terminal bonus which reflects recent good investment performance. If the policy matures in the middle of a stock market slump, the terminal bonus could be cut back quite sharply.

The management charges of an endowment policy are hard to identify and may be higher than for alternative types of investment. Where commissions are paid, they come out of the first year's premiums which are therefore unavailable for investment for the whole period of the policy. There are, however, some life assurance companies such as Equitable Life and London Life which do not pay commissions.

13. Advantages of a with-profits endowment policy.

(*a*) For standard rate tax investors:

(*i*) A low-risk investment with a guranteed minimum sum at the end of the policy term.

(*ii*) All proceeds are free of income tax and capital gains tax.

(*b*) For higher-rate tax investors:

(*i*) As in (*i*) for the standard-rate taxpayer.

(*ii*) All proceeds on redemption are free of capital gains tax. They are also free of income tax if it is a qualifying policy, otherwise they are liable to higher-rate income tax.

14. Disadvantages of a with-profits endowment policy.

(*a*) For standard-rate tax investors:

(*i*) There is no scope for investors to control the area of investment.

(*ii*) The charges are quite high and difficult to identify.

(*iii*) Investors must maintain the regular payment of their premiums. Early encashment of their policy or converting it to a 'paid-up' policy can involve a severe financial penalty and loss of capital invested. These disadvantages do not apply to a unit trust or investment trust savings scheme.

(*iv*) Investors are unable to utilize their annual capital gains tax exemption allowance. They could be used by saving with a unit trust or investment trust savings scheme and taking out term assurance to provide the life assurance required.

(b) For higher-rate tax investors:

(i)–(iii) As above for the standard-rate taxpayer.

(iv) The inability of investors to apply their annual capital gains tax exemption allowance to their life assurance policy will probably be irrelevant as these investors will have other investments which can be sold to utilize their allowance.

15. Investment in a unit-linked life assurance policy (regular premiums). This section considers the unit-linked life assurance savings plan which competes with the with-profits endowment policy and the unit trust savings scheme plus term assurance. Sections **18–20** will consider the single-premium unit-linked life assurance bond. The advantages of this type of policy compared to the with-profits endowment policy are:

(a) Investors can choose the fund of the life company in which they wish to invest. The financial pages of the *Financial Times* or the *Daily Telegraph* should be inspected to see the range of funds offered by different life assurance companies. Some offer a very restricted choice which make them less attractive if policyholders are active investors. The widest selection of all is provided by Skandia Life Assurance with ten funds run by their own fund managers, and nearly 150 funds managed by nine other fund management companies. This gives a range of choice as wide as unit trusts and only a foreign currency and a foreign bond fund are missing. Other life assurance companies have started to add these types of funds to their portfolios on offer. Unlike unit trusts, life assurance funds are allowed to offer units in a property fund investing directly in property, and a deposit fund if investors want to go liquid. Like unit trusts, however, they are not permitted to invest directly in commodities or gold. If investors want to leave it to the life assurance company's fund managers to select a wide spread of investments, they should choose a managed fund which will be invested in equities, fixed-interest securities and property.

(b) Investors can switch their savings and future premiums between the life company's funds either free of charge or for a low

10. Life assurance linked investments

fee. If investors change their opinion of the prospects for the life company's fund they have selected, they can redirect future premiums into an alternative fund and either leave past premiums in their existing fund or switch them too. The charges for switching vary slightly between the life assurance companies. In some cases, such as with Skandia Life, switching is free. More usual is one free switch per year and then a charge of 0.25 or 0.5 per cent of the funds switched. As the amount invested increases, a flat rate charge works out cheaper, e.g. the M & G Group charge £5 per policy with a minimum of £10. The switching fees are considerably lower than the 2.5–5 per cent charged by unit trusts, a distinct advantage if investors are active. Investors should also investigate how quickly they can make a switch as not all life assurance funds have daily dealings.

(c) The management charges are more clearly defined. There are three basic methods by which fund managers of unit-linked life assurance investments levy charges additional to an annual fee. Some use only one of the three methods, while others a combination of two of them.

(i) They allocate units to the policy-holder at one price, the *offer price*, and redeem them a lower *bid price*, the same as with unit trusts. The bid and offer prices are publicized daily in the *Financial Times* and *Daily Telegraph*, and the bid offer spread is typically 5–5.5 per cent, slightly less than for unit trusts. In addition, there is an annual management charge, typically equivalent to 0.75 per cent of the value of the fund, and again similar to the charging system of unit trusts. There will also be an annual policy charge which may be a further percentage deduction from the amount invested in units or a flat-rate annual charge.

(ii) The management operate a system of two types of units, *capital* and *accumulation units*. The first year or two of premiums are invested in capital units where high management charges are levied, for example 5 per cent per annum. Thereafter, the premiums are invested in accumulation units which have a lower management charge, for example 2 per cent per annum.

(iii) The third system involves varying the percentage of the premiums the managers receive that is invested in units. This may be done in addition to either of the first two methods of levying charges in order to give a discount to large investors or to charge higher premiums for older investors for whom the life assurance costs will be higher. It is because management charges are already being collected by one of the first two methods that it is possible for promotional literature to claim that more than 100 per cent of contributions are being invested in units in some cases.

However, other life assurance companies, such as London Life, use this method alone for deducting charges. In their case, only one price for their units is quoted in the financial press which is both the bid and the offer price. Their management charges are recouped by investing 97 per cent of the premiums received in units.

The total management charges that will be deducted can usually be calculated by careful reading of the life assurance company's brochure explaining their investment plans. In the event of uncertainty or ambiguity, investors should telephone the company for clarification. However, they should also remember that management charges are only one of the factors to be taken into consideration, and that differences in fund management performance can easily outweigh any differences in fund management charges between companies.

16. Advantages of a unit-linked regular-premium life assurance policy.

(*a*) For standard rate of tax investors:

(*i*) All proceeds on redemption are free of income tax and capital gains tax.

(*ii*) A wide choice of funds including property and sterling currency deposit funds.

(*iii*) Cheap switching between funds.

(*iv*) For those who want to hand over responsibility for switching between funds to professional investment managers, firms of insurance brokers and members of FIMBRA offer this type of service (discussed later in **23**).

(*v*) Can be combined with other types of insurance, for example family protection and health insurance.

(*b*) For higher-rate tax investors:

(*i*) All proceeds on redemption are free of capital gains tax, but are only free of higher-rate income tax if it is a qualifying policy.

(*ii*)–(*v*) As for the standard-rate taxpayer.

10. Life assurance linked investments

(*vi*) The proceeds of a qualifying policy can be left to grow tax-free or provide a tax-free income.

(*vii*) Their income tax liability is reduced as the life assurance policy pays no dividends and all the income received by the fund is reinvested. (Only unfranked income is subject to corporation tax.)

(*viii*) If the policy is not a qualifying policy, the proceeds can still be taken free of income tax if redemption is delayed until after the investor's marginal rate of income tax has fallen to the standard rate.

17. Disadvantages of a unit-linked regular-premium life assurance policy.

(*a*) For standard rate of tax investors:

(*i*) The charges are frequently higher than for unit trust investment. Investors should consider taking out term assurance and saving regularly with a unit trust scheme.

(*ii*) This method of saving is less flexible than saving with unit trusts. The regular payment of premiums must be maintained. Early encashment of the policy or converting it to a paid-up policy can involve a severe penalty and loss of capital invested.

(*iii*) The investment fund must make provision for capital gains tax. If investors are not going to use their annual exemption allowance, then this tax could be avoided by investing via unit trusts.

(*b*) For higher rate of tax investors:

(*i*) The disadvantages of (*i*) and (*ii*) above are less serious for the higher-rate taxpayers. The higher cost may be offset by the advantages of the fund's reinvestment of income received, especially in the case of a qualifying policy. The commitment to maintain premiums is not likely to be so important as this type of policy is likely to form only part of investors' total investments.

(*ii*) The disadvantage concerning the liability of the investment fund for capital gains tax is unlikely to be serious as investors paying higher-rate tax will probably be able to utilize their annual exemption by selling other of their assets.

18. Investment in a single-premium unit-linked life assurance bond. This type of policy is designed as an alternative to unit and investment trusts for the investor with a lump sum available for investment. The minimum amount varies between companies: Skandia Life's minimum is £3,000, that of London and Manchester Assurance £1,000. The full range of investment funds and the switching facilities available to the regular-premium policy-holders are also available to single-premium policy-holders. The management charges and the method of applying them varies between companies. Investors should read the prospectus of each company they are considering very carefully. For example, Skandia Life use a bid offer spread of 5–5.5 per cent and an annual management charge of 0.75 per cent. London and Manchester Assurance charge an annual management fee of 1.5 per cent for the first six years and 0.25 per cent thereafter.

The single-premium life assurance bond is not a qualifying policy (*see* **1** above), and so when surrendered, it is free of capital gains tax and income tax at the standard rate but not higher rates. Higher rates of income tax can be avoided if the bond is not surrendered until investors' marginal rate of income tax has reduced to the standard rate. If not, the top slicing rule explained in **10** above is applied. In the meantime, investors can withdraw up to 5 per cent of their initial investment tax-free each year.

19. Advantages of single-premium bonds.

(*a*) For standard rate of tax investors:

(*i*) All proceeds are free of capital gains tax and standard rate of income tax. With unit and investment trusts, dividends are paid net of the standard rate of income tax, and capital gains are liable to capital gains tax unless they are less than the annual exemption limit.

(*ii*) The charge of 0.25–0.5 per cent for switching between the different sector funds is cheaper than the 2.5–5 per cent charge for a unit trust. This is important if investors are active. (Note that some offshore umbrella funds have lower switching charges.)

(*b*) For higher rate of tax investors:

(*i*) Tax-free withdrawals of up to 5 per cent of the initial investment each year are permitted.

(*ii*) If surrendering the bond is delayed until the investors' marginal rate of income tax has fallen to the standard rate, all

10. Life assurance linked investments   213

proceeds are tax-free.

(*iii*) Cheap switching facility (as (*ii*) above).

(*iv*) Investment income is reinvested and thereby avoids the investors' high marginal rates of income tax. This benefit does not apply to unit trusts or investment trusts.

20. Disadvantages of single-premium bonds.

(*a*) For standard rate of tax investors:

(*i*) Investors should compare the charges with those of unit trusts and investment trusts.

(*ii*) The payment of capital gains tax by the life fund prevents investors from using their annual exemption to avoid or reduce their payment of this tax.

(*b*) For the higher rate of tax investors:

(*i*) As in (*i*) above.

(*ii*) The inability of investors to use their annual exemption of capital gains tax for this investment is unlikely to be important as they will have other investments which can utilize this tax allowance.

Investors' considerations when selecting life assurance linked investments

21. Key question. The key question investors need to ask is whether they wish to play an active investment role, choosing when to switch between the life assurance company's different funds, or whether they wish to hand over responsibility to professional investment managers.

22. Investors choosing to be actively involved with their investments. These investors will want unit-linked life assurance investments, either a regular-premium or a single-premium bond. Their choice of life company should be influenced by the following points:

(*a*) The investment record of the individual sector funds. These can be found in the tables at the back of the monthly magazines *Money Management* and *Planned Savings*. While past performance is no guarantee of future performances, it is still worth selecting from companies that have consistently appeared near the top of performance tables.

(b) The range of investment funds available. They should cover different geographical areas, a hedge against inflation such as an index-linked gilts fund and preferably a gold share fund, a fixed-interest fund, and a deposit fund for when they want to go liquid. Foreign currency deposit funds or bond funds are a bonus in case they wish to avoid a run on sterling, but few companies offer them.

(c) Free or low-cost switching facilities. If a charge is made, a small flat-rate fee will work out cheaper than a percentage of the value of the assets switched. They should find out not only the costs of switching, but also how quick and easy it is.

(d) Low management charges.

23. Investors wanting their investments to be professionally managed. There are two alternative ways in which investors' funds in life assurance linked investments can be professionally managed.

(a) By the fund managers of the life company. This can be achieved by investors choosing an endowment policy, or the managed fund of a unit-linked regular-premium policy or a single-premium bond. Their investment will be conservatively managed and spread between equities, fixed-interest securities and property.

(b) By making use of the services of one of the insurance brokers and members of FIMBRA which undertake to switch investors' insurance bonds between the different funds offered to policy-holders by a life assurance company. These types of investment managers advertise their services in the financial pages of the weekend press and the monthly magazines *Money Management*, *Planned Savings* and *What Investment*. The switching service is sometimes provided free for investors who have taken out their life assurance policies using the firm of investment managers as their broker.

Other types of insurance linked investments

24. Guaranteed income and guaranteed growth bonds. *Guaranteed income bonds* and *guaranteed growth bonds* are special types of single-premium bonds where the life company buys a portfolio of fixed-interest stocks, mostly gilts, with maturities equal to the term of the policy. By the redemption of the underlying stock coinciding

10. Life assurance linked investments

with the term of the bond, the rate of return can be guaranteed. The term of most bonds is three, four or five years but sometimes ten years. Income bonds produce a regular income net of basic rate tax paid out six-monthly or annually and then pay back the original capital at the end of the term. Growth bonds accumulate the interest and pay out all the proceeds at the end of the term, net of basic rate of income tax. As this is not a qualifying policy, investors should check carefully the details of the policy concerning their liability to higher rates of tax.

The guaranteed income bond is particularly attractive to investors seeking income when the rate of interest is expected to decline. This would cause their income from investments in bank, building society and National Savings deposits to fall. A guaranteed income bond enables them to lock into higher rates of interest for the term of the bond.

25. Annuities. Investors purchasing an annuity are purchasing a fixed income for the rest of their lives. The amount of income that the life company is prepared to pay depends upon:

(*a*) The amount of cash offered by the investor.
(*b*) The age and sex of the investor. The life company uses life expectancy tables to estimate the number of years that they will have to pay the income.

Different companies will offer slightly different rates. Examples of rates quoted by companies are given in tables each month at the front of *Money Management* and there are frequent reviews in *Planned Savings*. The policies also differ slightly in particular details. For example, some annuities make provision for an annual increase in payment to help offset any rise in the cost of living; some also guarantee a minimum payment in the event of early death. Annuities may be based upon a single life or upon joint lives of a husband and wife with payment not ceasing until the second death.

Annuities are regarded by the Inland Revenue as part capital repayment and part interest income. The income element will be subject to income tax, but the capital element will be tax-free.

A *home income plan* is a scheme designed for elderly home owners to release some of the capital tied up in their home. A mortgage is granted on their house and, with the proceeds, an annuity is bought.

Interest on the mortgage must be paid from the income received from the annuity, but the interest is eligible for tax relief on mortgages up to £30,000. The capital is repaid on death from the estate. Investors do not surrender ownership of their property and hence continue to benefit from any increase in its value. The borrower must legally be at least 65 years old, but the life companies giving an annuity often impose a minimum age of 70.

26. Investment with a friendly society. Friendly societies, like building societies, started as mutual, non-profit-making societies. Their objective was to help and protect their members in times of ill-health. Today, friendly societies provide the only opportunity to invest in a totally tax-exempt savings plan apart from a pension scheme, but without its disadvantages of having to wait until retirement to obtain the rewards and being unable to take all the proceeds in a cash lump sum. Several tax-exempt friendly societies advertise savings schemes which enable the income and capital gains that they earn to be rolled up tax-free, and then after ten years allow investors either to receive the proceeds tax-free in a lump sum, or withdraw an annual income tax-free, or leave the proceeds to continue growing tax-free. The various schemes on offer fall into one of two types.

(a) A scheme where all the savings are invested with a building society which pays a preferential rate to the friendly society tax-free, e.g. the Homeowners Friendly Society.

(b) A scheme where half of the savings are invested in a building society, or gilts, and the other half in equities via one of the low-risk unit trusts, e.g. the Lancashire and Yorkshire Assurance, a friendly society.

To qualify for tax exemption, the investor's savings plan is linked to life assurance, but in the 1984 budget, the Chancellor restricted the sum assured to £750 with a maximum annual premium of about £100. A married couple can assure both their lives and increase their savings to £200 per annum. The administrative costs for such a comparatively small scheme are quite high, but less than the benefits that they would receive from the friendly society's tax-exempt status. The main snag with this type of scheme is that it is a very illiquid form of saving. If investors cash in their policy within

10. Life assurance linked investments

seven and a half years, the society is prohibited by law from paying them back more than the total premiums they have paid.

27. Investment in a pension scheme. Life assurance companies are also involved in personal investments through the pension schemes they offer. Saving through a pension scheme is a highly tax-efficient form of personal investment. All income and capital gains in a pension fund are allowed to accumulate free of corporation tax and capital gains tax. There are two types of pension scheme available:

(*a*) *Occupational pension schemes* can only be provided by an employer so if investors are members of such a scheme and they wish to undertake further long-term savings for retirement, they should make enquiries of their employer whether it is possible to make additional voluntary contributions.

(*b*) *Retirement annuity contracts* are only available to people who are either self-employed or employed by a firm that does not have an occupational pension scheme. However, the earnings from a second job, e.g. consultancy, writing, or the marking of examination scripts can qualify for this type of contract.

These schemes restrict the amount of earnings that can be invested according to investor's year of birth. Appendix 2 gives details of the current maximum percentages of earnings that can be invested in pension schemes. If an investor is earning income but not participating in an occupational pension scheme, a retirement annuity contract should become one of their investments. With this type of scheme, investors can take their pension benefits at any age between 60 and 75 in the form of an annual income for the rest of their lives, and part of their investment may be taken as a tax-free lump sum.

Progress test 10

1. What was life assurance premium relief? (**1**)
2. What is a qualifying policy? (**2**)
3. What is the difference between an endowment policy and a low-cost endowment policy? (**5, 7**)
4. What types of unit-linked life assurance policies are available?

218 Professionally managed funds

What types of companies offer these investments? (**8**)

5. Which types of investments will require investors to pay income tax on the proceeds? (**10**)

6. What is the top slicing rule? To which types of investment does it apply? (**10**)

7. Are unit trusts and term assurance a better combination than insurance bonds? (**15–20**)

8. What are guaranteed income and guaranteed growth bonds? For what types of client are they most appropriate? (**24**)

9. For which type of investors are friendly society saving schemes most suitable? (**26**)

11
Other investments

Investment in land and property

1. Types of ownership. Land may be acquired by investors either *freehold* or *leasehold*. The acquisition of a leasehold restricts the use of the land to the period of the lease and the leaseholder may be constrained in the use of the land by the terms of the lease. The ownership of the freehold does not place any time restriction on ownership although the use of the land may be constrained by covenants and will be subject to local-authority planning controls. Property may also be acquired either with the freehold land or by virtue of a lease. If the property is purchased leasehold, it reverts back to the writer of the lease on the date that the lease expires.

A leaseholder will either pay a full commercial rent, which is often called a *rack rent*, or a large capital sum for a long lease, and then a small annual *ground rent*. Rack rents tend to be used for short leases which may also contain provision for a periodic rent review. Ground rents are sometimes found even attached to otherwise freehold land. This type of ground rent was sometimes attached by landowners in the nineteenth century to the new houses built on their land to provide an income for their spinster daughters!

2. Investment in property for owner-occupation. Many investors feel that their home has been their best investment with house prices rising by an average of about 11 per cent per annum over the last decade. These benefits have been made more widely available by the policy of successive governments of subsidizing the rate of interest payable on mortgages. Since April 1983, the form which this subsidization takes has been switched from adjustment of the house purchaser's PAYE income tax code which reduced taxable income by the amount of interest payable to a system of mortgage interest relief at source (MIRAS). Under MIRAS, the investor with a mortgage pays only 71 per cent of the gross interest rate to the lending institution. Higher rate income tax relief is also available. However, this tax relief on mortage interest applies to the first £30,000 only of the mortgage, and to the principal residence only.

3. Types of mortage. There are two types of mortgage.

(a) *Repayment mortgages.* Each monthly repayment consists of part interest and part capital repayment. In the earliest years of the mortgage, most of the monthly payment is interest as the loan outstanding is very large. Conversely, towards the end of the mortgage period, the repayment of capital constitutes a much larger proportion of the monthly payment. The borrower is usually required to take out a mortgage protection policy providing for the repayment of the mortgage in the event of the borrower's death. This is a type of term policy (*see* 10:**4**).

(b) *Endowment mortgages.* Two monthly payments are usually made, one to the financial institution providing the mortgage and the other to the life assurance company that is providing the endowment policy. The payment to the bank or building society providing the mortgage is interest only as it is intended that the capital borrowed will be repaid from the proceeds of the life assurance policy. There are two types of policy used in endowment mortages: the full endowment policy and the low-cost endowment policy. As the name suggests, the monthly premiums are lower for the low-cost policy as it is a combination of an endowment policy and term assurance (*see* 10:**7**). In the case of a full endowment policy, the investor can expect a larger lump sum available and hence surplus after redeeming the mortgage than in the case of a low-cost policy. Both types of policy provide full insurance for the repayment of the mortgage in the event of the death of the borrower.

4. Owner-occupation as an investment.

(a) *The arguments in favour*:
  (i) A high rate of return in recent years.
  (ii) The principal private residence is exempt from capital

11. Other investments

gains tax.

(*iii*) Mortgage interest relief is available on the first £30,000 at the borrower's marginal rate of income tax.

(*iv*) A real asset which will provide protection against inflation.

(*v*) When house prices are rising, a houseowner with a mortgage obtains the benefit of personal gearing. For example, a house is bought for £60,000 with a mortgage of £40,000. If the value of the house rises to £80,000, the equity stake in the house of the owner rises by 100 per cent to £40,000.

(*vi*) In addition to the financial arguments, investors are influenced by the greater choice of property available to buy compared to the rental market, and the greater sense of personal security and freedom that home ownership provides.

(*b*) *The arguments against*:

(*i*) In a recession, home prices can fall and, if the borrower has to move to obtain alternative employment, the house may have to be sold at a financial loss. If the house has been bought with a mortgage, the effect of the personal gearing is to increase the size of the owner's loss.

5. Other types of property investment. Besides home ownership, the other types of property investment are retail and office accommodation, factories, warehouses, agricultural land and buildings, second homes and holiday accommodation.

(*a*) *Retail and office accommodation, factories and warehouses.* Direct investment in these types of property will usually involve a large outlay beyond the means of most private investors. To be a profitable investment, the prospective return must allow for repairs and refurbishments, problems arising if the tenants have difficulty in meeting the rent payment, and the period of time that might elapse between tenants (some industrial premises may be specific to certain uses).

(*b*) *Agricultural land and buildings.* Investment in agricultural land and buildings also requires a large outlay. It was a popular investment with some financial institutions during the inflationary decade of the 1970s. Since then, the lower rates of inflation, the high level of real interest rates, and the large world agricultural surpluses and their effect upon farming profits have combined to produce a fall in agricultural land prices.

(*c*) *Second homes and holiday accommodation.* These investments may be justified in non-financial terms, e.g. investors wish to use the property for their holidays and perhaps to retire there. However, viewing property as an investment requires an assessment of its rate of return compared with alternative investments available. Since the rental income usually provides a low income yield, profitable investment is very dependent upon a continued appreciation in property prices. In times of inflation, property can provide an excellent rate of return and a safe hedge against rising prices. In times of deflation, it can involve investors in a severe loss and if the property is mortgaged, the effect of this personal gearing is to magnify the size of this loss.

A prospective investor in residential or holiday property should consider carefully the implications of the Rent Acts and the problems that can arise if tenants fall behind with their rent or apply to the Rent Tribunal for it to be reduced. Legal advice should be taken before this type of investment is undertaken. Allowance must also be made for repairs and maintenance of the property.

Rents other than from holiday lettings are considered by the Inland Revenue to be unearned income and hence wife's earned income allowance cannot be used to reduce the income tax liability. To qualify for holiday letting and hence recognition as earned income, the property must be available for letting to the public for at least 180 days during the season from April to October inclusive, actually let for at least 90 days, and must not be in the same occupation for continuous periods of more than 30 days.

6. Indirect investment in property. Investors not having the capital to purchase their own property or not wanting to bear the responsibility for managing the letting and upkeep of property can select a professionally managed property fund. The three main options open to investors are:

(*a*) The shares of a publicly quoted property company.

(*b*) The units of a unit trust property fund investing in the shares of publicly quoted property companies (*see* 8:**11**).

(*c*) The units in a life assurance company's unitized property fund which can be acquired either via a regular-premium policy or a single-premium insurance bond (*see* 10:**15, 18**).

(*d*) A B.E.S. connected with property (*see* **4:23**).

Investment in commodities

7. Classification. There are five main ways in which investors can invest in commodities: direct investment, futures, options, unit trusts, and offshore commodity funds. The investor should note that gains from any of these except authorized unit trusts will be liable to income tax.

8. Direct investment in commodities. This method requires investors to provide storage, insurance cover and protection against deterioration for as long as they own the commodities. During this time period, the commodities will provide no income. The large amount of money required to undertake direct investment rules out this form of investment for ordinary investors with the exception of small precious metal ingots and coins (*see* **13** below).

9. Commodity futures. A futures contract was defined in Chapter 7 as requiring the purchaser to take delivery of a specified quantity of a particular asset at the price agreed and on the date specified when the contract is purchased on a recognized commodity exchange. The seller likewise undertakes to supply the specified quantity of the particular asset at the price agreed and on the date specified. Futures contracts are available in a whole range of commodities with the most active markets located in London, New York and Chicago. Investors should find the page in the *Financial Times* with the heading 'Commodities and Agriculture' and examine the range of commodities available in these markets – everything from metals, 'soft commodities' like cocoa, sugar and coffee, to more unusual sounding markets like soyabean oil and pork bellies.

These markets developed to provide the opportunity for traders to reduce their risk. For example, a coffee producer can reduce or hedge the risk of a fall in the price of coffee before his crop is available for sale by selling coffee futures in the market. If the price of coffee rises, the profit the producer makes from the sale of the crop at a price higher than expected will be lost in buying back futures to close out the producer's position in the futures market. Since the gains/losses in the market for the commodity offset the losses/gains in the futures market, the trader can greatly reduce the risk that results from unknown prices in the future. Investors or 'speculators' play an important role when participating in the futures markets by making the market more liquid through their buying and selling activities and by assuming the risks which traders wish to reduce.

The investor who expects the price of a commodity to fall will sell futures in the expectation of being able to buy back the same number with the same expiry date more cheaply at a later date. This is called *going short* or *holding a short position*. Conversely, the investor who expects a commodity's price to rise will buy futures in the expectation of being able to sell them later at a higher price. This type of investment is called *going long* or *holding a long position*.

Investors wishing to buy or sell commodity futures must act through brokers dealing on the recognized exchange for the particular commodity, e.g. the London Metal Exchange, the London Cocoa Terminal Market Association, the Coffee Terminal Market Association of London. The broker will require the investor to supply *initial margin* and to make funds available for further payments of *variation margin* if the market quotation for the futures contract should subsequently move against the investor, i.e. a fall in the price of futures for a purchaser, or a rise in the price for a seller.

It is the fact that futures are traded on margin that makes them so risky for the ordinary investor. As seen in Chapter 7, the personal gearing effect of having to deposit only say 10 per cent of the underlying value of the contract magnifies the potential gains and losses. If the market moves against the investor, the size of the losses can be enormous. *Stop loss* instructions can be given to the broker to close out the investor's position if the price moves further than a specified amount against the investor. The high degree of risk attached to this type of investment makes it suitable only for wealthy investors, and then only when they have made a special study of the risks involved.

10. Options. The commodity brokers on each of the commodity exchanges may be able to negotiate option contracts for their clients. *Call options* (as discussed in Chapter 7) give the purchaser the right, but not the obligation, to buy a specified amount of a particular commodity on a specified date. Conversely, *put options* give the holder the right to sell a specified quantity on a specified date. However, these options are not tradeable, unlike the traded options market in the various securities on the Stock Exchange (see 7:4). The advantage of purchasing options is that the potential losses are restricted to the size of the premium paid for the option. The disadvantage is the size of the premium that has to be paid above the intrinsic value of the option.

Investors can combine options and futures as part of their investment strategy. For example, an investor buys an option contract to buy copper at £950 per tonne. The price rises to £1,050 per tonne, at which price the investor sells a futures contract for the same quantity of copper and the same delivery date as the option contract. This locks the investor into the profit. If the price of copper then falls back to £950 per tonne, the investor can buy back the futures contract in order to take the profits earned in the futures market, and continue to hold the option in the hope of another rebound in the copper price.

Like the commodity futures, commodity options are a specialized area and should be undertaken only by investors who can afford to sustain losses if they make the wrong decisions, and then only after careful study of the markets and the risks involved.

11. Commodity unit trusts. Unlike the first three investments considered, unit and investment trusts do not invest directly in commodities. Authorized unit trusts are not permitted to invest directly, only via investment in the shares of companies involved in the production and trading of commodities. There are several unit trusts specializing in gold shares, and both types of trust funds are also available specializing in oil-producing and exploration companies. Commodity unit trusts diversify their portfolios so that they contain companies involved in rubber, tea, mining, commodity trading and metal-forming industries, as well as oil, gas and precious metals. This type of investment is designed for the small investor who seeks exposure to the commodity markets without the higher levels of risk associated with futures and traded options. (For examples, see the page of authorized unit trust prices in the *Financial Times* or at the back of *Money Management*.)

12. Offshore unit trusts. There are two types of unit trusts investing in commodities located offshore. The first type is similar to the onshore authorized fund, investing in the shares of companies involved in the production and trading of commodities. The risk associated with this type of investment is therefore similar to its onshore equivalent.

The second type of fund is a managed fund dealing in commodity futures and options. These funds are therefore much riskier because they are trying to take advantage of the gearing available in these volatile markets. Examples of this type of fund are those managed by CAL Investments (IOM) Ltd and the Dunn & Hargitt Group whose prices are shown in the list of 'Offshore and Overseas' funds in the *Financial Times*. These investments fall into the very high risk category.

Investment in precious coins and chattels

13. The selection of coins. There are two types of precious coins that appeal to investors – those whose price fluctuates in line with the value of the precious metal from which they were minted, and those which sell at a premium due to their rarity. The first type are bought as a direct investment in the precious metal. Investors should recognize that this type of investment does not yield any income, so their price must rise on average by the rate of return on a similar risk investment if they are to make a profit. Furthermore, coins must be protected from both loss and damage, and so investors will be involved in insurance costs. It is usually safer to use the storage facilities offered by the bank or dealer from whom the investors have purchased the coins.

The market price of precious coins is shown in the *Financial Times* on the page with the heading 'Commodities and Agriculture'. Below the bullion prices will be found the dollar and sterling prices for gold and platinum coins. The most popular gold coin in the world until recently was the Krugerrand, but imports to the UK, the USA, the Commonwealth, Japan and much of Europe have been banned as they are produced in South Africa. A Krugerrand contains exactly one ounce of gold, and $\frac{1}{2}$ ounce, $\frac{1}{4}$ ounce and $\frac{1}{10}$ ounce ones are also available. Until the UK government agreed to an import ban, the Krugerrand traded at a premium over its intrinsic gold value, but this has now almost disappeared as demand

11. Other investments

has dropped. A premium still has to be paid for the Krugerrand's competitors, the Canadian Maple Leaf, the American Eagle, and the new Angel produced for the government of the Isle of Man, all of which also contain one ounce of gold. The British sovereign is only 0.2354 ounces of gold.

One of the major inconveniences of investment in gold and platinum coins is that purchases which result in delivery of the coins in the UK are liable to VAT. (The definition of the UK includes the Isle of Man but excludes the Channel Islands.) This means that their price must rise by more than 15 per cent before investors can expect to realize a profit. It is possible for investors to legally avoid the payment of VAT by having their coins stored abroad where there is no local VAT or sales taxes. The most popular locations for gold coins to be bought and stored are the Channel Islands and Luxembourg, neither of which levy taxes on the purchase or sale of coins. There are numerous banks, coin dealers, commodity brokers and stockbrokers in this country which can arrange for the purchase and storage of coins abroad.

Platinum has proved to be a more volatile investment than gold, reaching a peak of $1,000 an ounce in 1980 while gold reached only $850. The price then fell below that of gold, but has since risen above again. This has been the result of investors anticipating that disruption in South Africa, which accounts for 80 per cent of the world's new supply of the metal, will affect the platinum price more than that of gold.

A platinum coin called the Noble has been minted for the Isle of Man government and, as with gold coins, there are many banks and coin dealers that can arrange for the purchases and storage of platinum coins or ingots abroad to avoid VAT.

14. What makes coins a good investment? There are many factors which account for the prices of precious metals including the state of relations between the superpowers, the political situation in South Africa and the level of oil prices. However, the most important influences are the present rate of inflation and the expected future rate. Inflation destroys the value of paper money, and precious metals, particularly gold, are the traditional refuge from money. Hence it is no coincidence that the great surges in the gold price in 1974/5 and 1979/80 were associated with rising oil prices and accelerating inflation. Similarly, the decline in gold prices since 1980 has coincided with a period of disinflation. Investors should be wary of looking only at the dollar price of gold. A fall in the value of the dollar as has occurred in 1985/6 has naturally been associated with a rise in the dollar price of gold. To identify the underlying trend of gold prices, changes in price must be measured in other currencies as well.

The other type of precious metal coins that appeal to investors are the collectors' items which carry a premium over their intrinsic value because of their scarcity value. Investors would be advised to avoid these coins unless they have made a special study of the subject.

15. Investment in chattels. This type of investment consists of the collection of items like antiques, stamps or vintage cars which are valued by the collector because of their aesthetic appeal and rarity value. Like coins, they provide no income, and need protection and insurance against loss or damage. Unlike modern coins such as Krugerrands or the Maple Leaf, where there are millions of identical ones available, part of the attraction of collecting various chattels is their rarity or uniqueness. From an investment point of view, this may make them less attractive as it is difficult to establish their market value. If each antique is unique, its market value can only be determined by an auction, and then the market is restricted to the potential bidders who know of its existence.

These arguments lead to the conclusion that investment in chattels is only appropriate for those who derive pleasure from collecting and acquiring such rare items and who regard this satisfaction as part of the return they derive from their investment. Like gold, these investments have their greatest increases in value in times of inflation, when investors seek real assets as a refuge from the money assets which are losing their real value.

Progress test 11

1. Compare the advantages and disadvantages of investment for owner-occupation with other types of investment in property. (**2, 4, 5**)

2. Evaluate the methods of investment in commodities via

11. Other investments

futures and options. (**9, 10**)

3. What is the difference between onshore and offshore unit trust investment in commodities? (**11, 12**)
4. What is the case for investment in precious coins? (**14**)
5. What type of coins make the best investment? (**13**)
6. Do antiques represent a good investment? (**15**)

Part four
The successful selection of investments

12
Portfolio planning

Now that we have examined the major types of investment available, we shall review how the information provided in earlier chapters can be used to plan an investment portfolio and meet the special needs of different types of investors.

Taxation and the selection of personal investment portfolios

1. Introduction. Since the effect of taxation upon the returns earned by investors is one of the most important factors to consider when selecting investments (*see* 2:5), this review will focus on the investments most appropriate for investors with different marginal rates of income tax.

2. Investments for the investors who pay no income tax. These investors will be living on relatively low incomes and will probably also possess only limited investments. Their prime need from investment is likely to be a good income from secure investments which also provide ready access to their savings in case of need. These investors should consider the following points:

(*a*) The highest yields will be provided from the investments offered by the National Savings Bank through the Post Office since they pay interest gross. Banks and building societies are obliged to deduct composite rate tax which cannot be reclaimed from the Inland Revenue and so are unable to provide as high a rate of return as the National Savings Bank investment account.

(*b*) The National Savings Bank income bonds and deposit bonds offer an extra ½ per cent over the investment account. The income bonds provide a monthly income which may be very important. The deposit bonds pay no interest as it is added to the value of the bond.

(*c*) The rate of interest on National Savings Bank bonds can be varied after six weeks' notice, so that investors concerned that interest rates will fall and reduce their income should purchase high coupon medium-term gilts to lock into current yields. They should purchase the gilts from the National Savings Stock Register through the Post Office so that they receive the interest gross. If they purchase the gilts through a broker, interest will be received net of the standard rate of income tax, but the tax deducted can be reclaimed from the Inland Revenue.

(*d*) Other fixed-interest investments like local-authority bonds and term deposits with finance houses or banks are paid net of the standard rate of income tax. (This cannot be reclaimed in the case of term deposits.)

(*e*) If investors think that the rate of inflation is likely to accelerate they should consider index-linked gilts, and the National Savings Bank's indexed income bonds.

(*f*) If the investors need income from equities, they should identify shares with a good dividend yield or income-orientated unit trusts or investment trusts – not forgetting the income shares of split capital investment trusts. Many unit trust management companies offer trusts that provide a monthly income (*see* 8:**22**). Investment in equities has provided a better long-term protection of the value of investors' capital than fixed-interest securities or bank or building society deposits, but the higher level of risk means that they should be able to afford to view them as a long-term investment. Investors will be able to reclaim the tax that has been deducted from the dividends that they receive net of the standard rate of income tax.

3. Investments for the standard rate of income taxpayer. The following points should be considered:

(*a*) For the best rate of return from cash investments, investors should examine a table of net interest rates (*see* 3:**2** and Table 3A).

(*b*) If investors are seeking income and expecting interest rates to

12. Portfolio planning   235

fall, they should invest in medium-term gilts with the highest net interest and redemption yields. They should also compare their returns with guaranteed income bonds issued by life assurance companies.

(c) If investors expect rates to rise, they should sell their fixed-interest securities as a rise in yields will cause a fall in their market value. They should invest the proceeds in variable rate bank or building society deposits offering the highest net yields.

(d) To protect their capital against inflation, investors should consider index-linked gilts, index-linked National Savings Certificates and, if they need income, indexed income bonds from the National Savings Bank.

(e) For longer-term investments, they should invest part of their portfolio in equities, either directly or via unit trusts or investment trusts. If they are optimistic about the economic outlook, they should increase the proportion invested in equities. If they are pessimistic about the prospects for equities, they should concentrate their investments in cash and, if they think interest rates will fall, fixed-interest bonds.

(f) If investors have sufficient investments to utilize their annual capital gains tax exemption and wish to pursue an active investment policy involving fairly frequent switching between markets, they should consider single-premium insurance bonds. If they will not be fully utilizing their annual capital gains tax exemption, they would be better advised to use the low-cost unit trust opportunities, including offshore umbrella funds (*see* 8:**18**).

(g) For long-term investments they should also consider the Personal Equity Plan and Friendly Society investments to the advantage of their tax efficiency.

4. Investments for higher-rate taxpayers. The tax efficiency of investments is particularly important to this group of investors, and capital growth is going to be more important for most of them than income from their investments. These investors should consider the following points:

(a) The best return on cash investments should be found by examining a table of net of income tax rates of interest (*see* 3:**3** and Table 3A).

(b) They should take advantage of the tax-free investments that are available by purchasing their maximum entitlement of National Savings Certificates (£10,000 per issue), take out a savings contract with a friendly society (£100 per annum) and undertake the maximum National Savings Bank Yearly Plan (£2,400 per annum) and Personal Equity Plan (£2,400 per annum).

(c) The index linking of the index-linked savings certificates provides tax-free capital growth and makes these very attractive. The faster the rate of inflation, the greater the tax-free growth. Investors should purchase the maximum entitlement of £5,000 per issue.

(d) When investing in gilts, they should select the low coupon gilts which give the highest net of tax yield to redemption. All capital gains are tax-free.

(e) Index-linked gilts are particularly attractive to higher-rate taxpayers because a large part of their total return is in the form of a tax-free capital gain. The higher the rate of inflation, the more attractive these investments become.

(f) Investment in equities should aim for capital growth. The shares, unit trusts and investment trusts selected should therefore have a low dividend yield. The capital shares of split capital investment trusts may be particularly attractive.

(g) If investors are already using up their annual capital gains tax exemption on other investments and wish to pursue an active investment policy, they should consider single-premium insurance bonds which allow cheap switching between funds. These bonds allow up to 5 per cent of their initial investment to be withdrawn tax-free each year. The bonds pay no dividends so all income received by the fund is rolled up tax-free in the price of the unit. Offshore umbrella funds are a highly competitive alternative as there is no capital gains tax liability until the investment is withdrawn from the fund. However, income received by the fund is paid out by a fund with distributor status and hence liable to income tax at each investor's marginal rate. The capital gains on investments in an offshore fund which does not have distributor status are liable to income tax when the units are sold.

(h) A ten-year regular-premium life assurance policy which obtains the status of a 'qualifying policy' can reinvest all dividends and interest received by the life fund and hence avoid the payment of income tax. The proceeds on maturity are free of all income tax. This makes an excellent longer-term investment for investors already utilizing their annual capital gains tax exemption on other investments. If a policy is not a qualifying policy, the proceeds upon redemption will be subject to the top slicing rule.

(*i*) Wealthy investors may wish to consider some of the more risky investments. The Business Expansion Scheme is very tax efficient but a high-risk investment. Investment in traded options, futures and warrants provides the opportunity for an increase in personal gearing or risk.

(*j*) Investors should check whether it is possible to increase their pension contributions since these savings will be free of all tax. If the investors are already part of a pension scheme administered by their employers, they should enquire whether it is possible to make additional voluntary contributions (AVCs). If the investors are self-employed or their employer does not administer a pension scheme, or they have additional earnings, they should check that they are investing the permitted maximum of 17.5 per cent of earned income subject to tax, and that they have used their annual allowance for the last six years.

(*k*) If investors do not have a mortgage of £30,000 upon which they are claiming tax relief on the interest payable, they should consider obtaining or increasing their mortgage to invest the proceeds. Since the interest payments qualify for tax relief at the marginal rate of income tax, a mortgage is a very cheap source of funds and they can be invested to earn a higher rate of return risk-free in government securities or National Savings Certificates.

Investments for children

5. The tax position of children. Children are entitled to the single person's tax allowance (*see* Appendix 1) and so, for purposes of investment, are likely to be in the same category as non-taxpayers. However, if the money they invest has come from a parent, the income will be taxed as if that of the parent until the child is over 18 years or married. If the money has been provided by a person other than a parent, e.g. a grandparent or aunt or uncle, the income is regarded as that of the child.

A very tax-efficient way for relatives to give money to children is

238 Successful selection of investments

by deed of covenant. The agreement must last for more than six years, but the donor can deduct basic rate tax from the gift and the recipient can then reclaim it.

6. The selection of investments. Investments in shares and gilts and most unit trusts can only be undertaken by the child directly after attaining the age of 18 years. However, a parent or another adult can make an investment in the child's name. When the investment is made by a parent, so that the income counts as the parent's income, the investment must be tax-efficient for the parent's marginal rate of income tax. If the investment is a cash investment, the parent should consult a table of net of tax interest rates (*see* 3:2 and Table 3A).

When the investment is made by the child or on behalf of the child by a person other than a parent, the best gross rate of return should be sought until the child's personal allowance is fully utilized. For cash investments, National Savings Bank deposit bonds and the National Savings Bank investment account give the best rate of return. Gilts should be purchased through the Post Office so that the interest is received gross, and the tax deducted on dividends from shares and unit trusts should be reclaimed from the Inland Revenue.

Investments for retired people

7. Introduction. Investors who have retired should consider the points made for their appropriate marginal rate of tax in **2–4** above. They may also wish to consider the purchase of an annuity which would give them an income for the rest of their life (*see* **10:25**). This is not usually worth considering before the age of 70.

8. Inheritance tax. The Finance Act 1986 replaced capital transfer tax with inheritance tax. Transfers between husband and wife are exempt from the tax, as is the first £71,000 of the deceased's estate. The tax rate then starts at 30 per cent and rises to 60 per cent. A married couple making their wills should, if possible, avoid wasting their exemption allowances by leaving the whole of their assets to the surviving spouse. This point only applies where the size of the estate is more than sufficient to make adequate provision for the surviving spouse. Gifts to another individual or to an accumulation and maintenance trust are exempt if the donor survives seven years. If the donor dies during the seven-year period, a reduced rate of inheritance tax is payable with the reduction being greater the longer the period since the gift. For this rule to apply, the gift must be absolute. Thus a parent or parents giving their home to their child and continuing to live there rent-free do not take the house out of the estate as an interest in the gift is retained. To be exempt from inheritance tax, a market rent would have to be paid.

Other reliefs include:

(*a*) Gifts not exceeding £3,000 in a tax year. Unused relief can be carried forward one year if the relief for that year has been used in full.

(*b*) Outright lifetime gifts to any person in a tax year not exceeding £250 in value.

(*c*) Gifts and bequests to registered charities, certain public bodies and certain bodies concerned with the preservation of the national heritage.

(*d*) Wedding gifts by a parent to a child up to £5,000, by a grandparent up to £2,500 and by most other people up to £1,000.

(*e*) Lifetime gifts for the maintenance of children and dependent relatives and gifts which represent regular expenditure out of the transferor's income.

(*f*) There are reliefs on business assets, agricultural land, growing timber and works of art.

Portfolio planning and risk

9. Controlling exposure to risk. Investors must take steps to control their exposure to risk by:

(*a*) Ensuring that they have adequate liquidity to meet anticipated and unforeseen expenditure needs without having to sell off or cash in illiquid investments.

(*b*) Ensuring that they have adequate diversification to spread their risk. This is an advantage of managed investments like unit trusts and investment trusts for small investors as diversification can be achieved for them by the fund managers.

(*c*) Ensuring that they do not invest more in highly risky investments than they can afford to lose – if everything goes wrong.

(*d*) Being prepared to cut their losses and admit errors if things have gone wrong.

(*e*) Ensuring that they are protected against inflation risk if prices should start to surge upwards.

(*f*) Ensuring that they are not over-invested in equities or bonds if their prices are very high and the underlying state of the economy is likely to be unable to sustain them.

(*g*) Ensuring that their investments are not dependent upon the fortunes of a single currency, particularly if that currency is vulnerable to a fall in value.

13
The protection of investors

Legislation protects investors from the risk of loss due to malpractice by investment managers, such as fraud or deception.

1. The protection of bank and building society depositors. Under the provisions of the Banking Act 1979, only institutions recognized by the Bank of England may use the title of *bank*, and only such banks and licensed deposit takers recognized by the Bank of England may advertise or accept deposits. The Bank of England will only grant a licence if it is satisfied as regards the solvency and quality of the management of the applicant institution. A deposit protection scheme which is financed by all recognized banks and licensed deposit takers provides for the repayment of 75 per cent of deposits up to £10,000 in the event of loss.

The Building Societies Act 1986, which came into operation from 1 January 1987, gives building societies the opportunity to compete more keenly with the banks in the provision of financial services to the public. Societies with more than £100 million of assets are allowed to make unsecured loans and overdrafts to individuals provided the total is not more than 5 per cent of the society's assets and no individual borrows more than £5,000. These building societies may also give second mortgages, but the total amount of second mortgage and unsecured lending may not exceed more than 10 per cent of their total lending. Building societies may now offer accounts with cheque books, cheque guarantee cards, overdrafts and interest on credit balances in the accounts.

In the area of investment, these larger building societies are able to form subsidiaries through which they can run unit trusts and personal pension plans. They are able to establish and manage personal equity plans. They are also able to set up estate agencies and through them surveying, conveyancing and insurance services. The purchase of a house provides an excellent opportunity for the building society providing the mortgage to review with its clients its whole range of insurance services.

Other powers given to building societies include the ability to own, develop and manage land. This is likely to encourage some of the larger societies to venture into the provision of low-cost housing and the financing of housing associations. Building societies can also turn to the money markets to obtain more finance, but a minimum of 80 per cent of their liabilities must still come from retail deposits through their branch offices.

Building societies are now regulated by the Building Societies Commission which replaces the role formerly undertaken by the Registrar of Building Societies. The Building Societies Investors Board is responsible to the Commission and will manage the Investors Protection Fund. This fund will be financed from subscriptions levied from building societies, income from investments, payments made by the Commission for administrative expenses and, if necessary, money borrowed by the Board. The fund will be available to refund the depositors in the event of the failure of a building society. The maximum refund will be 90 per cent of the amount deposited or £10,000, whichever is the lower amount. The Act does provide, however, for two or more building societies to set up a voluntary fund to supplement payments from the Investors Protection Fund.

As an extra protection to the public, the building societies must provide an Ombudsman to deal with complaints and abide by his ruling.

2. The protection of investors in insurance policies. The Policyholders Protection Act 1975 provided a guarantee scheme to protect the policy-holders of an insurance company unable to meet its liabilities. The Insurance Companies Act 1982 made insurance companies subject to the Department of Trade and Industry's prudential controls which are aimed at maintaining solvency in the interest of policy-holders.

The Insurance Brokers (Registration) Act 1977 restricts the use

13. The protection of investors

of 'insurance broker' to those registered with the Insurance Brokers Registration Council and subject to its rules and code of conduct. The Insurance Companies Act 1971 provides that agents selling insurance must reveal their connection with any company and made the provision of false or misleading information an offence. The insurance company must also give its new policy-holders a period of 10 days in which they can cancel their policy without financial loss. These last two Acts have been superseded by the provisions of the Financial Services Act 1986.

3. The protection of investors in securities. The Prevention of Fraud (Investments) Act 1958 provided that any individual or firm dealing in securities had to be licensed by the Department of Trade and Industry (DTI). Some institutions were exempt from the need to obtain a licence – in particular, members of the Stock Exchange, building socieities, authorized unit trusts, insurance companies, banks and merchant banks. They were regulated, either by their own rules as in the case of the Stock Exchange, or separate legislation as in the case of building societies. The Act provided that insurance brokers, accountants, solicitors and others who wished to give investment advice were not allowed to recommend particular investments unless they had obtained recognition from the DTI as a licensed dealer. Members of the National Association of Security Dealers and Investment Managers (NASDIM, now part of FIMBRA) gained exemption from the Act because they were recognized as a self-regulatory body with power to create and administer its own rules, deal with complaints and the discipline of its members.

The 1958 Act nevertheless failed to provide sufficient monitoring to prevent several unfortunate incidents in which innocent investors suffered. In July 1981 the Secretary of State for Trade appointed Professor Gower to undertake a review of the existing statutory framework and to make recommendations concerning changes needed in the area of investor protection. Professor Gower's *Review of Investor Protection* was published in January 1984. His principal recommendations were embodied in a government White Paper published in January 1985 and in the Financial Services Act 1986. The main provisions are:

244 Successful selection of investments

(*a*) The Secretary of State for Trade and Industry is given powers to authorize and regulate investment businesses. Any organization or individual undertaking any investment business without authorization is committing a criminal offence. An investment business is defined to cover buying, selling or managing investments for other investors or giving investment advice. Investments are widely defined to include securities, rights to securities, options, futures, money market investments, collective investment schemes and certain life assurance contracts.

(*b*) The Secretary of State will not exercise these powers directly, but delegate them to the Securities and Investment Board (SIB). It was intended originally that its responsibilities would be shared with the Marketing of Investments Board (MIB) which would regulate the sale of life assurance and unit trusts to the public. However, the SIB and MIB decided to merge in mid-1986.

(*c*) The underlying principle of the new regulatory framework is *self-regulation*. The SIB will be responsible for authorizing all investment businesses but will in turn delegate this responsibility to self-regulating organizations (SROs) provided that they satisfy the SIB that they provide the same protection for investors as would result from direct authorization from the SIB.

(*d*) The main areas that the SIB and SROs will want to investigate are:

(*i*) That those carrying out investment business are 'fit and proper' and this will include consideration of capital adequacy. The investment business will be required to disclose its financial position and the amount of its liquid resources. Regulators will employ teams of inspectors to carry out snap inspections of businesses.

(*ii*) The segregation of client funds from those of the business.

(*iii*) That firms sign a customer agreement letter setting out the firm's functions, responsibilities and basis of remuneration.

(*iv*) That proper records are kept and a complaints procedure implemented.

(*v*) Adherence to high standards of integrity and fair dealing. An investment firm must not only act with skill, care and diligence, but also disclose its interests. This will require it to disclose in advance any material interest which it had in a proposed transaction and it must make clear whether it is acting as a principal or agent. Whenever an investment business acts as an agent it must follow the

13. The protection of investors

best execution principle which requires that it secure the best deal for its clients. It must also follow the *subordination of interest* rule so that a client's interest comes before those of the firm (e.g. no churning of portfolios to generate commission). No investment business should be recommended to a client unless such an investment is appropriate to the circumstances of the investor.

(*vi*) Provision will be made for the compensation of investors incurring a loss caused by an investment company ceasing to trade.

It is expected that there will initially be five SROs:

(*a*) *The Securities Association.* This was formed in September 1986 as a result of the merger of the Stock Exchange and the International Security Regulatory Organization (ISRO). This will be responsible for authorizing and subsequently monitoring any firm which wishes to deal in UK or international equities, UK bonds, or Eurobonds. There will be a liaison committee between the Securities Association's governing body and the Association of International Bond Dealers. This is the organization representing Eurobond dealers but, being based in Zurich and having an international membership, it cannot perform the role of an SRO.

(*b*) *The Investment Management Regulatory Organization (IMRO).* This will regulate professional fund managers such as members of the Accepting House Committee of merchant banks and the National Association of Pension Funds.

(*c*) *The Life Assurance and Unit Trust Regulatory Organization (LAUTRO).* This is responsible for the way in which life assurance and unit trusts are advertised and marketed.

(*d*) *The Financial Intermediaries Managers and Brokers Regulatory Association (FIMBRA).* This was formed as a result of the merger of NASDIM and the embryonic Life and Unit Trust Intermediaries Regulatory Organization (LUTIRO). This will also cover the work that has been undertaken by the Insurance Brokers Registration Council (IBRC) since the Insurance Brokers (Registration) Act 1977. This organization will license independent intermediaries selling life assurance and unit trusts.

(*e*) *The Association of Futures Brokers and Dealers (AFBD).* This organization will be responsible for regulating members of the London International Financial Futures Exchange (LIFFE) and other commodity exchanges.

Successful selection of investments

Those members of the professions who give investment advice which is incidental to their main activities (e.g. accountants and solicitors) will not need to apply to an SRO provided they belong to a recognized professional body (RPB). To achieve this status, the professional body will have to demonstrate to the SIB that it has rules governing the investment activities of its members which provide protection for the public equivalent to that required by the SIB for direct authorization.

14
The state of the economy and investment

Investment decisions cannot be separated from the state of the world economy and in particular the country in which the investments are based. If fixed-interest bonds are purchased just before a rise in the level of interest rates, investors will experience a capital loss. Similarly, the purchase of equities just before a large downward movement in the market will make investors wish they had purchased cash investments. Thus the monitoring of economic conditions and successful investment must go hand in hand.

Economic influences on share and bond prices

1. The rate of economic growth and the prices of stocks and shares. A faster rate of economic growth will produce higher levels of real income and higher profits. The higher levels of real income will in turn result in higher levels of consumer and capital expenditure and further raise company profits. Since dividends and share prices depend upon the profits of their companies, economic growth is usually good news for both share prices and bond prices. However, this must be qualified to the extent that the rate of economic growth is unsustainable. If the government is concerned that the rate of economic growth is outstripping the productive potential of the economy and threatens to produce an acceleration in the rate of inflation, you can expect the government to tighten interest rates. This will cause a decline in bond prices and, if investors expect government policy to succeed, also curb share price increases.

However, lack of confidence in the prospect for success in reducing inflation may make shares more attractive as a hedge against the fall in the purchasing power of money.

The main sources of statistics on economic growth are published in *Economic Trends*, a monthly publication of the Government Statistical Service which may be available in your nearest reference library. The latest figures are usually given in the financial daily newspapers the day after they are released by the Central Statistical Office. In particular, investors should look for:

(*a*) Cyclical indicators for the UK economy which attempt to identify the turning points in economic activity. The Central Statistical Office calculate monthly four cyclical indicators: longer leading, shorter leading, coincident and lagging.

(*b*) The annual percentage change in real terms of GDP, consumers' expenditure, gross fixed investment, general government consumption, imports and exports of goods and services, which are all calculated quarterly.

(*c*) The indices of output of the production, manufacturing and construction industries.

(*d*) The results of a quartelry survey by the CBI of the intended change in fixed investment by manufacturing industry. The figure given shows the percentage of firms expecting to authorize more capital investment in the next 12 months less the percentage expecting to authorize less. It is a useful lead indicator of fixed investment and the level of economic activity in the economy.

2. Inflation and the prices of stocks and shares. Inflation is bad news since it erodes the purchasing power of investors' wealth. This is particularly true if they have invested in fixed-interest securities where the redemption price is fixed. It was the high rates of inflation at the end of the 1970s that finally resulted in the introduction of index-linked gilts to protect the purchasing power of investors in government securities. Since the revenues and profits of companies can be expected to rise in step with inflation, investment in shares provides a better protection of their wealth. In times of falling inflation, bonds can provide investors with both a safe investment and a high real rate of return if they invest when nominal interest rates are still high before they start to decline.

14. The state of the economy

An increase in the rate of inflation is also bad news as it is likely to trigger the introduction of deflationary policy measures by the government. These might take the form of higher interest rates, higher taxation, or cuts in public expenditure which will be bad for both bond and share prices. The reasons why the government can be expected to react in these ways to higher inflation are that inflation reduces the country's international competitiveness causing the balance of payments to deteriorate, possibly even to the stage where the country incurs overseas debts which ultimately will have to be repaid out of future surpluses. Inflation also erodes domestic stability by undermining confidence in money, redistributing income between different sectors of society, and creating labour unrest as unions struggle to maintain the purchasing power of their members' incomes. The special problem with inflation is that if the government fails to tackle it resolutely, it can easily start to accelerate as a falling currency and higher wages push up prices to still higher levels resulting in an inflationary spiral.

Some of the main statistics on inflation in *Economic Trends* are as follows:

(*a*) There are price indices for the output of manufacturing industry, materials and fuel purchased by manufacturing industry (an important part of manufacturing costs) and various indices of retail prices.

(*b*) There are several measures of UK competitiveness in trade in manufactured goods. These include producer price indices and unit labour cost indices for the UK, the US, Japan, France and West Germany.

(*c*) The underlying increase in average earnings in the whole economy and manufacturing industry.

3. The balance of payments and the prices of stocks and shares. The balance of payments position of a country is a consequence of the fundamental economic conditions already considered. A high rate of growth of productivity and output combined with a low rate of increase in wages and prices are the conditions that are likely to create a strong balance of payments. International competitiveness resulting in a high volume of exports generates a high level of domestic employment, income and profits. Hence a strong balance

250 Successful selection of investments

of payments will normally be associated with high share and bond prices.

A weak balance of payments causes investors to anticipate deflationary policies from the government to protect its currency and help to reduce inflationary pressures. This will result in a fall in the profit expectations and hence share and bond prices.

Statistics on the balance of payments published in *Economic Trends* are:

(*a*) monthly volume indices for exports and imports;
(*b*) a quarterly analysis of the balance of payments showing oil and non-oil imports and exports, the balance of trade, and the import and export earnings from services.

4. The exchange rate and the prices of stocks and shares. The exchange rate or external value of a country's currency is both a cause and a consequence of the condition of the country's balance of payments. If the exchange rate is too high for a country to be competitive in international trade, there will be a deficit on the current account of its balance of payments and this will result in a weakening of its currency. The US economy is an example of this situation. The huge borrowing requirement created by the US Federal budget deficit has resulted in high levels of real interest rates and an inflow of capital on the capital account of its balance of payments. The deterioration in the US balance of trade and the increase in unemployment in manufacturing as a result of the high value of the dollar has caused the government to work for a lower dollar exchange rate to produce greater balance on the current account.

A lower exchange rate will normally result in an increase in the price of the shares of those companies which are expected to benefit from the increased competitiveness by higher sales and profits. Similarly, there will be a rise in the share prices of those companies which earn a large proportion of their sales and profits from the activities of their subsidiaries located abroad. A fall in the exchange rate results in a fall in share prices and bond prices when the market anticipates that it will result in higher interest rates, higher taxes or less tax cuts and hence lower profits for the companies operating in the domestic market. Thus a fall in the exchange rate of sterling can

14. The state of the economy

have contradictory results with some shares going up, e.g. export earners like ICI, Jaguar, BAT, and others coming down, e.g. the stores sector in anticipation of lower real consumer expenditure. Bond prices can be expected to fall in anticipation of the higher yields required to defend a weaker currency.

Conversely, a rise in the exchange rate can be associated with a rise in share prices – in the short run. The relationship is not, however, one of cause and effect. The direction of causation is rather from a strong or booming economy with a strong balance of payments to both higher profits and hence share prices and a stronger currency. In the longer term, a rising currency will depress domestic profits, both because of lower export profits and as a result of increased competition in domestic markets. Thus, in the longer term, a rising currency will restrain the growth in share prices. Bond prices should remain high reflecting the low level of interest rates normally associated with a strong and relatively problem-free economy.

The best guide to the strength of a country's exchange rate is its trade-weighted index which takes account of the global distribution of trade. Their values are shown daily in the *Financial Times* for sterling, the dollar and the Deutschmark on the page headed 'Currencies, Money and Capital Markets'. This page also gives a Bank of England Index with a base average of 1975 = 100 for twelve different currencies and the percentage change since 1980–2 calculated by Morgan Guaranty for the same currencies. The *Economist* publishes each week on its back page data of trade, exchange rates and foreign reserves for twelve countries. *Economic Trends* shows the monthly trade-weighted index of sterling and its value against six other currencies.

5. Interest rates and the prices of stocks and shares. Since interest rates and bond prices are inversely related, an increase in interest rates means lower bond prices. A high interest rate is also usually associated with low share prices. High interest rates reduce company profits, deter borrowing and spending by consumers and make bonds more attractive relative to shares. A high interest rate is also a sign that the economy faces problems, again a bad omen for company profits and share prices. The following factors may be responsible for a rise in interest rates:

252 Successful selection of investments

(a) An increase or an anticipated increase in the rate of inflation. The monetary authorities raise interest rates in the belief that it will reduce the demand for new loans from banks and that this will reduce both the amount of money in circulation and the amount of expenditure undertaken in the economy. This slowdown in spending is expected eventually to cool down the rate of inflation.

The monetary authorities are not alone in desiring a higher rate of interest when the rate of inflation increases. A faster increase in prices means a lower real rate of return for investors. Thus a higher money rate of interest is partly a response to maintain the level of saving and lending, and to ensure that the inflow of capital from overseas is not reversed. International investors are very conscious of comparative real rates of return, both actual and anticipated, when making their investment decisions.

(b) A fall in a country's exchange rate to defend the existing rate or at least moderate its rate of decline. The government's motive in defending its exchange rate is to prevent an upsurge in the domestic rate of inflation in response to the higher import prices that result from a fall in its exchange rate.

(c) A deterioration in the balance of payments. If a country is importing more goods and services than it is exporting, higher interest rates help to attract a capital inflow to finance the deficit on current account. They also help to depress the economy and hence the demand for such a high level of imports. A lower level of domestic economic activity not only reduces the demand for imports but makes productive resources and output available for firms to supply to new export markets.

(d) A high level of public expenditure relative to the government's income from taxation. The need to borrow large sums in the bond and bill markets will drive up interest rates in an attempt to attract lenders.

Statistics on interest rates can be found in the following sources:

(a) In the daily press: in the bottom left-hand corner of the front page of the *Financial Times*, the three-month sterling inter-bank rate is reported which is the rate at which banks lend to each other. Changes in this rate tend to lead to changes in bank base rates. Three-month US Treasury bill and long bond rates are also shown. Inside the newspaper on the page headed 'Currencies, Money and

14. The state of the economy

Capital Market', the interest rates for all the main currencies are shown. UK gilt interest rates are, of course, shown on the same page as all the share prices.

(b) *Economic Trends* gives details each month of a range of sterling interest rates. European, American and Japanese interest rates are published weekly on the inside back page of the *Economist*.

6. The money supply and the prices of stocks and shares. Given the monetarist orientation of governments since the late 1970s, it is hardly surprising that investors have watched carefully the official pronouncements of changes in the money supply. The level of interest rates and the rate of increase in the money supply are closely related. Until recently, governments have attached considerable importance to targets for the rate of growth of both narrow and broad money. Evidence that the rate of growth of the money supply was exceeding the target range resulted in a tightening of monetary policy and interest rates, which had the effect of depressing bond and share prices. Changes in individual and institutional habits concerning their holding of liquid deposits in banks and building societies have undermined the usefulness of monetary targets for the government as a means of controlling the economy. Now monetary targets are used as only one indicator of economic performance along with the exchange rate, inflation rate, rate of increase in wages, and level of economic activity. Even so, a larger than expected increase in the money supply figures can still be expected to have a depressing effect in the bond market, unless they also coincide with other indicators of a slowdown in the underlying rate of economic growth.

Statistics on changes in the money supply can be found in the following sources:

(a) Figures for the monthy changes in M0, sterling M3 and PSL2 are shown in *Economic Trends*. (M0 is a measure of narrow money and is composed of the bank notes and coin in circulation with the public and held by the banks, and the deposits that the banks have at the Bank of England which can be withdrawn as cash. Sterling M3, and PSL2 are measures of broad money. Sterling M3 measures notes and coin in circulation and total bank deposits. PSL2 is a measure of 'private sector liquidity' and includes notes and coin in circulation, bank deposits and building society and National Savings Bank deposits.) A quarterly commentary is published in the *Bank of England Quarterly Bulletin*.

(*b*) The latest annual rates of growth of narrow and broad money for other European countries, the US and Japan are shown on the inside back page of the *Economist*.

Summary

7. Good news. The following events are for the most part good news.

Events	*Good for share prices?*	*Good for bond prices?*
(1) Faster rate of economic growth	If sustainable	If sustainable
(2) An expected reduction in the rate of inflation	Yes	Yes
(3) A strong balance of payments	Yes	Yes
(4) A lower exchange rate	Yes, if exports are important to the company	No
(5) Lower interest rates	Yes	Yes
(6) A slower rate of growth of the money supply	Yes	Yes
(7) Lower oil prices	Yes: US, Europe, Japan No: UK	Yes: US, Europe, Japan No: UK
(8) Lower US budget deficit	Yes	Yes

8. Bad news. The following events are for the most part bad news.

14. The state of the economy

Events	Bad for share prices?	Bad for bond prices?
(1) Slowdown in the rate of economic growth	Yes	No
(2) An increase in the rate of inflation	Yes	Yes
(3) A weakening of the balance of payments	Yes	Yes
(4) A rising exchange rate	Yes, usually	No
(5) Higher interest rates	Yes	Yes
(6) A faster rate of growth of the money supply	Yes	Yes
(7) Strikes and industrial disruption	Yes	Yes
(8) Socialist policies of economic intervention	Yes	Yes

15
Prospects for investment in the world's stock markets

Having considered the economic influences which affect the prices of stocks and shares, the prospects for investment in four of the most important economies and stockmarkets for UK investors – the US, the UK, West Germany and Japan will now be reviewed.

Prospects for investment in the US

1. US Economic statistics. All data relates to the calendar year end and is taken from the Economic and Financial Indicators published weekly at the back of *The Economist* (*see also* **7, 12, 15**).

	1983	1984	1985	1986
Increase in GNP (%)	3.7	6.8	2.1	2.1
Balance of trade ($bn)	(69.4)	(123.3)	(148.5)	(169.8)
Current account ($bn)	(40.8)	(94.5)	(117.7)	(138.4)*
Consumer price inflation (%)	3.8	4.0	3.8	1.1
Trade-weighted exchange rate index	130.0	145.0	125.8	108.7
Government long-term bond yield	12.0	11.61	9.49	7.33
Dow Jones Stock Exchange Index	1,252.7	1,211.6	1,550.5	1912.1

*12 months to end of September

15. The world's stock markets

2. Background to the current situation in the US. The large increase in oil prices imposed by OPEC in 1979 resulted in a tightening of monetary and fiscal policies in the industrialized countries to limit its impact upon inflation. A recession followed in 1981/2 which was brought to an end in the US by tax cuts combined with large increases in government expenditure, particularly on defence. The budget deficit rose from $27 billion in 1981 to some $200 billion in 1985. The demand for credit resulting from the recovery of the economy combined with the enormous borrowing requirement of the federal government caused US interest rates to rise. These high returns attracted an inflow of capital from overseas to satisfy the domestic demand for dollars. The result was a rise in the value of the dollar compared with other world currencies.

The US economy was booming by the end of 1984 with the highest rate of growth for thirty-three years accompanied by a low rate of inflation. The US had become the world engine of economic growth with the demand for imports to the US accounting for some 70 per cent of economic growth in industrialized countries. The only problem was that US economic policy was unsustainable. The rapid economic growth and the strong dollar caused a deterioration in the deficit of the US balance of trade, from $43 billion in 1982 to $170 billion in 1986. The consequences of this trade imbalance are:

(*a*) A lopsided economy with some sectors booming while others are in decline. The sectors profiting are the beneficiaries of the high level of federal expenditure on military equipment and high technology, and the retail sector. Those suffering from intense competition from imports are the mature smoke stack industries of steel and engineering, electrical goods for consumers, and labour-intensive manufactured goods.

(*b*) A lower rate of economic growth which slowed from 6.8 per cent in 1984 to 2.1 per cent in 1985/6.

(*c*) An increase in the debts of the US to the rest of the world. At the beginning of 1985, the US became a net debtor for the first time since the First World War. This will reverse the inflow of interest and dividends which had made a positive contribution to the current account of the balance of payments.

In October 1985 the need for Congress to raise the federal government's debt ceiling to just over two trillion dollars (two million

million dollars) resulted in the passage of the Gramm Rudman Act. This Act provided for the federal deficit to be reduced from $200 billion dollars to zero by 1991. As a first stage, the budget deficit for October 1986 to October 1987 was to be reduced to $144 billion. If the President and Congress failed to reach agreement on how this was to be achieved, the Act provided for automatic spending cuts to be imposed on a narrow range of public expenditure areas. The Act was intended to force Congress and the President to compromise rather than allow its provisions to come into force since they would be so unpopular. However, the Act has been set aside by the Supreme Court which decided it was unconstitutional, and the US government still faces the problem of how to secure a better balance between income and expenditure.

The problem of the strength of the dollar was tackled in September 1985 when the finance ministers of the Group of Five (the US, Japan, Germany, France and the UK), meeting in New York at the Plaza Hotel, agreed on the need for an orderly depreciation of the dollar. In the following twelve months the dollar fell 10 per cent against the pound, 25 per cent against the French franc, 31 per cent against the Deutschmark and 37 per cent against the yen. The fall in the dollar was assisted greatly by the halving of the spot price of oil over the same period from which Japan, France and Germany will benefit most as they are more dependent upon imported oil. Interest rates also fell substantially as the Federal Reserve Bank was happy to encourage a weakening of the dollar as a means of both stimulating the US economy and easing the burden of the Third World debtors.

The US government and Mr Volker, Chairman of the Federal Reserve Bank, have pressed the governments of Japan and Germany, which have the largest balance of trade surpluses and low rates of inflation, to stimulate their domestic economies. This would help create a market following the fall in the dollar for some of the US exports necessary to correct its vast imbalance in trade. These proposals have not been welcomed by the Japanese and West German governments which have been wrestling throughout the 1980s to reduce their own public sector debt accumulated in the 1970s from trying to offset the deflationary effects of the first oil price shock of 1973/4.

Two of the factors that will be most influential in determining the future development of the US economy are:

(*a*) the effect of the lower dollar and lower interest rates upon the rate of domestic economic growth;

(*b*) the effect of the level of the dollar upon the level of interest rates and the rate of inflation.

There is both an optimistic and a pessimistic scenario for the future of the US economy, dependent upon the size of these two effects.

3. Optimistic scenario for the US economy.

(*a*) The effect of the lower dollar will soon be visible in rising exports and falling imports.

(*b*) The lower interest rates and improved international prospects will be encouraging domestic capital investment.

(*c*) Economic growth will accelerate and unemployment will fall.

(*d*) Lower oil prices will keep inflationary pressures under control and stimulate consumer and capital investment expenditure.

(*e*) Lower interest rates will assist the President and Congress in reducing the budget deficit (each percentage point decline in interest rate reduces the budget deficit by about $5 billion). A reduced budget deficit will allow interest rates to stay at lower levels. Growth elsewhere in the economy will offset the deflationary effect of a more balanced federal budget.

(*f*) The lower level of oil prices and interest rates world-wide will stimulate world economic growth. Growth will be strongest in the countries with the largest balance of trade surpluses, i.e. Japan and West Germany. This growth will help correct the US balance of trade deficit and offset the deflationary effect of a more balanced federal budget.

4. Pessimistic scenario for the US economy.

(*a*) The lower dollar fails to make a sufficient improvement in the balance of trade to raise economic growth. This might result from:

(*i*) lack of growth in demand for US exports from oil- and commodity-exporting countries whose economies are depressed;

(*ii*) lack of gain in competitiveness by US exports in South American and South East Asian countries whose currencies are linked to the US dollar;

(*iii*) world depressed demand for agricultural products resulting in low prices for US exports which are in competition with the subsidized surpluses of the EEC;

(*iv*) US industry's failure to provide adequate substitutes for imports that satisfy consumer tastes. This potential problem is aggravated by the tendency of US industry to invest in manufacturing capacity offshore where costs are lower thereby giving rise to some deindustrialization of the US.

(*b*) A failure by the US economy to respond to a lower dollar and lower interest rates, or a failure by the President and Congress to reduce the budget deficit could cause a further slide in the dollar and ultimately a rise in interest rates to curb its fall and its inflationary effects.

(*c*) Lower oil prices or lower prices for agricultural products and land, or the excess supply of property developments could create a crisis of confidence in the banking sector since some banks have very large loans outstanding to these sectors where the value of the assets acting as security for loans have fallen.

(*d*) Lower oil prices could create a loss of confidence in the ability of oil-producing countries to meet the interest and capital repayments on their debts. Higher interest rates for whatever reason would greatly increase this risk.

(*e*) If the US balance of trade and the level of economic activity fail to improve, pressure will be increased upon the US government to resort to greater protectionism. This would result in a reduction in world trade and a world recession.

5. Implications for investment in the US. At the time of writing, the optimistic scenario is that favoured by the market and reflected in the level of share prices. Brokers and bankers speak of a re-rating of equities as the prospects have improved dramatically with the fall in oil prices. Falling interest rates – whether to help the downward adjustment of the dollar, stimulate a weak economy or reduce pressure on Third World debtors – have fuelled a boom in the bond market. The future for investors depends upon whether future events reflect the optimistic or pessimistic scenario above. If there should be a swing from the optimistic to the pessimistic outlook, share prices will fall heavily, and while bond prices may

15. The world's stock markets

not be similarly affected, any fall in the dollar will result in some currency losses for investors. The future level of US interest rates and hence bond prices will depend upon both the level of economic activity in the US and confidence in the dollar.

6. Summary of good and bad news for investment in US equities.
The following checklist is intended to act as a guide to the events that are likely to cause a rise or fall in US equity prices:

(*a*) *Good news:*

(*i*) a rise in US profits, growth, output and employment;

(*ii*) an improvement in the US balance of trade;

(*iii*) the removal of barriers to free trade in the world;

(*iv*) reflation and faster growth in Japan and Western Europe;

(*v*) a slow, non-panic-inducing decline in the dollar to restore US competitiveness;

(*vi*) a fall in US interest rates;

(*vii*) measures to reduce the federal budget deficit;

(*viii*) modest growth of money supply within the Federal Reserve Bank's targets;

(*ix*) low inflation;

(*x*) debtor countries implement economic policies to repay debts;

(*xi*) low oil prices – but not sufficiently low to trigger a bad debt crisis among banks.

(*b*) *Bad news:*

(*i*) a fall in US profits, growth, output and employment;

(*ii*) a deterioration of the US balance of trade;

(*iii*) an increase in protectionism in world trade;

(*iv*) tight fiscal and monetary policy in Japan and Western Europe;

(*v*) either a large rise in the value of the dollar, or a rapid confidence-destroying fall;

(*vi*) a rise in US interest rates;

(*vii*) failure to control the federal budget deficit;

(*viii*) rapid growth of the money supply above the Federal Reserve Bank's targets;

(*ix*) an increase in the rate of inflation;

(*x*) debtor countries delaying or defaulting on repayment of interest and capital;

(xi) a further fall in oil, agricultural land or property prices which could trigger a bad debt banking crisis.

Prospects for investment in the UK

7. UK economic statistics. All data relates to the calendar year end (for source, see **1**).

	1983	1984	1985	1986
Increase in GNP (%)	3.3	2.1	3.3	2.6
Balance of trade ($bn)	(1.6)	(5.4)	(2.5)	(12.8)
Current account ($bn]	2.9	0.2	4.9	(0.3)
Consumer price inflation (%)	5.3	4.6	5.7	3.7
Trade-weighted index	82.2	73.0	78.0	68.9
Exchange rate (£/$)	0.70	0.86	0.69	0.68
Government long-term bond yield	10.55	10.92	10.64	10.52
FT Ordinary Share Index	771.8	952.3	1,131.4	1307.1

8. Background to the current situation in the UK. The government of Mrs Thatcher that was elected in 1979 inherited an economy suffering from a rapid rate of inflation and relative stagnation. Consumer prices during the 1970s had been rising at an average annual rate of 12.6 per cent compared with an average of 8.3 per cent for the other main industrial countries. Growth in productivity per employee had slumped to a barely positive rate of increase. Manufacturing output was experiencing an underlying rate of decline of 1 per cent per annum, and unemployment had doubled since 1974. To tackle these problems, the new government decided upon a tight monetary and fiscal policy to bring down the rate of inflation and a series of supply-side measures designed to improve the productive potential of the economy. The main contributions on the supply side were the shift of taxation from income to expenditure to encourage saving and enterprise, the denationalization of British industry, the restriction of the legal privileges of trade unions, and the abolition of government regulatory agencies such as

15. The world's stock markets

the Price Commission.

Unfortunately for the success of these new policies, they coincided with the large increase in world oil prices during 1979 and 1980 and the ensuing world recession. The inflationary effects of the switch of taxation from direct to indirect and the breakdown of the previous Labour government's wages policy resulted in unit labour costs rising by 15.2 per cent in 1979 and 22.2 per cent in 1980. The rise in world oil prices and the advent of the new Conservative government enhanced the attraction of sterling which appreciated sharply on the foreign exchange market. The combination of high interest rates from the government's tight monetary policy, the high exchange rate and the rapid increase in unit labour costs caused a slump in manufacturing output of 17.5 per cent between the second quarter of 1979 and the first quarter of 1981.

Although GDP by the end of 1986 was, in real terms, some 15.8 per cent higher than in 1980, manufacturing output was only 5.7 per cent higher and had still to regain its 1979 level. Lower inflation had been achieved but economic growth and unemployment figures have been very disappointing. During this seven-year period 1980–6, the structure of the UK's balance of payments underwent a radical change as shown in Tables 15A and 15B.

While the balance of trade in food and basic materials continued in deficit, fuel swung from a small deficit to a large surplus of £6.2 billion because of the exports of North Sea oil totalling £16 billion in 1985. 1986 saw a large reduction in the surplus due to the fall in oil prices. The improvement in the UK's balance of trade was more than offset by a deterioration in trade in manufactured goods from a surplus of £3.6 billion in 1980 to a deficit of some £8.5 billion in 1986. The rapid deterioration in the balance of trade during 1986 has been partially offset by a rise in invisible earnings, much of which is attributable to the growth in profits, dividends and interest payments received from overseas investments. From now onwards the surplus which the UK can expect to earn from exporting oil will fall as North Sea oil output declines, and it is expected that by 1993 the UK will again be a net importer of oil. If the UK is not to experience a substantial decline of living standards, there will have to be large readjustments in the structure of its economy as the need increases for a higher level of exports to pay for imports. Both the optimistic and pessimistic prospects for the ability of the UK

Successful selection of investments

Table 15A *Major items in the UK balance of payments*

Year	Balance of trade	Invisibles	Current balance	Major components of invisibles		
				Services	Interest, profits and dividends	Transfers
	£bn	£bn	£bn	£bn	£bn	£bn
1980	1.4	1.7	3.6	4.0	-0.2	-2.1
1981	3.4	2.9	6.2	3.9	1.0	-2.0
1982	2.3	1.7	4.0	2.6	1.0	-2.0
1983	-0.8	4.0	3.2	3.7	2.5	-2.1
1984	-4.4	5.3	0.9	4.2	3.3	-2.3
1985	-2.1	5.0	3.0	6.3	2.3	-3.6
1986	-8.7	8.5	-0.2	n/a	n/a	n/a

Source: Monthly Digest of Statistics, Central Statistical Office.

15. The world's stock markets

Table 15B *Major items in the UK balance of trade (visible exports − visible imports)*

Year	Food	Basic materials	Fuels	Manufactured goods
	£bn	£bn	£bn	£bn
1980	−2.9	−2.6	−0.4	+3.6
1981	−2.9	−2.7	+2.5	+2.6
1982	−3.3	−2.6	+3.8	+0.2
1983	−3.6	−3.2	+6.0	−4.8
1984	−4.2	−3.4	+5.0	−6.3
1985	−4.3	−3.2	+6.2	−5.8
1986	−4.6	−2.9	+2.4	−8.5

Source: Monthly Digest of Statistics, Central Statistical Office.

economy to adapt to these required changes will now be reviewed.

9. Optimistic scenario for the UK economy.

(*a*) The overseas earnings from North Sea oil which drove up the value of sterling was largely responsible for the deterioration of the balance of trade in manufactured goods. Hence, as the output of North Sea oil declines, the pound will depreciate and restore the competitiveness of British industry. This process has already commenced sooner than expected with the collapse of oil prices at the end of 1985. Since the Plaza agreement of the Group of Five Finance Ministers in September 1985, the pound has risen against the dollar and weakened against continental currencies. As most imports are paid for in dollars, the weakening of the dollar reduces manufacturers' costs and the rate of inflation. The fall against continental currencies has increased the competitiveness of exports.

(*b*) As the UK is a mature economy, it is to be expected that exports of manufactured goods will play a less important role in the balance of payments and the importance of the export of services should increase.

(*c*) Since the removal of exchange controls in 1979, the UK's net overseas assets have increased from £12 billion to £90 billion, the second largest of any country after Japan. This has changed a net outflow of interest, profits and dividends in 1980 to an inflow of about £3 billion per annum which will increase to about £4 billion per annum when the repatriation of profits earned in the North Sea by overseas operators decreases.

(d) Falling oil prices and inflation rates will increase real income in the major industrial countries and hence the rate of growth of world trade. This should provide the UK with markets for a higher volume of exports, provided the rate of increase in earnings in the UK slows down from its 8–9 per cent annual rate of increase, and British industry responds to the challenge by investing in new capital equipment and technology.

10. Pessimistic scenario for the UK economy.

(a) It will be extremely difficult for manufacturing industry to recapture its share of world exports markets. Even before North Sea oil, Britain was experiencing a faster rate of growth in the volume of imports than exports. Imported manufactured goods have risen as a percentage of total domestic spending on manufactured goods from 10 per cent in the early 1960s to 50 per cent. Furthermore, the recession in the early 1980s has resulted in the scrapping of manufacturing capacity so that large-scale investment will be necessary to increase the volume of output.

(b) The gap in the balance of trade that will be left by the run down of North Sea oil will not be plugged by an increase in export earnings from services. The share of services in total UK exports has fallen from 29 per cent in 1974 to 23 per cent in 1985. This was the result of a steep decline in UK earnings from shipping which the growth in earnings from air transport, tourism and financial services failed to offset. Financial services in the City have shown virtually nil growth of export earnings in real terms in the last decade. Many services are untradeable and those which are have been subject to the same competitive forces as manufactured goods and have been equally adversely affected by the high value of sterling.

(c) To adjust the economy to produce the goods and services necessary to replace North Sea oil will require a lower level of consumption and a higher level of saving to finance the necessary capital investment. Earnings growth will also have to be restrained to keep down the volume of imports. If these adjustments cannot be achieved at the existing level of employment, unemployment will increase.

15. The world's stock markets

11. Implications for investment in the UK

(*a*) The fall in the value of the pound necessary to make exports more competitive will raise the share prices of those companies with overseas earnings. However, if the exchange rate were to fall too rapidly, the market would become concerned about inflation and gilts in particular would fall.

(*b*) Once the exchange rate has adjusted to the effects of falling earnings from oil, the UK is likely to enter the European Monetary System. This will provide greater stability of exchange rate, exert downward pressure on wage increases and allow a lower level of interest rates.

(*c*) The UK economy will be very dependent upon the rate of growth in world trade. Any decrease in growth or increase in protectionism would be bad for equities.

(*d*) Lower rates of increase in prices and earnings will be necessary to maintain the competitiveness of British exports. High rates will be bad for equities and gilts.

(*e*) Lower inflation rates will reduce interest rates and be good for both equities and gilt prices.

(*f*) As the next general election approaches, overseas investors will watch carefully for signs of a change of government and economic policy. Any loss of confidence on their part will result in a drop in the value of the pound, share and gilt prices.

Prospects for investment in West Germany

12. West German economic statistics. All data relates to the calendar year end (for source, *see* **1**).

	1983	1984	1985	1986
Increase in GNP (%)	3.2	2.9	2.8	2.6
Balance of trade ($bn)	16.6	18.7	25.6	52.7
Current account ($bn)	3.2	6.0	13.6	36.3
Consumer price inflation (%)	2.5	2.2	1.8	(0.8)
Trade-weighted index	124.3	120.0	131.5	144.7
Exchange rate (DM/$)	2.76	3.15	2.46	1.94

Government long-term bond yield	8.35	7.10	6.80	6.25
Commerzbank Stock Exchange Index	1,060.6	1,107.9	1,951.5	2049.0

13. Background to the current situation in West Germany. West Germany is the largest and most important West European economy for investors (after the UK) and is therefore singled out for special attention. Its economy experienced negative rates of growth in 1981 and 1982 as a result of the deflationary policies in the Western world that followed the second large increase in oil prices in 1979/80. The expansionary policies of the US in 1982/3 created a surge in exports which, together with rising private sector capital investment, have provided the basis for its economic growth since 1982. The growth of capital investment has been financed by rising profits assisted by a low rate of increase in unit costs and low level of interest rates as a result of the government's tight budgetary policy. Thus the economic growth in West Germany has been more soundly based and sustainable than that in the US or the UK which have been much more dependent upon growth in domestic consumption.

The tight fiscal policy of the government has been criticized both at home by those seeking a faster reduction in the level of domestic unemployment and abroad by the US seeking assistance in the correction of its imbalance of trade. Although the government has introduced tax cuts of DM20 billion – DM11 billion in 1986 and DM9 billion in 1988, it has resisted pressure to bring forward the second instalment. The government is anxious to avoid a repeat of the reflationary policies that it agreed to at the Western economic summit meeting in Bonn in 1978. These increased interest rates, inflation, the public sector debt, and helped produce a deterioration in the balance of payments.

The fall in oil prices has reinforced the rise in the value of the Deutschmark, the fall in interest rates and the rate of inflation, and the increase in the balance of trade surplus. Being totally dependent upon imports of oil, the cost of these will fall by some $10 billion from the 1985 total of $22 billion if the oil price averages $15 a barrel. The rate of economic growth was maintained in 1986, helped by a stronger level of domestic demand and tax cuts, but has since started to slow.

15. The world's stock markets 269

The strength of the German economy and its balance of trade has been reflected in the rise of the Deutschmark against the dollar. While this has put pressure upon profit margins on exports to the US, this market accounts for only 10 per cent of German exports and their capital equipment exports are not highly price sensitive. The rise of the mark against other European currencies has been restricted by its membership of the European Monetary System. This has given German exports a competitive advantage in France and Italy which have experienced faster rates of inflation. However, the value of the lira was adjusted downwards in July 1985 and the mark was raised against the French franc and other EMS currencies in adjustments in April 1986 and January 1987.

14. Implications for investment in West Germany.

(*a*) The underlying strength of the German economy and the benefit it has received from low oil prices has made it a sound investment for equities. For this strength to endure in the longer term, Germany must succeed in keeping up with Japan and the US in the development and application of high technology. However, the rise of the mark against other currencies and its effect upon exports means that the stock market index is most unlikely to rise as fast as the increase of 71 per cent achieved in 1985.

(*b*) A fall in the rate of growth in the US and in the Dow Jones Index would be reflected in a fall in the German stock market. The future is therefore very dependent upon whether the optimistic or pessimistic scenario in the US comes about (*see* **3–4** above).

(*c*) The German stock market can be expected to retreat upon a further strengthening of the mark which would adversely affect the earnings of export-orientated companies.

(*d*) The low (even negative) rate of inflation makes the rate of interest high in real terms. The government's desire that the mark should not be more attractive than the dollar and the slowing of the German economy should combine to ensure a continued downward trend in interest rates. This makes Deutschmark bonds a good investment.

Prospects for investment in Japan

15. Economic statistics for Japan. All data relates to calendar year end (for source, see 1).

	1983	1984	1985	1986
Increase in GNP (%)	3.6	6.4	4.3	2.6 *
Balance of trade ($bn)	31.4	44.5	56.0	92.3
Current account ($bn)	21.0	35.0	49.5	85.8
Consumer price inflation (%)	1.6	2.7	1.8	NIL
Trade-weighted index	157.7	155.2	177.4	207.1
Exchange rate (yen/$)	232	252	201	159
Government long-term bond yield	7.11	6.53	5.81	
Nikkei Dow Stock Exchange Index	9,893.8	11,542.6	13,083.2	

*12 months to end September 1986

16. Background to the current situation in Japan. The first hike in oil prices in 1973/4 resulted in the restructuring of the Japanese economy away from the energy-intensive industries of steel, shipbuilding and chemicals towards the low-energy input, high-technology and electronics industries. In consequence, Japan suffered less from the 1979/80 oil price increase and the 1981/2 recession than the rest of the world and recovered rapidly as soon as the US reflated its economy. In 1984, exports accounted for 60 per cent of the growth in the Japenese economy, and 70 per cent of the increase in exports was to the US. Electronics-related goods accounted for 40 per cent of the growth in exports. The balance of trade surplus of $17.1 billion in 1982 expanded to $92 billion in 1986.

By 1986, Japan accounted for more than one-third of the US trade deficit. As the US economy slowed down, protectionist sentiments began to develop in the US along with accusations of unfair trading practices and demands that Japan open its domestic markets to facilitate a higher level of imports. Yet the fortunes of the US and Japanese economies have become closely interlinked. The rapid rate of growth in the US in 1983 and 1984 had been the result of the increase in the federal budget deficit and had caused the deterioration in the US balance of trade. Both of these were financed by large inflows of capital into the US, largely from Japan, attracted by

15. The world's stock markets

the high level in real terms of US interest rates. The level of saving by Japanese households is around one-fifth of their income, about three times the level in the US. This is in large part attributable to the ageing structure of the Japanese population and the small state provision for pensions. Thus Japan is in effect lending the US economy the money with which to purchase Japanese exports. The massive capital outflows from Japan to the US also helped to hold the value of the yen down against the dollar and thereby allow the trade deficit to continue.

The slowdown in the US economic growth rate in 1985/6 was mirrored by a slower rate of growth of Japanese exports. As exports to the US account for some 35 per cent of total Japanese exports, this in turn caused a reduction in the rate of growth of the Japanese economy. This was reinforced by a slowing in the rate of growth of exports to China, Japan's second largest export market. After doubling its exports in the twelve months to the middle of 1985, Japan suffered from the cutbacks imposed by the government of China alarmed by the rapid deterioration in its foreign exchange reserves.

International pressure on the Japanese government to redress its balance of trade surplus has added to these trends. In July 1985, the Japanese government announced an 'Action Program for Improved Market Access' designed to assist imports to Japan. The achievement of slow progress in this area has been partly due to the structural features of the Japanese economy. In particular, there are a very large number of independent retailers and wholesalers, and their strong ties with their local suppliers make it difficult for overseas suppliers to obtain business.

In September 1985, the meeting of the Group of Five Finance Ministers in New York agreed that the dollar should depreciate against other currencies including the yen, and that the Japanese government should boost domestic demand to help reduce trade friction. In the following twelve months, the yen rose some 37 per cent against the dollar. As this was greater than the rise of European currencies, the yen has also appreciated against them. Packages of measures to encourage domestic consumption and infrastructure expenditure were introduced in October 1985, April 1986 and September 1986 but these were unlikely to have a significant effect upon imports.

Although Japanese exports are declining in volume terms, this is not shown in the balance of trade figures measured in dollars for two reasons. First, most of Japan's imports are measured in dollars while 40 per cent of its exports are measured in yen which has increased in value terms against the dollar. Secondly, the fall in the oil price has reduced the value of Japan's imports. Oil accounts for some 30 per cent of Japan's imports and each dollar drop in the price of a barrel saves Japan some $1.2 billion a year.

The Japanese government has taken steps to stimulate the domestically orientated sector of the economy. These include the reduction of interest rates and the bringing forward of public investment projects. The government hopes that the lower oil prices which have increased consumer income in real terms and the lower interest rates will be sufficient to stimulate the domestic sectors of the economy and offset the effect of stagnant exports without major new public expenditure projects that would increase the budget deficit. Like the government of West Germany, the government of Japan is committed to trying to reduce the public sector debt burden on the economy incurred by the reflationary policies of the 1970s.

The Japanese and West German economies have much in common. Besides aiming to reduce their national debt, they have both relied upon exports and capital investment to produce economic growth. In contrast, the economies of the US and the UK have achieved growth by high consumption and low saving, despite their conservative governments' claims of fiscal responsibility. The consequences have been that the Japanese and West German economies have large trade surpluses, strong currencies and lower interest rates, while the American and British economies have experienced trade deficits, weak currencies and higher interest rates.

17. Implications for investment in Japan.

(*a*) Since the US is Japan's major export market, Japanese share prices will be strongly affected by Wall Street. A revival in US economic growth will be good news for Japanese equities. A recession in the US and/or the introduction of protectionist measures against Japanese exports would hit Japanese share prices hard.

(*b*) The shares of export-orientated companies have already suffered from the sharp appreciation of the yen. A further appreciation would continue to have an adverse effect upon share prices.

(c) A fall in Japanese interest rates will help weaken the yen and encourage domestic housing, consumer and capital expenditure. This is good news for domestically orientated shares, e.g. construction and also yen bonds.

(b) China represents an enormous potential market, and South East Asia and the Pacific rim is the fastest growing area in the world. The recovery of growth rates in these areas would greatly benefit Japanese equities.

(a) The huge Japanese current account surplus is balanced by an outflow of capital from the yen into the US dollar. Any dramatic loss of confidence in the dollar could result in a further sharp appreciation of the yen if this capital flow were to be reversed. UK investors would gain from holding yen bonds or yen denominated bank deposits. This situation might arise as a result of a US government failure to take adequate steps to tackle the size of its budget deficit.

(f) If the size of the US budget is not controlled the results could be:

(i) A dramatic relaxation of US monetary policy causing inflation and the depreciation in real terms of US government dollar bonds. This would create a flight into gold, the yen and strong currencies.

(ii) Higher US interest rates to protect the dollar and increase the attraction of US government dollar bonds. This would reduce the upward pressure on the yen, but the higher interest rates might result in a US recession and a Third World debt crisis.

Further reading

Now you have read this chapter, you should endeavour to follow developments in each of the major world markets. You may find it helpful to keep a notebook and record items of news which are going to affect investment performances in each stock market. Some useful sources of information that will assist you are listed below:

(a) The daily quality press: look out for the feature supplements which cover particular markets published fairly frequently in the

Successful selection of investments

Financial Times and *The Times*. Especially helpful are the reviews at the beginning of each calendar year and the annual budget analysis.

(*b*) Magazines: the *Economist*, the *Investors Chronicle*, and the American magazines *International Business Week* and *Fortune*. The statistics given at the top of the review of each major market can be updated by referring to the 'Economic and Financial Indicators' at the back of the *Economist* each week.

(*c*) The bank reviews produced by the major clearing and commercial banks – Barclays, Lloyds, Midland, National Westminster, Standard Chartered. Reports on different countries produced by banks, e.g. Lloyds. The *Bank of England's Quarterly Bulletin* is also important.

(*d*) Specialist economic reviews and surveys produced by international bodies such as the International Monetary Fund, the Bank of International Settlements, the Organization for Economic Co-operation and Development (*OECD Economic Outlook*).

(*e*) Specialist reviews and analyses produced by the Economist Intelligence Unit (individual country surveys), the National Institute for Economic Research (the *NIER Review*) and the London Business School (*Economic Outlook*).

Many of the reports produced by the specialist agencies in the last two categories of this list are summarized the day after publication in the financial press.

16
1988 update on the world's stock markets

All data in the tables that follow is taken from the Economic and Financial Indicators published weekly at the back of *The Economist*.

The United States

	1987		1987
Increase in GNP (%)	3.8	Trade weighted exchange rate index	93.0
Balance of trade ($bn)	-171.2	Government long-term bond yield	9.15
Current account ($bn)	-160.7	Dow Jones Stock Exchange Index	2031.5
Consumer price inflation (%)	4.4		

1. The US Economy in 1987/88. The US economy in 1987 resembled more closely the pessimistic rather than the optimistic scenarios described in 15.3 and 15.4. In February 1987, the group of seven Finance Ministers undertook, following the Louvre Accord, to co-operate in maintaining stability in the foreign exchange markets to allow international trade to adjust to the 35 per cent fall in the dollar's trade weighted index that had taken place in the preceding two years. However, the continued deterioration of the US trade figures resulted in further downward pressure on the dollar. Intervention by central banks to slow the decline resulted in their involuntary accumulation of over $100 billion as extra foreign currency reserves. As this was not neutralized by sales of government securities, it resulted in above target rates of growth in the European and Japanese measures of their money supply. This in turn was responsible for an upward trend in interest rates worldwide. The increased supply of liquidity fuelled a rapid rise in share prices. The Standard and Poor's Industrials Index rose by more than 40 per cent up to October to stand on a P/E ratio of over 24 and a dividend yield of less than 2.25 per cent. (The P/E ratio was 24 at the time of the 1929 crash!) A bad set of trade figures, a rise in US Treasury Bond yields above 10 per cent, and fears that further falls in the dollar would raise interest rates and trigger a recession in the US sparked a 508 point fall on the Dow Jones Stock Exchange Index on 19 October as investors suddenly realized that share prices anticipated an over-optimistic outlook for US profits.

The basic problem in the US economy remains an excessive level of expenditure both at government and household levels. Americans spend more than they earn. This behaviour results in the problems of the *twin deficits* - the budget deficit which results from the government spending more than it raises in taxes, and the trade deficit which results from Americans importing more than they export.

Although the budget deficit for the fiscal year 1986-7 declined from $220 billion to $159 billion, much of this reduction was due to one-off gains created by the 1986 tax changes. At the end of September 1987, President Reagan signed a revized Gramm Rudman Hollings Act which provides for a phased reduction in the budget deficit to balance by 1993, with most of the cuts to be imposed after the 1988 Presidential election. Like its October 1985 predecessor, the Act provides for automatic spending cuts if targets are not met, but it has been drafted to avoid the technicality that caused its predecessor to be declared unconstitutional by the Supreme Court. The budget deficit target for 1987-8 is a further reduction to $144 billion, but the Congressional Budget Office has predicted that large tax increases will be necessary in 1988-9 if the reductions are not to be reversed let alone if further progress is to be achieved in deficit reductions in line with the Gramm Rudman Hollings targets.

The US personal savings rate declined from approximately 7 per cent of disposable income in 1980 to 3 per cent in 1987. This increase in consumption combined with a large build-up in consumer debt has helped to produce the massive imbalance in US trade and its 1987 record deficit of $171 billion. Up to 1987, this was largely financed by private investors and institutions in the rest of the world holding an increased quantity of dollar denominated securities. In 1987, the collapse of the dollar was only

16. 1988 update on the world's stock markets

avoided by the intervention of the world's leading central banks. The US cannot afford to continue to run a current account deficit of $150 billion. The IMF estimated in 1987 that the continuation of such a deficit would cause the net indebtedness of the US to rise from less than 10 per cent of GNP to 15 per cent by 1991 and 22 per cent by 1995. The consequences would be a falling dollar, higher interest rates, and probably higher inflation and recession.

The continued fall of the dollar in 1987 failed to produce any really significant improvement in the US trade position. Although US exports increased in volume by over 16 per cent, imports continued to grow by 3 per cent in volume. The US trade deficit increased in dollar terms because of the J curve effect, the name given to the deterioration in the terms of trade when a currency depreciates. While the deficit with Western Europe fell by $2.15 billion to $30.2 billion, that with Japan rose marginally by $1.2 billion to $59.8 billion and the deficit with low cost producing Taiwan, South Korea, and Hong Kong increased by $6.2 billion to $35.4 billion. Rising exports are providing a stimulus to the economy which, if not matched by a fall in consumer expenditure, could increase inflationary pressure. However, as exports contribute only 11 per cent of US GNP against consumer spendings's 67 per cent, the effects of a major slowdown in consumer spending could not be offset by rising exports.

2.   The investment outlook in 1988/89. Investment prospects depend upon the size of the change in the expenditure/savings imbalance in the US economy. There are three major alternative scenarios.

(a) Domestic demand remains buoyant with the result that there is higher inflation and no significant improvement in the current account. The most likely consequences would be a falling dollar, higher interest rates, and a repeat of the falls in the stock market seen in the autumn of 1987.

(b) Sluggish consumer expenditure combined with strong export growth could produce modest rates of economic growth and inflation, and some improvement in the balance of trade leading to greater stability of the dollar. These events would cause interest rates to remain fairly steady and underpin the equity market without causing any dramatic movements in either direction.

(c) A sharp fall in consumption would lead the US into recession. This would cause a fall in interest rates, a rise in bond prices, a fall in equity prices, and a widening of the US budget deficit which could further weaken the dollar.

The United Kingdom

	1987		1987
Increase in GNP (%)	4.8	Trade weighted index	75.4
Balance of trade ($bn)	-16.3	Exchange rate (£/$)	0.55
Current account ($bn)	-4.6	Government long-term bond yield	9.63
Consumer price inflation (%)	3.7	FT Ordinary Share Index	1437.1

3. The UK economy in 1987/88. The UK experienced one of the most rapid rates of growth amongst industrialized countries during 1987 with manufacturing output up 5.6 per cent, 22 per cent higher than in the recession in the early 1980s and 3 per cent higher than its previous peak in 1979. The output of the motor vehicle industry, for example, grew by 16 per cent. The mainstay of the UK's growth performance continued to be consumer expenditure which grew at an annual rate of 5.7 per cent in real terms as against a real personal disposable income growth of 3.4 per cent. Consumers have been financing their increased expenditure partly by a fall in the personal savings ratio and partly by borrowing that has been rising at an annual rate of 20 per cent. The growth of the economy was also assisted by an 8.5 per cent increase in the volume of exports stimulated by the depreciation of the pound against the Deutschemark and European currencies in the autumn of 1986. However, the partial recovery of the pound during 1987 and the high level of consumer expenditure caused the volume of imports to rise by 11 per cent and the trade balance to deteriorate by £1.25 billion. The deficit in manufactured goods continued to widen from £5.5 billion in 1986 to £7.25 billion in 1987.

The economy was giving cause for concern in early 1988 that it may be 'overheating'. The balance of trade deficit in the final quarter of 1987 was at an annualized rate of £6 billion. The supply of broad money was growing at an annual rate of 22 per cent and house prices were rising at an annual rate of 15.5 per cent with faster

16. 1988 update on the world's stock markets

rates in the south of the country. The rate of growth of earnings was beginning to accelerate and had reached an annual rate of 8.5 per cent. High earnings growth had not caused inflationary increases in labour costs per unit of output during 1987 because they had been matched by equally rapid gains in productivity. However, fears that output growth may slow down during 1988 and with it productivity gains meant that a continued rapid rise in earnings would become inflationary. The constraints on growth in the UK in 1988 are expected to be a slower rate of growth in the world economy and the effect of the rise in the value of the pound during 1987 and early 1988.

4. The investment outlook in the UK 1988/89. The investment prospects depend upon the extent to which the economy moves towards one of the following scenarios.

(a) Consumer demand remains too buoyant, partly as a result of the rate of increase in earnings, and inflation starts to increase and the balance of trade to deteriorate rapidly. The government will act to reduce these inflationary forces by raising interest rates and this will depress gilt prices and equities. The drawback with raising interest rates is that it may cause the pound to appreciate further above the £1=DM3 barrier adopted by the government in 1987. Appreciation of the pound would assist in the reduction of inflationary pressures, but would be bad for the equities of companies dependent upon international trade.

(b) If there were a sharp slowdown in world trade in the second half of 1988 or 1989 which reduced income growth and the threat of inflation, the government would move rapidly to encourage lower interest rates and possibly a lower pound to bolster the economy. Gilts would perform well in this environment, but not equities.

(c) The most optimistic scenario for investment lies between (a) and (b) and would involve a slower but more sustainable rate of growth of domestic demand and output, and no slowdown in world trade. Since exports comprise 26 per cent of the UK's GDP, with 58 per cent of its visible exports going to Western Europe and 17 per cent to North America, UK equities are vulnerable to any deterioration in export earnings. Gilts would also perform well with interest rates in a downward trend helped by the negative PSBR for 1988-9.

Successful selection of investments

West Germany

	1987		1987
Increase in GNP (%)	2.4	Trade weighted index	151.2
Balance of trade ($bn)	65.8	Exchange rate (DM/$)	1.63
Current account ($bn)	44.6	Government long-term bond yield	5.90
Consumer price inflation (%)	1.0	Commerzbank Stock Exchange Index	1284.5

5. The West German economy 1987/88. Economic growth slowed in 1987 but because of the strengthening of the Deutschemark, the balance of trade and current account continued to improve in value terms. Inflation continued at a very low level. The government came under a great deal of pressure during 1987 from the governments of the US and other countries to stimulate its domestic economy to help prevent a slowdown in the world economy when the US balance of trade starts to improve. The government cut taxes by DM 14 billion at the beginning of 1988, but it has been suggested that the proposed cuts of a further DM 20 billion in 1990 should be brought forward to 1989. However, the government is already concerned that the combined central, state, and local government deficit has risen from DM 42 billion in 1986 to DM 70 billion in 1988. The 1988 deficit is equal to 3.5 per cent of GNP, a larger percentage than the US budget deficit, and a faster rate of increase than in 1978-80 when West Germany undertook the role of the 'locomotive of world growth'.

The weakness of the dollar during 1987 forced West Germany to buy dollars to moderate its fall. This caused the money supply to grow above the target range of 3-5 per cent set by the Bundesbank. As a result, there was upward pressure on interest rates during 1987 up to the October stock market crash, since which time the short-term interest rate has been cut to 2.5 per cent, its lowest level since 1948.

There is widespread concern that exports which have been the engine of economic growth will stagnate as a result of the high value of the currency during 1988. Although only 11 per cent of West Germany's exports go to the US, these are concentrated in particular sectors. Some 25 per cent of West German motor industry exports go to North America

16. 1988 update on the world's stock markets

and 32 per cent to the dollar area. With a high domestic savings rate, consumer and investment expenditure seem reluctant to expand to fill the void. Investment has fallen from 16 per cent of GNP in 1970 to only 8 per cent in 1987. The dilemma of the West German economy is that its dependence upon exports (33 per cent of GNP) has depressed investment, which in turn has further depressed growth and tax revenue. The growth in the budget deficit has then deterred government tax cuts that would have been aimed at increasing incentives and boosting growth.

6. *The investment outlook in West Germany 1988/89*. With economic growth in 1988 widely expected to be in the range 1 to 2 per cent, the implication is that the equity market will remain depressed. Once the Bundesbank is satisfied that recession poses a greater threat than inflation, bond prices may rise since their real rate of return is still excessively high in historical terms. The strong balance of payments is likely to continue to underpin the value of the Deutschemark.

Japan

	1987		1987
Increase in GNP (%)	5.3	Trade weighted index	240.6
Balance of trade ($bn)	96.1	Exchange rate (Yen/$)	127
Current account ($bn)	86.7	Government long-term bond yield	4.45
Consumer price inflation	1.0	Nikkei Dow Stock Exchange Index	21,575

7. *The Japanese economy 1987-88*. In response to pressure from the US government to stimulate domestic demand and to offset some of the adverse effects of a soaring yen, the government boosted spending by 7.4 trillion yen in 1987, equivalent to 2.25 per cent of GNP. Domestic demand rose by 5 per cent in 1987 as a result of the government's public works programmes and a private sector housing boom. The strength in the construction sector, consumer spending, and corporate investment are expected to remain the engine of growth in 1988. The continued rise in the yen failed to make much impression on the balance of trade surplus which declined by only 3.5 per cent in 1987. Exports increased in value by 9.6 per cent while imports rose by 18.2 per cent, partly as a

Successful selection of investments

result of the rebound in oil prices. Japan's trade surplus with the US grew marginally, while that with the EEC rose by $3.43 billion to $20.12 billion, and with South East Asia by $2 billion to $14.34 billion. Although Japan is importing much more from low cost South East Asia it is currently offset by the export of capital goods as Japanese firms relocate their low value added products and components in low wage locations. These figures are likely to result in a further rise in the yen against the dollar in 1988, especially if the US demand for imports fails to moderate significantly. While Japan could do much more to reduce barriers to imports, the cost to US exporters has been estimated by the Institute for International Economics in Washington to be as low as $5-8 billion, which is largely offset by the effects of US non-tariff barriers against Japanese goods, particularly cars, steel and textiles.

The robustness of the Japanese economy was one of the reasons why its stock market suffered less than other world stock markets in October 1987. Other factors that contributed to its more modest decline were the small percentage of shares in the hands of overseas investors (approximately 3 per cent) and the low proportion of personal wealth held in shares by Japanese individuals. Since most of the shares are, therefore, held by institutions and companies with interlocking shareholdings, government pressure on the large institutions and broking firms to buy those shares that were offered for sale during 'the crash' was effective. The government also succeeded in stemming the sale of equities by *tokkin funds* in January 1988 by allowing them to avoid reporting losses on their investments by valuing them at cost rather than market value.(Tokkin funds provide the opportunity for companies and insurance companies to invest cash surpluses in shares, and have provided a means for companies experiencing depressed profits to boost them by gains on the Tokyo Stock Exchange – a process called *zaitech*, which means financial engineering.)

8. The investment outlook in Japan 1988/89. With economic growth based upon domestic expansion expected to continue, the investment outlook for Japan in 1988 remains fairly attractive. However, a potentially dangerous scenario could develop as a result of any further dramatic strengthening of the yen. Despite the fact that Japanese industry has been highly successful in adjusting to a 20 per cent rise in 1987 and a 50 per cent rise since 1985, a further substantial rise could hit Japanese industry and

16. 1988 update on the world's stock markets

the equity market. Even after the Autumn fall in the market, the Tokyo P/E ratio was 55 in January 1988 compared with 14 in New York. A fall in the Tokyo market may trigger forced selling by companies involved in zaitech, and by individuals who have bought shares on margin which also presents a large market overhang. A recession in the US would again not leave the Tokyo Stock Exchange immune. Although exports are only 15 per cent of Japan's GDP, over one third of these go to the United States.

17
Investment for trust funds

1. The investment powers of trustees. A trust can be
established to transfer the ownership of assets from one
person (the settlor) to another (the trustee) to look
after for the benefit of another person (the beneficiary)
until the occurrence of a specified event. A common
example is the husband who leaves some of his investments
in trust to his children, but specifies that the income
shall be paid to his widow during her lifetime.

The deed setting up a trust usually specifies the
investment powers of its trustees, and frequently gives
them authority to select the investments they consider
appropriate. Where no investment powers are specified or
the trustees are holding assets for the heir of a person
who died intestate, the trustees must follow the
procedures specified in the Trustees Investments Act 1961.

In carrying out their responsibilities trustees must
always act in the best interests of the beneficiary.
Where there is more than one beneficiary the trustees must
ensure they are treated equally, and if their interests
are in conflict the investments must be chosen to produce
a reasonable compromise. In the example given above the
need for capital growth for the children must be tempered
by the need for income during the lifetime of their mother.

2. The Trustees Investments Act 1961. The object of the
provisions of the Act is to ensure that the trustees
achieve a balance between secure investments and the more
risky investments which offer the prospect of capital
growth and a greater return in the longer term. The Act
specifies that the investments may be divided between up
to three classes of investment: special-range,
narrower-range and wider-range investments. If the
trustees do not make a division, then all the investments
must belong to the narrower-range.

17. Investment for trust funds

3. Special-range investments. These are investments which the trustees are specifically authorized to acquire and hold by the trust deed. An example would be shares in the family firm. Without specific authorization by the trust instrument, the trustees are barred from holding such assets as land and buildings, shares and debentures in non-UK companies, units in offshore and unauthorized unit trusts and shares in private companies. However, if the investments specified qualify as narrower-range investments, they are not allocated to the special-range category but included with other narrower-range investments.

4. Narrower-range investments. These are investments which are intended to provide security and income. They fall under two headings: those which can be undertaken by the trustees without advice, and those which can only be made with advice. The advice must be sought from a stockbroker or solicitor or other person experienced in financial matters, and the advice must be given or confirmed in writing. The advice must cover whether the proposed investment is appropriate, given the circumstances of the particular trust, and whether the degree of diversification of investments is also appropriate. Obtaining advice is unnecessary where one or more of the trustees is suitably qualified.

(a) Narrower-range investments - not requiring advice:

   (i) Deposits with the National Savings Bank and most major banks.

   (ii) National Savings Certificates and their Northern Ireland counterparts, National Savings Income Bonds and Deposit Bonds.

(b) Narrower-range investments - requiring advice:

   (i) Other fixed interest securities issued by the United Kingdom, Northern Ireland or Isle of Man governments, Treasury Bills and Tax Reserve Certificates.

   (ii) Other securities where the payment of interest is guaranteed by the UK or Northern Ireland governments.

Successful selection of investments

(iii) Fixed interest securities issued in the UK by any public authority or nationalized industry.

(iv) Fixed and variable interest securities issued and registered in the United Kingdom by any Commonwealth government or local authority.

(v) Fixed and variable interest securities issued and registered in the United Kingdom by the International Bank for Reconstruction and Development (the World Bank), the Inter-American Development Bank, the European Coal and Steel Community, or by the European Investment Bank.

(vi) Fixed interest securities, secured and unsecured, which are registered in the UK and issued by a company incorporated in the UK. (The company's total issued and paid-up share capital must exceed £1 million and it must have paid a dividend on all its shares in each of the five years preceding the year in which the investment is made.)

(vii) Stock of the Bank of Ireland.

(viii) Debentures issued by either the Agricultural Mortgage Corporation or the Scottish Agricultural Securities Corporation.

(ix) Loans to any local authority in the UK charged on revenues of that local authority, and fixed interest securities of any local authority in the UK.

(x) Debenture, guaranteed, and preference stocks of water boards which have paid a dividend of not less than 5 per cent on their ordinary shares in each of the ten years immediately preceding the year in which the investment is made.

(xi) Deposits with building societies which have trustee status.

(xii) Mortgages on freeholds, or leaseholds of sixty years or more, in England, Wales or Northern Ireland, and on heritable security in Scotland. The Trustee Act 1925 provides that no more than two-thirds of the professional valuation of a property may be advanced as a mortgage.

17. Investment for trust funds

(xiii) Perpetual rent charges on land in England and Wales or Northern Ireland, and fee-farm rents, and feu-duties or ground annuals in Scotland.

5. Wider-range investments. These are investments which involve a higher level of risk but greater prospect of capital growth. These investments may only be undertaken after advice has been received. The following investments are classified as wider-range investments.

(a) Securities registered in the UK, and not within the narrower-range, that have been issued by a company incorporated in the UK (whose total issued and paid-up share capital exceeds £1 million and which has paid a dividend on all its shares in each of the five years preceding the year in which the investment is made).

(b) Shares in building societies which have trustee status.

(c) Authorized unit trusts.

Under the Trustee Act 1925 trustees in England may invest in bearer securities provided the issuer meets the requirements for authorized registered securities.

6. The selection of investments. The Act provides for a once only division of the trust fund between the three ranges of permitted investments. This would apply if the trustees wanted to include equities or unit trusts among their investments. The trustees must undertake the following steps.

(a) Set special-range investments on one side.

(b) Divide the remainder of the fund into two equal parts - the narrower-range part and the wider-range part. This is a once for all division and changes in capital values will rapidly cause the equality of their values to diverge. In dividing the trust fund into two equal parts narrower-range investments may be included in the wider-range part, but wider-range investments may not be included in the narrower-range part. Any investment not authorized as a narrower or wider-range investment must be sold and the proceeds reinvested in authorized investments.

Once the fund has been divided the sale of investments in the narrower-range part may only be replaced by other narrower-range investments, but investments in the wider-range part may be replaced by either narrower or wider-range investments. Investments may, however, be transferred from one part to the other provided they are matched by the movement of assets of equal value in the opposite direction. This means that it is possible to dispose of narrower-range investments and purchase wider-range investments (provided an equal amount of narrower-range investments currently in the wider-range part are transferred to the narrower-range part).

Additions to the trust fund such as bonus or rights issues of shares are added to the part of the fund in which the assets are held. If the settlor of the trust provides extra funds they are divided equally between the two parts.

The proceeds from the sale of either narrower-range or wider-range investments may be used to acquire special-range assets. The proceeds from the sale of special-range assets may be used to acquire other special-range assets if permitted by the terms of the trust instrument, otherwise they must be divided equally between the narrower and wider-range parts of the fund.

Any withdrawal from the trust fund, e.g. when a beneficiary attains the age of 18, may be taken from either part of the fund without a compensating transfer.

7. Investments for charitable trusts. The investment powers of the trustees are either specified in the trust deed or else are subject to the same legislation as private trusts. The only differences therefore from private trusts are the following.

(a) Charitable trusts are exempt from all UK taxes.

(b) The requirements of the trust are likely to necessitate investments providing income.

(c) The proposed life of the trust is probably indefinite.

The Charities Act 1960 provides for the operation of managed *common investment schemes* or unit trusts in which charities could invest. Examples of funds which qualify as narrower-range investments by virtue of their investment in deposits and gilt-edged stocks are Charinco and M & G's Charibond. The 'sister' funds to these two examples, Charishare and M & G's Charifund, invest in equities and convertibles and are designed as wider-range investments.

A number of fund managers operate *exempt* unit trusts which because of their tax free status are restricted to charities and pension funds and are classified as wider-range investments.

8. Pension fund investment. The object of pension fund investment is to provide income for existing pensioners and capital growth for future pensioners, so that they in turn can enjoy a good income in their retirement. High yielding investments like gilts are appropriate for the first group. For those still in employment, investments must aim to achieve growth in real terms so that the income that they can eventually provide will match the pension fund's future liabilities. The liabilities of a pension fund will depend upon its principle of operation. There are two types of pension scheme currently available.

The first type of scheme is where the pension paid is calculated on the basis of the final earnings before retirement. Here, the employer takes the risk that if the pension fund performance fails to match the required income payments the employer will be asked to make additional contributions to the fund. Conversely, where the actuary of the pension fund estimates that there are adequate funds to meet future liabilities the employer may be able to make reduced contributions.

The alternative type of pension scheme is where the pension payments are linked to the investment performance of a pension fund. Here, it is the contributor to the pension fund who carries the risk of the variability in the potential returns of the fund's investments. Since a pension fund's liabilities are not, therefore, fixed in nominal terms, investment cannot take the form of simply investing in gilts that mature in the years when liabilities are expected to arise. To obtain growth in real terms pension funds must include index linked gilts, UK and international equities, and property in their portfolio.

The trust deed of a pension fund will usually allow for the investment policy to be left to the trustees, after consulting the company and its investment advisors. If there is no statement covering investment policy in the trust deed the terms of the Trustees Investments Act 1961 will apply, which will restrict the range of investment available (property and shares in overseas companies being excluded by the Act). The day-to-day investment decisions are taken by the fund managers, who are usually either employees of the company or a financial institution like a merchant bank or insurance company.

Successful selection of investments

Pension funds benefit from exemption from corporation tax and capital gains tax. This allows their investments to grow more rapidly and will also influence the selection of some investments. In the case of gilts, those which offer the highest *gross* yield to redemption will be the most attractive. Pension funds also benefit from a regular inflow of contributions. This allows fund managers to make marginal adjustments to the composition of the fund without having to sell investments. Thus the liquidity of the fund can be increased by not investing new contributions and not reinvesting interest and dividend payments received. This policy may be adopted when the fund managers take a bearish view on the prospect for equities, or when they expect a rise in long-term interest rates to produce a fall in gilt prices. Purchases of securities at regular intervals by the fund managers also produces the benefit of 'pound cost averaging' (see **8:21**). Pension funds can also invest in the special 'exempt' unit trusts that are managed by unit trust management companies for charities and pension funds that are not liable to corporation tax on their investment income.

18
Personal pensions

1. Historical background. Personal pensions are paid from two sources – state schemes and private sector schemes. The government not only determines the details of the state schemes but also regulates the framework within which private pension schemes can operate. The state pays a basic flat rate pension to women over the age of 60 and men over the age of 65 (commonly referred to as 'the old age pension') who have paid sufficient national insurance contributions. This is irrespective of whether they have been employees or self-employed and whether they receive any other pension. In 1978, the government introduced the *State Earnings Related Pension Scheme* (SERPS) to provide an additional pension related to the size of former earnings and hence contributions. Contributions to SERPS are compulsory for all employees who do not participate in a *'contracted out pension scheme'* operated by their employers. In order to obtain the status of a 'contracted out' scheme, the Inland Revenue and the Occupational Pensions Board (an independent board appointed by the government) have to verify that the scheme matches the benefits obtainable from SERPS.

Up until 1 July 1988 the provision of pensions for those working full-time fell into one of four categories.

(a) Employees contributing to their employer's contracted out scheme who were not therefore required to contribute to SERPS.

(b) Employees contributing to their employer's scheme that was not classified as contracted out (and hence was deemed to be *'contracted in'*) who were required to contribute to SERPS.

(c) Employees working for employers with no pension scheme who were therefore required to contribute to SERPS.

(d) The self-employed, who were not permitted to contribute to SERPS.

Categories (c) and (d) were permitted to make provision for their pension by contributing to Retirement Annuity Contracts (sometimes referred to as Section 226 policies) offered by life assurance companies (see **10:27**).

2.   The situation since 1 July 1988. As a result of the Social Security Act 1986 and the Finance Act (No 2) 1987 important changes have been made in the operation of SERPS and in the regulations covering the provision of private sector pensions. The government was concerned by the burden of operating SERPS by the late 1990s and wanted employees who were not members of a 'contracted out' pension scheme to take a greater responsibility for the future provision of their pensions. Hence it is encouraging contributors to SERPS to take out one of the *'personal pension plans'* which became available from 1 July 1988 (see **18.6**). It has announced changes to SERPS that would make its benefits gradually less generous. It has also provided a financial incentive to any employee currently contributing to SERPS to contract out and join a personal pension plan (see **18.7**). To increase flexibility and choice in pension provision, the government made it illegal from April 1988 for an employer to make membership of the company's pension scheme compulsory, so that members of contracted out pension schemes can switch to a personal pension plan if they wish. However, unless employees change their jobs they may not be able to transfer their past contributions to their employer's pension scheme into their personal pension plan, and the employer may not be willing to make future contributions to it. To increase competition and the range of choice of pensions available, personal pension plans can be offered not only by insurance companies, but also by unit trusts, banks, building societies and friendly societies.

3.   Changes in SERPS. For the first ten years of its operation SERPS was designed to provide men at 65 and women at 60 with up to a maximum of 25 per cent of their average inflation-adjusted *band earnings* over their best twenty years. Band earnings are defined as earnings between the Lower Earnings Limit and Upper Earnings Limit, which are redefined each year to equal approximately the single person's basic pension and 1.5 times the national average earnings respectively.

18. Personal pensions

Example: the band earnings for 1988-9 are £2,132 and £15,860. If an employee's earnings for this year were £10,000 and this year was part of the best twenty years' earnings, its contribution to the final pension before adjustment for inflation would be 25 per cent of (£10,000 - £2,132) ÷ 20.

The Social Security Act 1986 provides for a reduction in the benefits obtainable from SERPS for employees retiring after March 1999. The new maximum entitlement will be 20 per cent of the inflation-adjusted band earnings *taken over the whole working life* starting from the age of 16. The lower figure of 20 per cent will be phased-in over the ten years from March 1999 to March 2009 at the rate of a reduction of 0.5 per cent per annum, but any band earnings from 1978-88 will be protected at the 25 per cent rate.

Example: a male reaching the age of sixteen and commencing employment in 1980 will be entitled to eight years of 25 per cent of his average inflation-adjusted band earnings. Thus, when he retires 49 years later in 2029, he will receive 25 per cent of 1/49 of each year's inflation-adjusted band earnings up to 5 April 1988, and only 20 per cent of 1/49 of each year's inflation-adjusted band earnings from April 1988 to his retirement in 2029.

People who reached the age of sixteen on or after 6 April 1988 will therefore find that the maximum percentage of their band earnings that they can receive from SERPS is only 20 per cent. To obtain this, the individual must work continuously until retirement age which rules out either post-sixteen continuing education or retirement before the state retirement age. By basing SERPS on average lifetime earnings rather than the best twenty years, the value of the pension will be lower. Contributions do not attract tax relief and higher rate taxpayers also suffer from the fact that SERPS does not take account of earnings above the Upper Earnings Limit.

The provision of pensions by the private sector

4. Contracted out pension schemes. These schemes may be either '*self administered*' by the employer, or '*insured*' if administered by an insurance company. Two types of scheme are acceptable for contracting out.

(a) *Guaranteed minimum pension schemes* (GMP). These provide specified benefits which are not linked to the investment performance of the pension fund. They are frequently referred to as *'final salary'* schemes as the benefits depend upon the number of years of 'pensionable service' worked and the final salary. The maximum benefit upon retirement is 2/3 of final salary, but this is reduced if part of the benefit is taken as a tax free lump sum. This type of scheme is sometimes referred to as an *'occupational pension scheme'*. Besides the provision of a pension upon retirement, they usually contain additional benefits covering death in service, a widows pension and dependents' allowances, and early retirement due to ill health. The employer and employees usually jointly contribute to the fund to provide these benefits. There is a maximum contribution for employees of 15 per cent of their gross earnings. There is no maximum for employers except that pension schemes may not be *'overfunded'*, i.e. have funds greater than required to produce the maximum permitted benefits. However, if the investment performance of the fund is thought to have been inadequate to provide for the future liabilities, it is the employer who is expected to make up the shortfall.

(b) *Money purchase schemes*. These schemes specify the maximum contributions of the employee and employer to the pension fund, but not the pension benefits. These are determined by the investment performance of the pension fund. This type of scheme was permitted from 6 April 1988. It is a scheme that is more attractive to employers as their commitments are limited to their annual contributions. This is less of a financial risk than providing for guaranteed future pensions on retirement. Part of the contributions may be used to provide insurance giving a lump sum death benefit.

5. *The tax advantages of a pension scheme.* Approval by the Inland Revenue of a pension scheme carries valuable tax advantages.

(a) The employee's contributions are made from pre-tax income so that they enjoy tax relief at their marginal rate of tax.

18. Personal pensions

(b) The employer's contributions may be charged against taxable profit so that they also enjoy relief against corporation tax.

(c) The income received and capital gains made by the pension fund are exempt from tax. UK tax deducted from dividends received by the fund can be reclaimed by the fund's managers.

(d) Restricted lump sum payments may be made tax free upon retirement, but the pension is treated as taxable income.

6. The new personal pension plans. These schemes became available from 1 July 1988 and should be considered by:

(a) the self-employed since the retirement annuity contract (or Section 226 policy) ceased to be available with the introduction of the personal pension plan.

(b) employees who are contributing to SERPS, either because their employer does not offer a pension scheme or because the employer's scheme is not contracted out. These employees can use the personal pension plan to contract out of SERPS, in which case it is called an '*appropriate personal pension plan*'.

(c) employees who are members of a contracted out pension scheme but who may nevertheless prefer to arrange their own pension using the personal pension plan.

The basis of these plans is the investment of contributions to the plan until retirement, which may be taken at any age between 50 and 75. At this time, up to 25 per cent of the value of the plan may be taken out as a tax free lump sum with a maximum for each pension arrangement of £150,000. The remainder of the value of the pension plan must be used to purchase an annuity from an approved insurance company. The value of the lump sum and income from the annuity therefore depend upon the investment performance of the pension plan selected. Three types of investments are available via a personal pension plan.

(a) *With-profits schemes*: offer a basic guaranteed lump sum with bonuses dependent upon the fund management's investment performance.

(b) *Unit-linked schemes*: allow the investor to choose between a range of investment funds. The value of the plan is the surrender value of the units.

(c) *Deposit schemes*: offer a risk free, tax free rate of return that varies with the level of interest rates.

While there are no limits on the benefits from the personal pension plans, contributions are restricted by the Inland Revenue as follows.

Age at beginning of tax year (6 April)   % of earnings

50 or less	17.5
51-55	20.0
56-60	22.5
61-74	27.5

These percentage limits include any premiums payable to existing retirement annuity contracts and contributions paid by employers. Any unused tax relief for the previous six years may also be used. Up to 5 per cent of earnings may be used to pay the premiums to secure additional death benefits.

7.   Appropriate personal pension plans. These special schemes are available only to employees who are contributing to SERPS to encourage them to contract out. Both the employer and employee continue to pay the full 'contracted in' National Insurance contributions. At the end of each tax year the DHSS will pay into the employee's pension scheme a rebate of the difference between the full National Insurance contributions paid and the lower contracted out rates. In addition, the DHSS will pay the tax relief at the standard rate on the employee's rebate which it will receive from the Inland Revenue. As an extra inducement the DHSS will pay an incentive payment of the larger of 2 per cent of the employee's earnings or £1 per week until 5 April 1993. An employee starting an appropriate pension plan on or before 5 April 1989 can also backdate it to start from 6 April 1987 to obtain a maximum of six years of incentive payments.

The contributions of the DHSS to an appropriate personal pension plan are called '*protected rights*' and special conditions attach to their investment. They may not be taken as a lump sum, but must be used at the state retirement age to purchase an annuity. The value of the annuity must increase annually by the lower of the rise in the RPI or 3 per cent, and must on the death of the person

18. Personal pensions

receiving the annuity pass to the widow or widower for their lifetime at 50 per cent of the annual amount.

If the likely pension obtainable from the appropriate pension plan is not considered adequate by investors, they can make additional contributions to the plan which will be subject to the same rules as the pension plan described in **18.6**. **This will also increase the** investor's flexibility as these contributions can be converted into a lump sum as well as an annuity at any time after age 50 (see **Figure 1**).

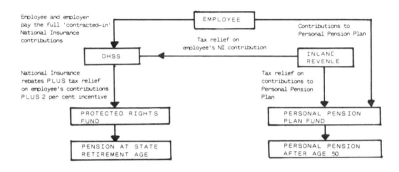

Figure 1   The appropriate personal pension plan contracting out of SERPS.

8. Advantages of personal pension plans v final salary pension schemes.

(a) There are no limits to the benefits from a personal pension plan, so if the investment performance is very favourable the income on retirement could be higher from this scheme.

(b) Portability means that frequent job changes do not involve withdrawing contributions from different schemes. However, providing at least two year's contributions have been made, employees leaving an employer may have their pension preserved in the scheme, but the trustees are only required to ensure that the preserved benefits increase by the lower of 5 per cent or the increase in the RPI.

(c) The contributor to the personal pension plan has a choice of investment managers and types of investment.

(d) The personal pension plan protects the value of the pension against the effects of a fall in income in the final years.

9. Disadvantages of personal pension plans v final salary pension schemes.

(a) The pension benefits depend upon the investment performance of the plan managers and the annuity rates at retirement, and may be less than under a final salary scheme.

(b) Other benefits available in a final salary scheme, such as death in service, will require extra insurance under a personal pension plan.

(c) Employers may not be willing to contribute to personal pension plans.

(d) Administration charges and commissions deducted from a personal pension plan are likely to be higher.

10. Additional Voluntary Contributions (AVCs). While many occupational pension schemes had previously permitted additional voluntary contributions, since April 1988 all pension schemes have had to offer '*in scheme*' AVCs to their members. This now provides employees with the choice between 'in scheme' AVCs and '*free standing*' AVCs which have been available since October 1987 from insurance companies and building societies. Total contributions to an employer's scheme and AVCs must not exceed 15 per cent of gross earnings. For the self employed contributing to a retirement annuity contract or now a personal pension plan, additional lump sum investments or increased contributions to the pension scheme have always been permitted provided the total contributions do not exceed the annual percentage of income limits fixed by the Inland Revenue (i.e. 17.5 per cent up to the age of 50).

AVCs started since April 1987 may only be used to increase pension benefits and provide life insurance cover. They may not be used to provide a tax free lump sum upon retirement.

18. Personal pensions

The advantages of taking out AVCs are as follows.

(a) They are a very tax efficient form of saving. Contributions benefit from income tax relief and the investment funds are exempt from all taxes. However, since they may not be drawn out in cash they should not be compared with ordinary forms of savings.

(b) For employees who are a member of an occupational pension scheme which is 'contracted in' and hence participates in SERPS, an AVC may be used as an 'appropriate personal pension plan' to contract out of SERPS and obtain the incentives offered by the DHSS.

The disadvantages of AVCs are as follows.

(a) The total benefit from an employer's pension scheme and AVCs must not exceed the Inland Revenue limits of 2/3 of final salary.

(b) AVCs started since April 1987 may only be used to enhance income on retirement, and may not be taken as a lump sum.

11. Pension Mortgages. A pension mortgage is a loan to purchase or improve a property where the repayment is to be made from the tax free lump sum available on retirement from the borrower's pension scheme. Pension mortgages have been made available by some employers for their employees participating in their pension scheme. They have also been obtainable against 'retirement annuity contracts' (Section 226 policies), and now against personal pension plans. Since April 1987, new AVCs have been unable to provide lump sums and so they are no longer an investment vehicle to meet the repayment of a mortgage.

The advantages of a pension mortgage are as follows.

(a) Low cost compared to repayment mortgages as the regular payments to the lender consist of interest only (as in endowment mortgages).

(b) They are more tax efficient than endowment mortgages as the investments can grow free of all taxes in the pension fund and the contributions qualify for tax relief.

The disadvantages of a pension mortgage are as follows.

(a) The size of the pension available will be reduced by the repayment of the mortgage unless other saving has been undertaken.

(b) Early retirement, redundancy or a change of job may present problems.

19
Recent developments in investment

Giving Investment Advice

1. The Financial Services Act 1986. The Act provided for rules to be drawn up governing the conduct of investment business. The Securities and Investment Board has published '*conduct of business rules*' which apply to those persons which it directly authorizes. Each SRO and RPB (see 13.3) is required to provide equivalent protection for investors.

2. The 'know your customer' rule. This is one of the SIB's conduct of business rules and requires firms to obtain information from customers, other than execution-only customers, concerning their investment objectives, attitudes to risk, financial resources and tax position. Firms must determine into which of the following four categories customers fall.

(a) *Business investors*: persons who are not employed in an investment activity that would require authorisation under the Act but nevertheless customarily buy or sell investments, eg the treasury department of a manufacturing company using currency futures and options to hedge their foreign exchange exposure.

(b) *Professional investors*: persons who are employed in an investment business, eg a pension fund manager.

(c) *Experienced investors*: persons who have actively managed their investments for more than a year and exposed their portfolios to significant risks and can therefore be expected to appreciate the risks involved in investment.

(d) *Ordinary investors*: persons who do not satisfy any of the above conditions.

Firms are required to obtain the necessary information to make this categorization and draw up an appropriate *customer agreement* before undertaking any investments. They must also have reasonable grounds to believe that the customer has the means to meet any liabilities incurred.

3. *Written customer agreements*. These are required before investments, other than for execution – only customers, are undertaken by all firms except registered life offices and the operators or trustees of regulated collective investment schemes such as authorised unit trusts. Customer agreement forms should take one of three forms:

(a) *terms of business letter*

(b) *full customer agreement*

(c) *occasional customer agreement*.

Each of these types of agreement must contain the following basic information.

(a) Details of the firm's investment business.

(b) The types of investment services offered.

(c) The method and frequency of remuneration of the firm by the customer, and whether commissions received by the firm, e.g. from unit trust management companies, will be passed on to the customer.

(d) A warning that purchases of units in collective investment schemes and single premium life assurance policies cannot be cancelled, except by mutual agreement.

(e) Whether the customer agrees to the firm making unsolicited calls to the customer and the circumstances in which such calls may be made. An occasional customer agreement must state that no unsolicited calls will be made.

4. *Terms of business letter*. This is used by firms for business, professional and experienced investors. It must specify the types of investment for which the customer will be considered to fall into these categories, eg a business customer using currency options and futures may not be considered in this category for other types of investment.

19. Recent developments in investment

5. *Full customer agreement*. This must provide the following details:

(a) The investment objectives of the customer, e.g. income or capital growth.

(b) Any restrictions on investment in particular markets.

(c) A warning of the risks involved where investments are not readily realizable.

(d) The arrangements by which the customer can give instructions and receive advice.

(e) Details concerning the holding of money and investments, and accounting for them to the customer.

(f) In the case of a managed portfolio, its initial composition, and the frequency with which statements of account will be provided.

(g) How the customer can terminate the contract without incurring any penalty charges.

The firm may not deal in futures and options unless specifically permitted by the customer agreement, in which case the following additional points must be covered.

(h) A warning of the risk involved in these investments.

(i) An explanation covering when deposits and extra payments of margin associated with these investments will be required.

(j) Details of the circumstances in which the firm may close out existing contracts without referring to the customer.

Where the investment firm will undertake the discretionary portfolio management of its customer's funds, it must also obtain specific permission to do the following.

(k) Invest the money in funds managed by the firm.

(l) Invest in other investments in which the firm is involved.

(m) Gear up by borrowing.

(n) Gear up by selecting investments where only an initial margin is required.

Investments may only be undertaken for a customer after the customer agreement has been signed and returned to the investment firm.

6. *An occasional customer agreement*. This is required where the investment firm believes the investment relationship to be on a one-off basis. It must provide details of the following.

(a) The advice given by the firm to the customer.

(b) Any instructions given by the customer to the firm.

(c) Any investments in single-premium life policies or units in recognized investment schemes (e.g. unit trusts).

The agreement must be signed by the customer and returned to the firm before any transactions are undertaken.

7. *Polarization*. Another part of consumer protection introduced under the SIB rules is *polarization*. This is the requirement that firms are either totally independent of all life assurance and unit trust companies or else are tied to selling the investment products of one particular company. Until the implementation of the Financial Services Act, there were a number of firms operating in the 'middle ground', giving the impression of independence and yet selling the products of a small number of companies which may have been selected on the basis of the commissions paid, the size of contributions made towards the cost of office overheads, or other incentive payments. If a firm is to be an independent intermediary, it must only recommend a particular investment if it is satisfied that no other life or unit trust company offers a better one. If the firm is not an independent intermediary, it must represent a single life assurance and unit trust group and disclose this to prospective clients and on business letterheads.

The polarization rules presented problems for the major high street banks which owned both independent broking companies and their own life and unit trust companies. The SIB insisted that the branches of banks should act either as part of their independent broking operation or

19. Recent developments in investment

as a representative for their life and unit trust companies and must make it clear to customers which role they have adopted. In the event, the banks, other than the National Westminster Bank, have opted for company representative status. The National Westminster Bank, which did not own a life assurance subsidiary, decided to sell its unit trust subsidiary to MIM Britannia and to act as an independent intermediary. Amongst building societies, the norm is to act as an independent intermediary, but the Abbey National Building Society has opted to act as a representative for Friends Provident's investment products.

Investor Protection

8.   Legal penalties of the Financial Services Act 1986.
Any person convicted of carrying on an investment business in the UK without authorization is guilty of a criminal offence and is liable to imprisonment for up to two years, or a fine, or both. Any investments undertaken by an unauthorized person are unenforceable against the customer. The customer is entitled to recover any money or other property handed over and to compensation for any loss sustained. To induce a customer to undertake an investment by knowingly making a false or misleading statement is also a criminal offence punishable by imprisonment for up to seven years, or a fine, or both.

If investors believe that they have been wrongly advised or the investment transaction has been executed unsatisfactorily, they can complain to the ombudsman of the appropriate SRO who will investigate and has the power to propose compensation. Investors can also seek compensation for damages in the civil courts. In the event of an authorized firm failing, compensation is available from the compensation fund of 100 per cent of the first £30,000 and 90 per cent of the next £20,000.

9.   The Companies Securities (Insider Dealing) Act 1985.
The objective of this act is to maintain the integrity and efficiency of the operation of financial markets by protecting the principles of equal access to price sensitive information for both buyers and sellers. The Act makes it a criminal offence for an individual who has acquired unpublished price sensitive information in confidence within the preceding six months to do the following.

Successful selection of investments

(a) Deal in the securities of that company.

(b) Advise any other person to buy or sell the securities of that company.

(c) Pass on the unpublished price sensitive information to any other person whom he or she knows, or has reasonable cause to believe, will make use of the information.

A *tippee* is a person who obtains confidential information from an individual who has been connected with the company in the past six months. If the tippee knows that the information was in confidence and that it is price sensitive, then the tippee is also prohibited from dealing.

Exemptions from these rules apply to the following.

(a) Individuals who have a duty to deal in the company's shares, eg receivers, liquidators, and trustees in bankruptcy.

(b) Market-makers on the Stock Exchange and dealers in any other recognized stock exchange or recognized investment exchange.

(c) Anyone who acts without the intention of profiting from the inside information, e.g. to raise cash to meet a financial commitment.

A person convicted of an offence under this Act is liable to imprisonment for up to two years and/or a fine for which there is no limit set. The transactions concerned are not voidable.

The Financial Services Act 1986 extended the rules on insider dealing to the officers of the SIB, SROs, and Recognized Investment Exchanges who may have access to price sensitive information while fulfilling their duties. The Act also gave the Secretary of State power to appoint inspectors to investigate suspected insider dealing offences. The inspectors have the power to require any person to produce documents in his or her possession, to give evidence under oath and render all reasonable assistance. They also have power to enter premises to search for evidence. Anyone refusing to co-operate can be held in contempt of court, and in the case of an authorized person, restrictions can be imposed on their ability to continue their authorized business. The Director of Public Prosecutions may bring criminal

19. Recent developments in investment

proceedings under the Companies Securities (Insider Dealing) Act 1985 as a result of the investigation.

10. The Banking Act 1987. The Act provides for the continuation of the Deposit Protection Board which administers the statutory Deposit Protection Fund that was set up by the Banking Act 1979. The Fund is financed from levies from authorized institutions and compensation is payable in the event of the insolvency of an authorized institution of three quarters of a deposit and accrued interest, with a current ceiling on the protected deposit of £20,000.

11. Shareholders' pre-emptive rights. It is a principle embodied in the Companies Acts that existing shareholders have the right to subscribe for any new shares that are issued, unless the shareholders' approval has previously been obtained in a general meeting. These rights are called the shareholders *pre-emptive rights.* If they are not observed and new shares are issued at a discount to the market price, a transfer of value takes place from the existing shareholders to the new investors. It was the occurrence of a number of these non pre-emptive share issues in overseas capital markets (and hence not available to existing shareholders) that caused representatives of industry, institutional investors, and the International Stock Exchange to investigate the situation. In October 1987, they produced the following guidelines for the protection of shareholders' pre-emptive rights.

(a) Listed companies will still be required to obtain annual approval from shareholders for a special resolution to disapply pre-emptive rights. A limit of 5 per cent of issued ordinary share capital shown by the latest published annual accounts will apply. Companies will be expected to apply an additional limit of 7.5 per cent of issued ordinary share capital shown by the latest published annual accounts in any rolling three year period.

(b) The discount at which equity or deferred equity (convertibles and warrants) is offered to investors other than shareholders should not exceed 5 per cent.

(c) Any issues beyond the annual pre-emption approval by the shareholders will always require shareholders prior authority at an EGM.

A *vendor placing* can also dilute the holding of existing shareholders in their company and deny them the opportunity to purchase new shares at a discount. A vendor placing occurs when a company pays for the acquisition of the shares or assets of another company by an issue of its own shares at a discount. The vendor may then place these shares with institutions to obtain cash. The share issuing companies have used this method of raising finance as they have considered it more convenient than conducting a rights issue to their existing shareholders.

Other Developments in Investment

12. Changes in the powers of building societies. The government announced in February 1988 an extension of the powers of building societies after reviewing Schedule 8 of the Building Societies Act 1986. Their main business must remain raising funds from the public for lending on house purchase. (The minimum of retail deposits was lowered from 80 per cent to 60 per cent in November 1987, thereby giving building societies greater access to cheaper wholesale deposits to enable them to compete with banks on more equal terms.) The new changes will affect their lending policies by the following.

(a) Increasing the limit on unsecured lending to an individual from £5,000 to £10,000.

(b) The ceilings on non-traditional lending are to be raised by stages. The maximum permitted unsecured lending is to rise from 5 per cent to 7.5 per cent in January 1990, to 10 per cent in January 1991 and to 15 per cent in January 1993. The maximum permitted second mortgage *and* unsecured lending is to rise from 10 per cent to 17.5 per cent in January 1990, 20 per cent in January 1991 and 25 per cent in January 1993.

The type of financial services provided by building societies is to be further extended by allowing building societies to do the following.

(a) Take a minority equity stake in both life and general insurance companies.

(b) Take a minority equity stake in stockbrokers, but not undertake market making.

19. Recent developments in investment

(c) Undertake fund management of unit trusts as well as pensions.

13. New rules for the prices of unit trusts. In the past, some unit trust fund managers have calculated the prices at which they are prepared to buy and sell units to investors on the previous day so that they can be quoted in the morning paper. Others have calculated each day's dealing prices during the same day and printed the previous day's prices in the morning paper (see 8.24). In the second case, it has meant that any investor wanting to deal before the prices for the day have been calculated had the option of 'dealing blind', ie dealing without knowing the price at which the units would be bought or sold, or waiting until the price had been fixed. It is also a system that is fairer to other unit investors since the dealing price reflects the latest available prices, and in the case of North America and South East Asia, a complete day's extra trading that took place during our night.

In the interests of fairness to existing investors, the Securities and Investment Board, which has taken over from the DTI the responsibility for the authorization and supervision of unit trusts, proposed a new system of *forward pricing* in draft rules released in October 1987. Forward pricing means that the dealing prices are not calculated until the close of business each day, so that investors are forced to deal blind. Unit trust fund managers objected that this would deter investors, but were forced to adopt the system of forward pricing during the October stock market crash as the only way of being able to calculate a price in such volatile markets.

After further consultations, new regulations to be operative from 1 July 1988 were announced in January 1988 and permit managers to use forward pricing or backward pricing. However, if they deal on a *backward pricing* basis, i.e. quoting prices based on the latest valuation, the managers must do the following.

(a) Inform the trustee of the dealing prices at the start of each dealing period.

(b) Deal at these prices unless:

(i) they know or have reason to believe that the value of the fund has moved by 2 per cent or more.

(ii) the transaction is large (i.e. in excess of £15,000).

(iii) the investor requests to deal at a forward price.

Three further changes have been introduced with regard to the pricing of unit trusts.

(a) The rounding adjustment of the lesser of 1.25p or 1 per cent that was formerly added to the offer price of units has been abolished.

(b) The Unit Trust Instrument Duty which was levied at the rate of 0.25 per cent on the asset value of newly created units and included in the offer price calculation was abolished in the 1988 budget.

(c) Unit trust information in the press has had to show since 1 July 1988:

   (i) the offer, bid, and cancellation prices at the most recent valuation available. The *cancellation price* is the minimum bid price which represents the break-up value of the unit trust fund divided by the number of issued units (see 8.3).

   (ii) the initial charge in percentage form at least once a week.

14. New rules for the creation and cancellation of units. A unit trust management company is not only responsible for the investment portfolio of the funds under its control, but also acts as a retailer of its units, buying in from investors who wish to sell and reselling to investors who wish to buy. The management company's float of units available for sale is called its *box* of units. When buyers exceed sellers, the managers buy newly created units from the trustee in exchange for cash, which increases the total size of the trust fund. When sellers exceed buyers, the managers sell units back to the trustees and investments may have to be sold to pay for the cancellation of these units. In the past, some fund management companies have made a useful profit at the expense of their unit holders by buying or cancelling units from the trustee at prices ruling up to a week

19. Recent developments in investment

before. The new rules introduced on 1 July 1988 require managers, within two hours of a valuation, to inform the trustee of the number of units which they wish to create or cancel. This system has increased the risk for managements operating on a backward pricing basis.

15. *The introduction of new types of unit trusts.* The Department of Trade and Industry published in November 1987 proposals for new unit trust rules and types of unit trust to be introduced later in 1988. Four new types of fund are proposed.

(a) Money Funds - will invest in cash or new cash instruments.

(b) Futures, Options and Commodity Funds - there will be a lower limit on the proportion of the fund that must be kept in cash to reduce risk.

(c) Property Funds - will invest directly in property, but at least 20 per cent of the fund must be kept liquid and no single investment may account for more than 15 per cent of the fund at the time acquired.

(d) Mixed Funds - will invest in at least three of the following sectors: equities; government securities; debt instruments; property; options, futures and commodities.

These new funds will be able to use traded options, futures and forward currency transactions to hedge against adverse exchange rate or interest rate movements. They will also be permitted to borrow up to 10 per cent of the fund on a temporary basis, eg to anticipate cash due to the fund but not received from the sale of investments. Fund managers are hoping that these new trust funds will be given a different title than unit trusts, in recognition of the higher level of risk involved.

16. *Property Income Certificates (PINCS).* PINCS are to be another method of investing in property which was to become available to investors during the autumn of 1987, but was postponed due to the uncertain market conditions and the delays encountered in the implementation of the Financial Services Act. A PINC will be a security or unit representing a direct investment in property that can be traded on the Stock Exchange using the SEAQ dealing system and TALISMAN settlement system. PINCS will be sold initially by the owner or developer of a large commercial property to transfer part ownership and entitlement to the income from the property to other investors. A PINC will consist of two inseparable elements.

(a) An Income Certificate entitling the holder to a share of the property's rental income.

(b) An Ordinary Share in the management company responsible for the management of the property and the collection of rents.

The market value of a PINC will reflect the property's investment potential since ownership will provide a proportionate share in all the income and capital growth benefits of ownership of the particular property.

The main advantages of the introduction of PINCS are the provision of the following.

(a) A means for smaller direct investments in commercial property which will permit more investors to participate.

(b) The opportunity for investors to reduce their risk by spreading their investment over a range of properties by investment in a portfolio of PINCS.

(c) Greater liquidity to the commercial property market as it is anticipated that PINCS will be bought and sold on the Stock Exchange in the same manner as other securities.

(d) A means for the market valuation of property investment reducing reliance upon subjective professional valuations.

(e) An extra source of long term finance for large development projects once they have been completed.

17. Gilt-edged stock auctions. The two traditional ways of issuing new gilt-edged stocks are the *minimum price tender* method and the *tap stock* method. In the case of the tender, the Bank of England sets a minimum price at or near the market price on the Friday before the Wednesday tender. All those allocated stock pay the same price, either the minimum price or the price at which the quantity of bids is sufficient to cover the issue. Any unsold stock is taken up by the Bank, who thereafter will deal only with gilt-edged market makers (GEMMs). When it believes the market would not absorb a new issue, the Bank will issue a tap stock consisting of *tranchettes* of existing stocks. The Bank sells these to the GEMMs.

19. Recent developments in investment

The auction method of issuing gilts was first tried in May 1987. The initial experiment was three auctions in May and September 1987 and January 1988, at which £2.8 billion was raised compared with more than £10 billion during the same period through tap issues and minimum price tenders. In an auction the Bank sets no minimum price, and apart from exceptional circumstances, all the stock are allocated. The price paid by those allocated stock is the price bid by the investor. This causes the range of bids to be much narrower than in a tender offering. All the GEMMs are expected to participate in the auction on their own account as well as on behalf of clients. The minimum application is for £1,000 of stock. Most bids are submitted to the Bank of England via a GEMM rather than directly to the Bank of England by hand, since GEMMs are allowed to make up to three telephone bids in the last 15 minutes before the auction. This means that fixing the bid can be delayed to take account of last minute news that may influence prices in the 'after market'. There is a facility to make a *non-competitive bid* for up to £100,000 of stock which will be allocated in full and involves payment of the average accepted price. To protect themselves against adverse price movements, GEMMs try to have purchasers for new stock lined up in advance to avoid having to take all their allocation on to their own books. There is also a *when issued* market in advance of the auction which provides the opportunity to buy or sell stock in advance.

The gilt-edged auction has shown itself to be a workable alternative method of issuing new stocks but, given the small amount of new stock that needs to be sold, is unlikely to be used very frequently.

18. The FT-Actuaries World Indices. The *Financial Times* has added a world stock market index and a set of 24 country and 10 regional indices to those it already publishes. These are compiled by the *Financial Times*, Goldman Sachs and Wood Mackenzie, in conjunction with the Institute of Actuaries and the Faculty of Actuaries. The indices are calculated after the close of business in New York for publication the following day in the *Financial Times*. All the index values are shown as of the close of the prior business day, except for Mexico which is subject to a time lag of one day. There are three indices for each national and regional market measured in terms of the US dollar, the pound sterling, and the local currency. Each index has a base value of 100 on 31 December 1986.

314 Successful selection of investments

Further information is provided on the dollar index: the day's percentage change, the gross dividend yield, the high and low values of the index for the year, and its value a year ago. The indices are calculated to give weighted arithmetic average values for at least 70 per cent of the aggregate market value of all the shares listed on each stock exchange.

19. Stamp Duty Reserve Tax. On 27 October 1986, the date of Big Bang and when stamp duty on share purchases was reduced from 1 per cent to 0.5 per cent, a new Stamp Duty Reserve Tax of 0.5 per cent was introduced to apply to the following.

(a) Shares which are bought and sold before they are legally transferred to the new investor, eg investors buying and selling in the same Stock Exchange Account.

(b) The purchase of renounceable documents. Renounceable share certificates are issued to existing shareholders when a company makes a capitalization issue. The shareholder can either keep or sell or give away part or all of the allocation of new shares. The renounceable certificate is similar to an allotment letter in that it has a form of renunciation printed on the back that has to be completed and returned to the Registrar if there is to be a change of ownership. If the shareholder wishes to keep the new shares, no action needs to be taken, and after a period the Certificate will cease to be renounceable and will become the document of title.

(c) Shares which are registered in the name of a nominee who acts for both the purchaser and the seller, e.g. shares purchased by a US bank in order to issue American Depository Receipts (ADRs). The rate of Stamp Duty Reserve Tax levied on these purchases is 1.5 per cent.

Appendix 1
The 1988 budget

1. Income tax.

(a) Tax rates for 1988/89.

Band of taxable income	Marginal tax rate	Cumulative income tax at upper limit
£	%	£
0-19,300	25	4,825
Over 19,300	40	-

(b) Tax rates for 1987/88.

Band of taxable income	Income in band	Marginal tax rate	Cumulative income tax at upper limit
£	£	%	£
0-17,900	17,900	27	4,833
17,901-20,400	2,500	40	5,833
20,401-25,400	5,000	45	8,083
25,401-33,300	7,900	50	12,033
33,301-41,200	7,900	55	16,378
Over 41,200	-	60	-

(c) Personal allowances.

	1988/89	1987/88
Single person's allowance	2,605	2,425
Wife's earned income allowance	2,605	2,425
Married man's allowance	4,095	3,795
Additional personal allowance and widow's bereavement allowance	1,490	1,370
Single age allowance (age 65-79)	3,180	2,960
Married age allowance (age 65-79)	5,035	4,675
Single age allowance (age 80 and over)	3,310	3,070
Married age allowance (age 80 and over)	5,205	4,845
Age allowance income limit	10,600	9,800

(d) Notes.

(i) For taxable income above £10,600, the age allowance is reduced by £2 for every £3 of extra income until it is reduced to the level of the appropriate ordinary personal allowance.

(ii) Wife's earnings election. It will only be worthwhile electing for separate taxation if the couple's continued income before deduction of allowances and reliefs in 1988/89 is at least £28,484 including wife's earned income of at least £6,579.

(iii) Separate taxation of husband and wife will apply from 6 April 1990.

(iv) The composite rate of tax was reduced in April 1988 from 24.75 per cent to 23.25 per cent.

(v) Mortgage interest relief. The tax relief available on the interest on mortgages up to £30,000 for the purchase of a property used as the borrower's only or main residence was changed for purchases after 1 August 1988. Tax relief ceased to apply to each borrower and now applies to the residence irrespective of the number of persons borrowing to purchase it. Tax relief on the interest on loans for home improvements was abolished on new loans with effect from 6 April 1988.

2. Capital gains tax.

(a) The 30 per cent rate of capital gains tax was abolished. Taxable capital gains (i.e. gains after the application of allowances) will be treated in the same way as additional income and taxed at the investor's marginal rate of income tax. However, the rate of capital gains tax is 25 per cent for investors with a nil marginal rate of income tax. In the case of a husband and wife living together, the gain is treated as investment income and until 6 April 1990 will be assessed as part of the husband's income. If taxable gains cause taxable income to exceed £19,300, the excess will be taxed at the higher rate of 40 per cent.

Example: Taxable income = £15,000
Taxable capital gains = £5,000
Capital gains tax payable at the standard rate = (£19,300-£15,000) x 25% = £1,075
Capital gains tax payable at the higher rate = (£20,000-£19,300) x 40% = £280
Total CGT payable = £1,355

(b) The annual exemption allowance is reduced from £6,600 to £5,000 for 1988/89.

Appendix 1

(c) The base date from which capital gains are taxable is changed from 6 April 1965 to 31 March 1982, the same date as used for the indexation calculation. This means that any gains on investments made before 31 March 1982 are exempt until this date, and gains that have been made since are only taxable after the application of the indexation allowance and the annual exemption limit (see 2:8).

Example: an investment made in 1960 for £10,000 increased in value to £20,000 on the 31 March 1982 and was sold for £40,000 in January 1988.

(i) Calculation of inflation adjusted base date value:

Inflation adjusted base date value =

Market price at 31 March 1982 x $\frac{\text{RPI for month of sale}}{\text{RPI for March 1982}}$

£20,000 x $\frac{407.5}{313.4}$ = £26,005

(ii) Taxable gain = sale value − inflation adjusted base date value

= £40,000 − £26,005 = £13,995

Less annual exemption allowance = £13,995 − £5,000
= £8,995

(iii) Tax payable is calculated by treating the £8,995 as additional taxable income (with a minimum rate of 25 per cent).

NOTE: for investments purchased before 31 March 1982, there are additional rules that apply where the new regulations would increase the amount of the taxable gain or allowable loss.

(i) If the value of the investment at 31 March 1982 was below its purchase price so that the new rules would increase the taxable gain, the old rules may be applied, i.e. the indexation allowance may continue to be calculated on the investment's initial cost rather than its 31 March 1982 value.

Example: an investment made for £20,000 in 1960 decreased in value to £10,000 on 31 March 1982 and was sold for £40,000 in January 1988.

(i) Calculation of indexation allowance:

Indexation allowance =

Purchase price $\times \dfrac{\text{RPI for month of sale}}{\text{RPI for 31 March 1982}}$ − Purchase price

$= £20,000 \times \dfrac{407.5}{313.4} - £20,000 = £6,005$

Taxable gain = £40,000 − (£20,000 + £6,005) = £13,995

(ii) Where the capital loss is greater when calculated using the new rules rather than the old, the old shall apply, i.e. the allowable loss is based upon purchase price, not 31 March 1982 value.

(iii) Where an investment's value increased up to 31 March 1982 but since that date has recorded a loss, the asset will be neither liable to tax not eligible as an allowable loss.

(d) The rate of capital gains tax chargeable to companies remains at their corporation tax rate. The special 30 per cent rate for gains made for policyholders by life assurance companies investments is unchanged.

3. Inheritance tax. The threshold above which inheritance tax becomes payable was raised from £90,000 to £110,000. The four rates of tax ranging from 30 to 60 per cent were replaced by a single rate of 40 per cent.

4. The Personal Equity Plan (PEP). The annual limit was raised from £2,400 to £3,000 and applies to all plans taken out in 1988 (see **8:25-27**). The limit for investment in unit trust or investment trust shares has been raised to the greater of £150 or 25 per cent of the total investment (which gives a maximum of £750).

5. The Business Expansion Scheme (BES). A limit of £0.5m was imposed on the amount that any company can raise under the scheme in any one year. Exceptions were made in the cases of businesses concerned with ship chartering and the letting of residential property on the new assured tenancy terms, where the ceiling is £5m in any one year. The normal BES restriction on the proportion of a firm's assets that may be comprised of land and buildings will not apply to companies providing private rented housing (see **4:23**).

6. Other changes from the 1987 budget.

(a) Taxation of conventional options: any gains or losses from conventional options are now treated in the same way as

Appendix 1

for traded options and are subject to the capital gains tax rules, not those of income tax (see 7:12 for the earlier position).

(b) Investment in friendly societies: the limit on eligible friendly society policies was raised from a £750 sum assured to an annual premium of £100. This means that an annual premium of £100 could provide a man aged 30 years with life assurance of £4,500 over a 35 year term.

SOME IMPLICATIONS OF THE 1988 BUDGET FOR INVESTMENT

7. The higher rate taxpayer. The biggest gainers are investors whose marginal rate of tax formerly exceeded the current top rate of 40 per cent. Since their net yields are higher, this has made income from investments marginally more attractive, a trend reinforced by an effective increase in the capital gains tax rate from 30 to 40 per cent. The following points should therefore be considered.

(a) National Savings Certificates and the Yearly Plan, which credit interests free of tax, have lost some of their relative attraction compared to building society and higher rate bank deposits.

(b) Equity unit trusts and investment trusts that combine income and capital growth objectives have become more attractive.

(c) Gilts and UK corporate bonds acquired after 13 March 1984 which are exempt from CGT have become more attractive.

(d) PEP's are relatively more attractive as a shelter for capital gains.

(e) Life assurance linked investments are less attractive as a means of rolling up income to avoid payment of higher rate income tax. However, the 30 per cent capital gains tax on life assurance funds is now lower than the 40 per cent payable by the higher rate taxpayer.

(f) Offshore umbrella funds which permit investors to switch between funds without liability for capital gains tax have increased their tax advantage over authorized unit trusts where gains are taxable when a switch is made between funds.

8. The standard rate taxpayer. The tax rates on capital gains and income are now equal at 25 per cent, but the reduction was greater for capital gains. The following points should be considered.

(a) Investment for capital growth still benefits from the indexation allowance and the £5,000 annual exemption. This means that many standard rate taxpayers can avoid any liability for capital gains tax.

(b) Capital gains in excess of the allowances may cause

the marginal rate of tax to rise to 40 per cent. Investments that are exempt from CGT may therefore be important to such investors.

(c) Life assurance linked investments continue to be liable for a higher rate of capital gains tax at 30 per cent than the 25 per cent now payable by the investor on alternative investments.

Appendix 2
Passing examinations on investment

If you are preparing for an examination on investment, probably the most important ingredient of success in your course is the degree to which you become personally involved in the subject of investment. If you learn and practise everything asked of you in this book, you should pass the examination; but investment can be so much more interesting and exciting than a mere syllabus for an examination that has to be passed. It is an absorbing, rapidly changing subject that can become a lifelong interest and provide you with enormous pleasure, and profit! If you have not already found this for yourself, I have tried to offer you a gateway to this world through this book. Your success in your examination and in the future therefore depends upon:

(a) Studying each chapter and, where appropriate, using the progress test at the end to ensure that you have understood its main points.
(b) Where the chapter asks you to find the latest figures in the newspaper, undertaking the task and repeating the calculations. You will learn best by doing!
(c) Becoming familiar with the layout and information provided in the financial press, particularly in the Financial Times. Where the chapter tells you to look for particular information, use this as an opportunity to familiarize yourself with that part of the newspaper.
(d) Studying the syllabus carefully in the Chartered Institute of Bankers' Regulations, Syllabus and Tuition Guide. Tick off the topics as you study them.
(e) Preparing answers to past examination questions. You will find a selection at the end of this text. Refer to the magazine Banking World for a discussion of past examination questions and up-to-date information on items appearing in the syllabus.

When the time comes for the examination itself, you should prepare for it by making a careful study of the table of available interest rates in the Investors Chronicle or Saturday edition of the Financial Times (see Chapter 3). Revise carefully all the types of investment appropriate for investors in different income tax bands (see Chapter 12).
The May 1988 examination was the first in a new format.

(a) Section A consists of up to 20 short answer or multiple choice questions. All are to be attempted by the candidate and the questions may range over the whole

322 **Appendix 2**

syllabus. The section carries 20 marks.

(b) Section B consists of four questions, of which the candidate must attempt two. These are essay type or extended questions and again may be taken from any area of the syllabus. This section carries 40 marks.

(c) Section C covers investment advice and consists of four questions of which the candidate must attempt two. One of these four questions deals with the practical aspects of investment by trusts and charities.

You should bear in mind the following additional points when preparing for and sitting the examination.

(a) Candidates will be required to obtain pass marks both for the overall paper and for Section C.

(b) The tax rates and allowances that candidates are expected to use will be provided at the front of the examination paper.

(c) You should divide your time between questions in proportion to the marks allocated. Thus you should not spend more than 36 minutes on any question giving 20 marks. It also means that five marks is worth up to nine minutes of your time.

(d) Never start answering a question until you have identified all the relevant points. Arrange them in a logical sequence and decide on the amount of time you think you should devote to each.

(e) Always think carefully about which points are <u>really relevant to the actual question asked</u>. Too often students either write down all they know about a topic, or answer the question that they wish the examiner had set.

(f) Now you can start writing. You should write concisely; you may write in report format and use the listing 'technique', i.e. give headings and number the points you make. The examiners will appreciate a well laid out, easy to read answer (do not, however, write in note format, i.e. abbreviated words, incomplete sentences, etc.).

(g) While answering a question, watch your timing. You should check after approximately 20 minutes that you are more than halfway through your answer. If not, you must consider how you can answer the rest of the question more concisely to avoid over-running the time available for that question.

Appendix 3
Examination questions

The following questions on investment were taken from the Banking Diploma examinations and have been reproduced from Examiners' Reports which are published annually by the Chartered Institute of Bankers.

Chapter 2 The investor's needs

1. What tax advantages and/or disadvantages do the following types of investment have for a private investor? Comment as appropriate on the income tax and capital gains tax aspects.

   (a) A single-premium managed bond. (8)
   (b) A National Savings Bank ordinary account. (4)
   (c) A building society share account. (4)
   (d) A low-coupon dated British government stock. (4)
   (Total marks for question – 20)
   September 1985

Chapter 3 Investment in cash assets

1. The Finance Act 1984 contains provisions which will require a composite rate of tax to be paid to the Inland Revenue in respect of bank interest paid on and from 6 April 1985 to individuals resident in the UK.

   (a) What is meant by 'composite rate?' (5)
   (b) Describe the effects of the introduction of composite rate tax on the following investments: interest-bearing personal accounts with clearing banks; the National Savings Bank; building societies; pension funds. How will this new legislation affect the competitiveness of the interest-bearing accounts? (15)
   (Total marks for question – 20)
   April 1985

Chapter 4 Investment in shares

1. Takeover bids are an almost daily feature in the activities of the Stock Exchange in London. Spectacular battles, involving vast sums of money, often result.

Required:
(a) What measures are available for the protection of the UK investor who has shares in a company involved in a takeover bid? What penalties can be imposed on companies involved in takeover situations? (10)
(b) Outline the main items which should be contained in the offer document. (10)

(Total marks for question - 20)
April 1986

2. The revolution in the Stock Exchange in London, sometimes known as the 'Big Bang', has been discussed at length in the financial press. Describe the main changes proposed to the rules and regulations and outline how these changes are likely to affect the operations of the Stock Exchange in London. (20)

April 1986

3. Write notes on <u>three</u> of the following:
(a) a placing;
(b) an introduction;
(c) a rights issue;
(d) a bonus issue. (20)

September 1985

4. Since November 1980 companies seeking a quotation have had a choice of two main markets in the UK: either the traditional 'full' listing in the Stock Exchange Daily Official List or in the Unlisted Securities Market (USM) which is also operated by the Stock Exchange.

(a) What is an unlisted security? (13)
(b) Compare the costs of obtaining a quotation in the USM with those of obtaining one of the Official List. (7)

(Total marks for question - 20)
April 1985

5. Describe the main features of the <u>Financial Times</u> Industrial Ordinary Share Index, the <u>Financial Times</u> - Actuaries Indices, and the <u>Financial Times</u> - Stock Exchange 100 Index. How may these indices be of use to the investor? (20)

September 1984

Chapter 5 The selection of shares

1. The capital structure of Herbert Clay plc, a long-established brick-making company, is as follows:

    £375,000 $7^1/_2$% debenture stock 1988/91
    £530,000 $5^1/_4$% (net) cumulative preference £1 shares
  £1,200,000   Ordinary stock units of 50p each

Appendix 3 325

The profit after debenture stock interest and corporation tax for the year ended 31 December 1984 was £225,937. A dividend of 9.8 pence per ordinary stock unit has been paid.

<u>Required</u>:
Calculate the income priority percentages showing the cost of interest or dividend, the capital priority percentage and the overall cover for each class of stock or shares. (20)
NOTE: Base your calculations on corporation tax rate of 50 per cent and basic rate tax of 30 per cent.

September 1985

2. (a) Describe briefly the use of 'filter' rules with reference to the 'Hatch' system. (6)
(b) Distinguish between line charts, bar charts and point-and-figure charts. (6)
(c) Describe the following chart patterns commonly identified by technical analysts and say how they are usually interpreted:
  (i) line;
  (ii) head and shoulders. (8)

(Total marks for question - 20)
April 1983

3. In assessing the ordinary shares of a quoted public company, what importance would you attach to the following factors:
(a) earnings;
(b) net asset value;
(c) management? (20)

April 1983

Chapter 6 Investment in gilt-edged and fixed-interest securities

1. A customer has received notification of impending conversion dates in respect of two convertible unsecured loan stocks:

(a) ABC plc 12 per cent convertible unsecured loan stock 1995 is convertible into 25 pence ordinary shares on 25 May each year from 1983 to 1993 inclusive at the rate of 30 shares for every £100 stock. The market price of the ordinary shares is 280 pence. The market price of the convertible stock is £105. Net dividends per ordinary share in respect of the year ended 31 March 1983 totalled 9.8 pence.
(b) XYZ plc 5 per cent convertible unsecured loan stock 1990 is convertible into 25 pence ordinary shares on 28 May

each year from 1974 to 1983 inclusive at the rate of 38 shares for every £100 stock. The market price of the ordinary shares is 370 pence. The market price of the convertible stock is £142. Net dividends per ordinary share in respect of the year ended 31 March 1983 totalled 7.77 pence.

(a) Calculate the conversion premium (or discount) in each case. (3)
(b) What action would you advise your customer to take? Give your reasons for your advice and show any relevant calculations. (12)
(c) What are the advantages of convertible unsecured loan stocks from the point of view of the issuing company? (5)
(Total marks for question – 20)

April 1983

2. The following information relates to six British government stocks on a particular day in September 1983:

Stock	Price (£)	Accrued interest (£)	Yield Interest (%)	Yield Redemption (%)
10 1/2% Exchequer convertible stock 19 May 1986(1999)	99 1/2	4.242	10.553	10.695
2 1/2% Exchequer stock 24 February 1987	81 9/16	0.185	3.065	8.841
8 1/4% Treasury loan 15 June 1987/90	90 1/4	2.192	9.369	10.771
14% Treasury stock 22 January 1996	118 1/2	2.301	12.048	11.490
3 1/2% War loan 1 June, 1 December	36	1.064	10.018	
2% Index linked Treasury stock 30 March 1988	103 1/4 clean	-0.60	2.125	2.909 [*] 3.278 [+]

[*] Assumed rate of inflation 10 per cent
[+] Assumed rate of inflation 7 per cent

Outline the main features which are common to all six stocks and describe the special characteristics of each stock, indicating how it would meet the needs of particular types of investor. (20)

May 1984

Chapter 7 Warrants, traded options and futures

1. Write short notes on <u>four</u> of the following:

(a) Warrants. (5)
(b) Traded options. (5)
(c) Gearing. (5)
(d) Guaranteed income bonds. (5)
(e) Reverse yield gap. (5)
(f) Current cost accounting. (5)

(Total marks for question - 20)
April 1986

Chapter 8 Investment in unit trusts

1. The competing attractions of authorized unit trusts and single premium investment bonds have long been debated by financial writers and planners.

(a) Describe the similarities between these two types of investment. (6)
(b) Describe the taxation differences. How do these affect the individual investor? (8)
(c) What other differences are there between the two types of investment? (6)

(Total marks for question - 20)
September 1986

Chapter 9 Investment in investment trusts

1. (a) In what ways are unit trusts and investment trusts similar? (6)
(b) Discuss the various differences between unit trusts and investment trusts which make unit trusts the more popular with the small investor. (14)

(Total marks for question - 20)
September 1987

Chapter 10 Life assurance linked investments

1. In assessing the merits of a life assurance policy it is helpful to disentangle three of the main features - life cover, investment, taxation. Discuss the relative importance of these factors for the following major types of policy:

(a) a managed bond;
(b) a mortgage protection policy;
(c) a regular premium with profits endowment policy;
(d) a guaranteed income bond. (15)

May 1984

Chapter 11 Other investments

1. What are the advantages and disadvantages for the

private investor of the purchase of:

(a) residential freehold property for owner occupation. (10)
(b) freehold shop property to provide a regular income. (10)

Total marks for question - 20)
April 1987

Chapter 12 Portfolio planning

1. Your customer, Mr Dogood, a widower aged 53 years with no children, informs you that he has decided to go to Africa for the next twelve years to help a well-known charitable organization. He has retired early from the company where he has been employed for twenty years. He will receive a deferred pension at the age of 65 and this pension together with his state pension, he feels, will enable him to live comfortably in due course. Meanwhile his house is up for sale and he will receive £100,000 for it after clearance of the mortgage and payment of all costs. He will need a spending income of £7,000 a year for the next twelve years. He will receive no payment from the charitable body for his work.
He requires your advice. He wishes to keep the real value of his capital as intact as possible, in order to purchase a house in which to live in retirement when he returns to the UK at the end of twelve years. However, he recognizes that it may not be possible for him to purchase a house of the same standard as the one he is selling.
Required:
(a) How should his funds be managed to achieve his aims and what investment policy should be followed? Give reasons for the course of action you propose and point out the advantages and the risks involved. (25)
(b) Prepare a portfolio showing types of investment and how this required level of spending income can be achieved. (15)

(Total marks for question - 40)
April 1986

2. Your customer, Mr Price, supplies you with details of investments which he has recently inherited from his late mother. These are as follows:

		Price	Net dividend per share
£5,000	Transport 3% 1978/88	£ $81^{5}/_{8}$	
£3,600	Exchequer 11% 1989	£ $96^{15}/_{16}$	
£2,450	Exchequer $10^{1}/_{4}$% 1995	£ $92^{5}/_{8}$	

Appendix 3

500	Allied Lyons ordinary	173p	6.81p
700	Imperial Chemical		
	Industries ordinary	852p	24.00p
1,500	Racal Electronics ordinary	196p	2.89p
945	Sainsbury ordinary	306p	3.75p

Required:

(a) From the information given, calculate the values, gross yields and, additionally, in the case of gilt-edged securities, the approximate gross yields to redemption. (18)

(b) Your records show that Mr Price is aged 40 with a wife and two young children. He is a house owner with a property worth £70,000 on which he has a mortgage of £35,000 with your bank. He currently pays income tax at basic rate but has been promised promotion in six months' time, which will make him liable to income tax at 45 pence in the pound after income from the inherited investments has been taken into account. After promotion, he calculates he will have adequate spending income without resort to his investment income. Advise Mr Price whether:

(i) He should retain the inherited investments. Give reasons and suggestions for any alternative forms of investment.
NOTE: Candidates are not expected to comment on individual companies. (18)

(ii) He should take any steps to reduce his mortgage. (4)

(Total marks for question - 40)
September 1985

3. You have been consulted by four customers (briefly described below) about their investment problems.

(a) Customer A is a young man aged 20. He is unmarried and lives with his parents. He earns £6,500 gross per annum and plans to save £50 monthly. He has no assets at present and wishes to build up reserve for the future, although he has no specific plans. (10)

(b) Customer B is a married man aged 35. His salary is £14,000 per annum. His wife earns £7,000 per annum. They have two children aged 2 and 4. They have just returned to the UK after working overseas for four years. They own their house which is woth £40,000 subject to a £25,000 mortgage. They have £25,000 cash which they wish to invest on a longer-term basis, and they also plan to save about £150 per month. (10)

(c) Customer C and his wife are both aged 60. Mrs C receives a retirement pension of £1,771. Mr C has just retired and will receive a pension of £8,000 per annum, together with a lump sum of £14,000. In addition, he has bank and building society accounts amounting to £11,000. His house is paid for and the children are independent. He estimates that he and his wife will need a net income of approximately £170 per week. (10)

(d) Customer D is a widower aged 80. He lives in a council flat. His only income is a state pension of £34.30 a week. He has no investments, but has just inherited £10,000 which he wishes to invest for maximum income.

Required:
Draft a note for the file setting out the investment portfolio structure which you consider appropriate in each case, detailing suitable types of investment, and giving your reasons. (10)

(Total marks for question - 40)
September 1984

4. (a) Mr Y is taking early retirement at the age of 58. He and his wife, who is aged 56, are both in good health. They have two sons, both of whom are married and have good jobs. Mr and Mrs Y jointly have National Savings Certificates worth £3,000 and £5,000 in a building society. Mr Y will receive a pension from his former employers of £6,000 per annum, together with a lump sum of £15,000. They expect to be able to manage on the pension, but are rather worried about future inflation. Mr Y raises the following questions with you:

(i) He has an outstanding mortgage on his house of £1,000 and is wondering whether to pay it off. What points would you make for and against this course of action? (7)

(ii) He asks whether it would be wise to purchase an annuity with part of his lump sum. Outline the characteristics of this type of investment and your reply to Mr Y's question. (7)

(iii) He mentions index-linked investments and asks whether any of these are available. Outline your reply, giving a brief description of the available investments of this type, and say whether you consider them suitable for Mr Y. (7)

(iv) What other types of investment would you consider appropriate for Mr Y's requirements? Give reasons, and set out a brief investment scheme for the sum of £15,000 showing the approximate amount of gross annual income expected. (9)

(b) One of your customers, a young man aged 24, has received £50,000 as compensation for an industrial injury.

He is still working, but is concerned that a future deterioration in his physical condition might affect his earnings adversely. He is quite unaccustomed to dealing with amounts of this size and asks for your advice about investment. Outline the reply you would give him. (10)

(Total marks for question - 40)

May 1984

Appendix 4
Useful addresses

The Unit Trust Association. Park House, 16 Finsbury Circus, London EC2M 7JP; 01-638-3071
A free booklet <u>Explaining Unit Trusts</u> is available on request.

The Association of Investment Trust Companies. Park House, 16 Finsbury Circus, London EC2M 7JJ; 01-588-5347
A free booklet <u>Explaining Investment Trusts</u> is available on request. <u>How to make IT. The 1987-88 Guide to Investment Trusts</u> is available by post, £5.95.

The Options Development Group. The Stock Exchange, London EC2N 1HP; 01-588-2355 ext. 28727
A series of excellent booklets is available free on request. Their titles are <u>Introduction to Trade Options, Traded Puts, FT-SE 100 Index Options, Options in Gilts</u> and <u>Currency Options</u>.

The London International Financial Futures Exchange Ltd, Royal Exchange, London EC3V 3PJ; 01-623-0444
A free introductory leaflet is available on request.

The Securities and Investment Board (SIB). 3 Royal Exchange Buildings, Cornhill, London EC3V 3NL; 01-283-2474
A booklet <u>Financial Services - A Guide to the new Regulatory System</u> is available.

Financial Intermediaries, Managers and Brokers Regulatory Association (FIMBRA). 22 Great Tower Street, London EC3R 5AQ; 01-929-2711
A booklet is available on <u>Its future role in the regulation of investments</u>.

Appendix 5
The investment advice question

1. Introduction. Candidates must score pass marks for both Section C of the examination paper and the whole paper to pass the subject. As the Section C investment advice question gives the most trouble to candidates, a 'model answer' to a recent question is presented below. Candidates should note the following points when preparing for the examination.

(a) The tax rates and personal allowances will be provided on the examination paper. However, you are required to know the latest yields available from National Savings investments, and the approximate yields currently available on building society and bank deposits. UK equities, preference shares and loanstocks, gilt-edged stocks, and overseas equities. On the last Saturday before the examination, you should familiarize yourself with current yields by studying the table printed in the quality press (see 3:3). The average yield on equities can be obtained by referring to the gross dividend yield of the FT-Actuaries All Share Index (see Fig. 4.2). Candidates are not required to recommend or quote the returns of specific shares, but they should know what types of shares give higher or lower yields, and why. The yields available on gilts, company debentures and loanstocks, and preference shares can be found in the <u>Financial Times</u> in the table printed immediately below the FT-Actuaries Indices. The yield available from international equities can be found from the yields given in the <u>Financial Times</u> for international unit trust funds.

(b) While investment advice questions may require candidates to provide an investment portfolio, they should bear in mind that in this type of question there is no one right answer. For example, the examiner is not looking for 'correct' percentages of a portfolio to be distributed between cash investments, fixed interest securities, and shares. What the examiner seeks in the answer are the following.

(i) Logical analysis of the question, making use of the information provided.

(ii) Sensible, practical advice on the types of investment that would be suitable.

334 Appendix 5

(iii) A reasoned explanation as to why these particular investments have been selected and of the proportion that each investment contributes to the total portfolio.

(iv) Accuracy in the yields that different investments provide and in the calculation of the income and tax payable by the investor.

(v) A clearly presented answer. The investments selected should be presented in a tabular form showing the expected yield and income or whatever is required by the question. Beneath this table, a precise explanation should be given for each investment selected. Tax calculations should also be set out clearly in tabular form. To make explanations clear, avoid over-long sentences and paragraphs.

At the time of writing, the May 1988 examination paper is not available and so an investment advice question from the autumn 1987 examination will be discussed. Although this question is twice as long as the new Section C questions since it is for 40 marks, it can been seen that parts (c)(i) and (c)(ii) of the question could easily have been used for a new 20 mark Section C question.

2. The question from the examination paper.

Mrs Y, a widow aged 42 with two children aged 11 and 14, has recently inherited the following securities, following the death of her father:

		Price	Value £	Gross Yield %
£48,000	Treasury 8% 2009	84½	40,560	9.47 (flat) 9.80 (redemption)
£2,000	McCarthy and Stone 7% Convertible Loan 99/04	141	2,820	4.96 (flat)
6,000	Marks and Spencer Ord. 25p	196	11,760	2.81
3,000	Barclays Bank Ord. £1	516	15,048	4.93
3,000	Lloyds Bank Ord. £1	497	14,910	5.06
5,000	Green Circle Ord. 50p	323*	16,150	9.73
2,000	M & G High Income Unit Trust	698.7	13,974	3.88

Appendix 5

	Price	Value £	Interest Rates (net) %
Halifax Building Society:			
£3,000 Deposit Account	-	3,000	5.00
£12,000 Share Account	-	12,000	5.25
£2,000 'Extra Interest' Account	-	2,000	6.75

* Private company - Inland Revenue valuation for Inheritance Tax purposes.

Mrs Y earns £15,000 p.a. as a civil servant and also receives pensions (including the state widowed mother's allowance) amounting to £10,000. Her house was paid for by the proceeds of an endowment policy on her late husband's life. Her own savings (some £3,500) are invested with another building society. She also has substantial life assurance to cover her children's maintenance and education in the event of her own death.

(a) She poses two specific questions about the investments:

(i) 'My father used to work for Green Circle Ltd. The shares cost him nothing since he received them under a profit-sharing scheme, so I think I should keep them. Do you agree?'

(ii) 'Please explain the reasons for different interest rates paid by the building society.'

How would you reply to each of these questions? (6)

(b) Comment on the safety of the convertible loan stock on the basis of the data provided. What further information would you require to enable you to comment more fully on this investment? (8)

(c) She then asks you for investment advice.

(i) What criticisms would you make of the structure of the inherited portfolio? (8)

(ii) Suggest a portfolio <u>structure</u> which you consider would meet her needs better. (Limit your choice of investments to the <u>types</u> of investment in the existing portfolio but do not mention any specific securities by name.) (8)

(iii) Tell her briefly about the principal investment products and services offered by or through the UK high street banks to personal investors. (10)

(Total marks for question - 40)

3. A Model Answer. In this answer, the tax rates, personal allowances and other announcements in the 1988 budget that will affect investments will be used.

Section (a)(i)

Since Green Circle is a private company, its shares may be difficult to sell as they may not be sold on the Stock Exchange to other investors. There may be some restrictions on the transfer of shares specified in the Articles of Association of the company. Since there is no market price for the shares, a price will have to be negotiated with a prospective purchaser.

The fact that the shares were free to Mrs Y's father is irrelevant now to her investment planning. Past expenditures are what accountants call <u>sunk costs</u>. What is important is how the shares are likely to perform in the future compared with any alternative investment - the <u>opportunity cost</u> of continuing to hold the shares. Assuming that Mrs Y does not wish to hold these shares for purely sentimental reasons, the relevant points that should be considered when deciding whether to sell them are:

(a) Whether the shares can be sold and at what price.
(b) The yield obtainable if the shares are retained. If their market value is close to their Inland Revenue valuation, the shares are giving a very high yield - comparable to the gilts in the portfolio. Does this high yield mean that the investment is very risky, or that the company has no growth potential, or that the shares are difficult to sell? One would certainly expect the first and third of these explanations to apply to small private companies.
(c) What are the future growth prospects for the company and its share price?
(d) How do the income and growth prospects of the shares compare with alternative investments?
(e) What proportion are the shares of the total portfolio? The market value of the portfolio is £132,222, so the Green Circle investment constitutes 12.2 per cent, which is a fairly large percentage and probably more than would normally be prudent for this type of investment.

Section (a)(ii)

There are three building society accounts shown.

(a) The Deposit Account. This is the lowest risk account offered by a building society and hence earns the lowest rate of interest. Deposits in this type of account are viewed as creditors rather than shareholder investments in the event of the liquidation of the building society.
(b) The Share Account. This is the ordinary share account and since the investor is a shareholder, the account bears

a marginally greater risk which explains the extra 0.25 per cent interest shown. In the event of the failure of a building society, the Building Societies Investors Protection Fund, established by the Building Societies Act 1986, will refund the lower of 90 per cent of the amount deposited or £10,000. This account offers the second lowest interest rate as it provides investors with the convenience of immediate access to their money and a minimum deposit of only £1.

(c) The 'Extra Interest' Account. This is also a share account, but earns a higher rate of interest because it will require a minimum investment and probably a minimum period of notice of withdrawal.

Section (b)

The convertible loan stock is at a premium of 41 per cent compared to its redemption value if it is not converted. Furthermore, since its coupon is only 7 per cent, if it were valued as a straight loanstock, its value would be well below par. (The Treasury 8 per cent 2009 is valued at £84 and this has a higher coupon and much lower risk). The high premium of the convertible over its loanstock value suggests that investors regard it as a higher yielding method of investing in the shares, and that the price of the convertible will fluctuate more or less in line with the ordinary share price.

Factors that reduce the risk of this investment are:

(a) There are still many years left in which conversion can take place.
(b) The income from the convertible is almost certainly greater than from the ordinary shares.
(c) In the event of the company being forced into liquidation, the convertible loanstocks would be redeemed before the ordinary shareholders would be returned any of their investment.
(d) The convertible represents only 2.1 per cent of the investment portfolio.
(e) Provided the company is not forced into liquidation, the price of the convertible will not fall below that of a straight loanstock issued by a company of similar risk.

Further information required to commment more fully on this investment is:

(a) The terms of conversion.
(b) The times when conversion can take place.
(c) The price of the ordinary share. Information in answer to points (a) and (c) would enable the <u>conversion price</u> and the <u>conversion premium</u> to be calculated.

(d) The dividends paid on the ordinary shares. This would enable the income from the two investments to be compared.
(e) The prospects for the ordinary share.
(f) The yield on straight loanstocks of companies of comparable risk.

Section (c)(i)

The composition of the £132,222 inherited portfolio can be summarized as follows:

Cash deposits	12.9%
Gilt-edged stocks	30.7%
Convertible loanstocks	2.1%
Equities	54.3%
	100.0%

The distribution between cash, fixed interest and equity investments is fairly prudent, but the following criticisms can be made of the specific investments made in each area.

(a) Income could be increased with virtually no increase in risk by transferring most of the building society deposits into the Extra Interest Account.
(b) The investment in Green Circle is too large a proportion of the investment portfolio.
(c) An amount of £41,718, or 31.6 per cent of the portfolio, is invested in only three companies. Furthermore, the two largest of these investments (22.7 per cent of the portfolio) are high street banks which represents too high a level of dependence upon one specific investment sector.
(d) There is no diversification into overseas investments and no index-linked investments to secure a positive real return in the event of an acceleration in the rate of inflation.

Apart from these criticisms, these investments may have been appropriate for Mrs Y's father, who would have been retired and in need of income earning investments, but they are not as appropriate for meeting Mrs Y's investment needs since her income and tax position is different.

Section (c)(ii)

Mrs Y's income and tax position is shown below.

	£	£
Salary from civil service		15,000
Pension		10,000
Total Income (excluding investment income)		25,000
Personal allowance	2,605	
Additional allowance	1,490	
Less Total allowances		4,095
Taxable income (excluding investment income)		20,905
Less maximum income taxable at the standard rate		19,300
Total income subject to higher rate tax (excluding investment income)		1,605

The calculation above shows that all of Mrs Y's investment income will be subject to the 40 per cent higher rate of tax. Since the mortgage has been redeemed by her husband's endowment policy and there is substantial life assurance to cover the children's maintenance and education in the event of Mrs Y's death, we will assume that Mrs Y has no particular need of extra income, and that her investment requirements are capital growth with no more than a normally acceptable level of risk.

Since Mrs Y is a higher rate taxpayer, realized capital gains on her investments will also be subject to tax at 40 per cent once the annual exemption has been used. This makes low coupon and index linked gilts attractive investments because much of the return is in the form of tax free capital growth.

Mrs Y will have an investment portfolio worth approximately £135,700 when her own building society deposits are included. A suitable portfolio structure for Mrs Y, limiting the types of investment to those in the existing portfolio, would be:

Appendix 5

Percentage of portfolio	Approx amount £	Type of investment	Yield %	Income £

Cash investment

1	1,500	Building society ordinary account	5.25	79 (net)
5	6,500	Building society 'extra interest'	6.75	439 (net)

Fixed interest investments

10	13,500	Medium date low coupon gilt	8.5	1148 (net)
10	13,500	Long date low coupon gilt	8.5	1148 (flat)
10	13,500	Medium date index linked gilt	2.5	338
10	13,500	Long date index linked gilt	2.5	338

Equity investments

27	36,500	A spread of UK equities (at least 12) or UK equity unit trust aiming at capital growth	3.5	1278
27	36,500	International unit trust aiming at capital growth to obtain diversification and exposure to the world's stock markets	2.5	913

When the building society interest is grossed up to give an equivalent gross income of £691, the total gross income from the portfolio can be calculated to equal £5,854, a gross yield of 4.3 per cent. This compares with a gross income of £9,140 from the £132,222 portfolio of Mrs Y's father which gave him a yield of 6.9 per cent.

Appendix 5

Notes on recommended portfolio.

(a) All portfolios must have a liquid or cash reserve. It is assumed that £8,000 is adequate, and most of it is invested to earn the highest rate available.
(b) The gilts are chosen to give capital growth by selecting low coupons with more than five years to maturity (medium and long dated issues were selected). The index linked gilts not only provide capital growth but also protection against inflation.
(c) The equity part of the portfolio was divided between the UK and international funds so that the professional fund manager can invest where the growth prospects are thought to be best.

If the portfolio had not been restricted to investments in the existing portfolio, the following investments would have been included.

(a) 33rd Issue National Savings Certificates. The maximum investment is only £1,000 but the yield is 7.0 per cent tax free if held for five years.
(b) Index Linked National Savings Certificates. The maximum investment is £5,000 and the yield is an average of 3.7 per cent above the rate of inflation tax free if held for five years.
(c) A Personal Equity Plan would allow £3,000 to be invested in equities which will be exempt from income tax and capital gains tax provided the plan is maintained throughout the year following that in which the investment is made.
(d) Life assurance bonds would allow Mrs Y to avoid paying higher rate tax on her investment income which would be rolled up in the price of units. Capital gains tax paid by the fund managers is at 30 per cent, compared with Mrs Y's personal rate of 40 per cent.
(e) The capital shares of a split capital investment trust would give Mrs Y the prospect of a faster rate of capital growth in return for zero income from this type of investment. These shares could be sold and the proceeds reinvested at the end of any tax year in which the annual capital gains tax exemption allowance has not been utilized.

Section (c)(iii)

The principal investment products offered by or through the UK high street banks to personal investors are:

(a) High interest deposit and term accounts.
(b) Unit trust: lump sum investment and saving schemes.
(c) Regular premium life assurance: endowment and unit linked.

(d) Life assurance single premium bonds.
(e) Pension schemes and annuities.
(f) Personal equity plans.
(g) Stocks and shares and fixed interest securities available from the Stock Exchange.
(h) Offshore funds, especially gilt funds which pay interest gross.
(i) Foreign currency accounts.

The principal investment services offered by or through the UK high street banks to personal investors are:

(a) Investment advice.
(b) Discretionary management of clients' investment portfolios.
(c) Stock Exchange dealing service.
(d) Trust investment management.
(e) Inheritance tax and estate planning.

Index

'A' ordinary shares 32
acceptances 61
account day 40
accounting ratios 91
accumulation units 26, 209
accumulator trusts 164
acid test 107
advance corporation tax 117, 136
advance/decline line 97
AFBD 245
agency brokers 37
agricultural land and buildings 221
allotment letter 57
alpha stocks 38, 97
American depository receipts 35
American Eagle 227
analysts card 91
Angel 227
annual card 90
annual exemption limit 14–15
annual general meetings 63–5
annuities 215–16
antiques 228
arbitrage 155
articles of association 62

back to back loans 171
balance of payments 249–50
balance sheet 102–7
bank deposits 19
Banking Act 1979 241

bear market 96
bed and breakfasting 15
best execution rule 37, 39
beta stocks 38
bid basis, unit trusts 163
Big Bang 33–40
Block Order Exposure (BLOX) 40
Bonds and Stock Office 132
bond washing 168
bonus issue 58
box in charts 92
British government stocks 31
broker dealers 37
brokers transfer form 41
Building Societies Act 1986 241
building society bonds 134
Building Societies Commission 242
building society deposits 19
Building Societies Investors Board 242
bulldog bonds 39, 117
bull market 96
Business Expansion Scheme (BES) 50–51, 223

call options 144, 148–50, 225
Canadian Maple Leaf 227
capital asset pricing model 74
capital gains tax 14–16, 58, 61
capitalization issues 58

Index

capital priority percentage 110, 135
capital shares 183–4
capital units 209
cash investments 9
chairman's statement 101
Channel Islands 25
charts 91
chattels 228
children 237–8
City Code on Takeovers and Mergers 60
class meeting 63
closed end fund 184
coins 226–8
commission 34, 37
commodities 223–6
commodity unit trusts 225
Companies Act 1985 61, 63
company 61
company debentures 31, 134
company loan stocks 31, 134
company meetings 63–4
company's annual report and accounts 101–13
composite rate tax 12
contract note 44–5
contracts (traded options) 144
conventional option 150–51
conversion discount 137
conversion premium 137
conversion price 137
convertible gilts 131
convertible loan stock 31, 136, 194–5
convertible preference shares 32
Coppock indicators 97
corporation loans 117, 134
cost of sales adjustment 111
coupon rate of interest 116
covenants 237–8
cumulative preference shares 32, 194

current accounts 19
current cost accounting 110
current cost operating profit margin 114
current ratio 108

debentures 134
debtor turnover ratio 109
declaration day 151
deep discounted rights issues 58
delta stocks 38
deposit accounts 19
Director General of Fair Trading 60
distributor status 25, 165
dividend cover 78, 106
dividends 102
dividend yield 78, 86–8
double option 150
dual capacity 37

earnings per share 102
economic growth 247–8
efficient market hypothesis 98–100
endowment life assurance 201
 without profits 201
 with profits 201, 206–8
endowment mortgage 220
equities 32
Eurobond market 35
Eurobonds 118
ex cap 58
exchange rate 250–51
ex div 77, 119, 121
exercise price 143
extel cards 89–91
extraordinary general meetings 64
extraordinary resolutions 64

factory investment 221
FIMBRA 243, 245
finance house deposits 22

Index

Financial Services Act 1986   243–6
fixed debentures   31, 134
floating debentures   31
flotation   52
foreign currency deposits   24
foreign currency traded option contracts   147
franked income   117, 164
freehold   219
friendly society   216
FT 30 share index   65–6
FT-Actuaries share indices   66
FT-Stock Exchange 100 index   67
FT-SE traded option contracts   147, 149
fundamental analysis   75
funds flow statement   107
futures contracts   151–6
   arbitrage   155
   hedger   156
   initial margin   154
   program trading   155
   quotation   152
   trader   154
   variation margin   154

gamma stocks   38
gearing   73, 105–6, 186–8, 192
gearing adjustment   114
gilt-edged stocks   31, 115–39
gilt traded option contracts   147
going long   224
going public   51
going short   224
gold   226–8
Gower, Professor   243
gross dividend yield   119
gross interest yield   119
gross redemption yield   119
gross yield   12
grossed-up net redemption yield   24
ground rent   219

guaranteed growth bonds   214–15
guaranteed income bonds   214–15

hatch system   98
head and shoulders   96
hedging risk   149, 154, 171, 223
high interest cheque accounts   19
historical dividend yield   88
historical P/E ratio   88
holiday accommodation   222
home income plan   215–16

IMRO   245
income bonds   22
income priority percentage   110, 135
income shares   183–4
income tax   12–14
indexation allowance   14–15
indexed-income bonds   23
index linked gilts   129–31
index linked savings certificates   24
indices of stock markets   65–8
inflation   127, 248–9
inheritance tax   238–9
initial margin   154, 224
insurance bonds   202
Insurance Brokers (Registration) Act 1977   242
Insurance Companies Act 1982   242
inter-dealer brokers   40
interest cover   106, 135
interest rates   251–2
interest yield   119, 121
intrinsic value
   of traded options   145
   of warrants   141, 196
introduction   46, 55
inverse yield curve   126
investment company   182
investment trusts   181–97

346 Index

    convertible loan stocks 194–5
    debentures and loanstocks 194
    discount to net asset value 185–6
    gearing 186–8, 192
    preference shares 194
    split capital trusts 183–4
    warrants 195–7
investor protection 50, 241–6
Isle of Man 25
ISRO 37
issue by prospectus 52

jobber 33
jobbers turn 33

Krugerrand 226–8

London Options Clearing House 145
LAUTRO 245
leasehold 219
letter of acceptance 54
levels 1, 2 and 3 of SEAQ 38–9
level of resistance 92, 94, 95
level of support 92, 94, 95
life assurance investments 198–217
    capital and accumulation units 209
    endowment 200, 206–8
    guaranteed growth bonds 214–15
    guaranteed income bonds 214–15
    level term 199
    low-cost endowment 201
    premium relief 198
    qualifying policies 198, 202
    single premium 202, 211–13
    taxation 202–6
    term assurance 199, 206
    top slicing rule 204–6
    unit linked 201, 208–13
    whole life 200
LIFFE 151, 245
Line charts 91
liquidity 107
Listing Agreement 52
loanstock 31, 134
local authority bonds 31, 134
London Share Service 76
London Stock Exchange 34–50
low cost endowment assurance 201

margin 148
market makers 37–40
market risk 72
memorandum 61
merger 59
momentum 96
monetary working capital adjustment 114
money supply 253–4
Monopolies and Mergers Commission 60
monthly income scheme
    unit trusts 177
monthly savings scheme
    investment trusts 193
    unit trusts 176
mortgage debentures 31, 134
mortgages
    endowment 220
    repayment 220
moving averages 97

naked debentures 31
naked options 148
NASDIM 243
National Debt 115
National Savings Bank Ordinary Account 22
National Savings Certificates 23
National Savings Bank Investment

Index

Account 22
National Savings Stock Register 132
net asset value 109, 185
net interest yield 123–4
net redemption yield 123–4
net yield 12
new issues 51
new time 41
news card 90
nil paid share 57
Noble 277
nominal value 116
notification of interest 63

occupational pension scheme 217
offer basis, unit trusts 163
offer for sale 53–4
offer for sale by tender 54
office accommodation 221
Office of Fair Trading 34
offshore bank deposits 25
offshore currency funds 25
offshore unit trusts 164–5, 226
Old Court Currency Fund 25
open-ended fund 184
option money 150
options 225
ordinary business 64
ordinary resolutions 64
ordinary shares 32
overseas share indices 67
over the counter market (OTC) 48

parallel markets 35
participating preference shares 32
partial surrender 205–6
partly paid gilts 132
partly paid shares 55
pension schemes 217
personal equity plan (PEP) 178–80
personal gearing 55, 58, 132

placing 47, 54
platinum 226–7
point and figure charts 92–3
Policyholders Protection Act 1975 242
portfolio 10
Post Office 22–6, 132
pound cost averaging 176
preference dividend cover 136
preference shares 32, 135–6
premiums 143
Prevention of Fraud (Investments) Act 1958 243
price earnings ratio 78, 86–9
price volatility 126
prices, unit trusts 163
priority percentages 110
private company 61
profit and loss account 102–7
profit before tax 102–3
profit margin 103
program trading 155
property 219–23
prospective dividend yield 88–9
prospective price earnings ratio 88–9
prospectus 52
provisional allotment letter 57
proxy 64
public company 61
put options 144, 149–50, 225

qualifying policies 198, 202
quick ratio 107
quorum 65
quotation, futures contract 152

rack rent 219
random walk 99
range and close charts 91–2
real rate of return 127
reducing term assurance 199
rectangle 92, 94

Index

redemption of company shares 65
relative strength 96
repayment mortgage 220
representative at shareholder meetings 64
Restrictive Practices Act 1956 34
retail accommodation 221
retired people 238–9
retirement annuity contract 217
return on capital employed 104–5
return on shareholder funds 105
reverse takeover 59
reverse yield gap 86
reversionary bonuses 200
rights of shareholders 62–3
rights issues 55–8
risk
  control 239–40
  definition 10, 71–3
  gilts 126
risk premium 72
roll up funds 165

same account trading 41
Sandilands, Sir Francis 111
savings scheme
  investment trusts 193
  unit trusts 176
scrip issue 58
SEAQ 38–40
second homes 222
Secretary of State for Trade and Industry 60
Securities and Investments Board (SIB) 244–6
Securities Association (SA) 245
Self-Regulating Organization (SRO) 244–6
semi-annual redemption yield 119
separation of capacity 34
SEPON 42
settlement day 40
shareholders meetings 63–5
shares 31
simple debentures 31
single capacity 37
single-premium policies 202, 204–6, 211–13
sinking fund 129, 135
sources and application of funds statement 107
special business 64
special resolutions 64
specific risk 72
speculator 224
split capital trusts 183–4
SSAP 16 114
stags 54
stamp duty 34
stamps 228
stockbroker 33
Stock Exchange account 40
Stock Exchange Daily Official List 78–86, 117, 135
Stock Exchange flotation 51
Stock Exchange money brokers 40
stock market indices 65–8
Stock Transfer Act 1963 41

takeovers 59–61
Talisman 42
taxation
  futures 156
  gross 12
  investment trusts 181–2
  life assurance investments 202–6
  net 12
  pension schemes 217
  traded options 156
  unit trusts 163–5
  wasting assets 151
taxes
  capital gains 14–16
  composite rate 12

Index

income 12–14
technical analysis 91–8
term assurance 199, 206
term deposits 19
terminal bonus 200
theoretical ex rights price 56
Third Market 49
time value
   of traded options 145
   of warrants 142
top slicing rule 204–6
traded options 143–50
   call options 144, 148–50
   contracts 144
   exercise price 143
   foreign currency contracts 147
   FT-SE Index contracts 147
   gilt contracts 147
   hedging 149
   margin 148
   naked options 148
   premiums 143
   put options 144, 149–50
   time value 145
   uncovered options 148
   writer 144
trader of futures 154
trading profit 102
trading rules 98
traditional option 150–51
transaction costs 10
trend lines 92, 94, 95
triple bottom 96
turnover 102
two box reversal 92

umbrella funds 174
unconditional bid 61
uncovered options 148

undated gilts 128
underwriters 53
unitized funds 201
unit linked life assurance 201, 208–13
unit trusts 161–180
   accumulator trusts 164
   buying and selling 177–8
   charges 175
   commodity 225
   distributor status 165
   hedging 171–2
   monthly income scheme 177
   offshore funds 164–5, 226
   prices 163
   roll up funds 165
   rules 162–3
   saving schemes 176
   switching discount 175
   umbrella funds 174
USM 42–8

variation margin 154, 224
vintage cars 228

warehouses 221
warrants 32, 140–3, 195–7
wasting asset 151
weekly rule 98
whole-life assurance 200
writer of options 144

yearlings 134
yearly plan 24
yield curves 125–6

zebra 133–4
zero coupon bond 133–4

M&E Handbooks

Law

'A' Level Law/B Jones
Basic Law/L B Curzon
Cases in Banking Law/P A Gheerbrant, D Palfreman
Cases in Company Law/M C Oliver
Cases in Contract Law/W T Major
Commercial and Industrial Law/A R Ruff
Company Law/M C Oliver, E Marshall
Constitutional and Administrative Law/I N Stevens
Consumer Law/M J Leder
Conveyancing Law/P H Kenny, C Bevan
Criminal Law/L B Curzon
Equity and Trusts/L B Curzon
Family Law/P J Pace
General Principles of English Law/P W D Redmond, J Price, I N Stevens
Jurisprudence/L B Curzon
Labour Law/M Wright, C J Carr
Land Law/L B Curzon
Landlord and Tenant/J M Male
Law of Banking/D Palfreman
Law of Contract/W T Major
Law of Evidence/ L B Curzon
Law of Torts/J G M Tyas
Meetings: Their Law and Practice/L Hall, P Lawton, E Rigby
Mercantile Law/P W D Redmond, R G Lawson
Private International Law/A W Scott

Business and Management

Advertising/F Jefkins
Basic Economics/G L Thirkettle
Basics of Business/D Lewis
Business Administration/L Hall
Business and Financial Management/B K R Watts
Business Mathematics/L W T Stafford
Business Organisation/R R Pitfield
Business Systems/R G Anderson
Data Processing Vol 1: Principles and Practice/R G Anderson
Data Processing Vol 2: Information Systems and Technology/R G Anderson
Economics for 'O' Level/L B Curzon
Human Resources Management/H T Graham
Industrial Administration/J C Denyer, J Batty
International Marketing/L S Walsh
Management, Planning and Control/R G Anderson
Managerial Economics/J R Davies, S Hughes
Marketing/G B Giles
Marketing Overseas/A West
Microcomputing/R G Anderson
Modern Commercial Knowledge/L W T Stafford
Modern Marketing/F Jefkins
Office Administration/J C Denyer, A L Mugridge
Operational Research/W M Harper, H C Lim
Production Management/H A Harding
Public Administration/M Barber, R Stacey
Public Relations/F Jefkins
Purchasing/C K Lysons
Retail Management/R Cox, P Brittain
Sales and Sales Management/P Allen
Statistics/W M Harper
Stores Management/R J Carter